CATHERINE OF SIENA

Catherine of Siena by Andrea Vanni

CATHERINE OF SIENA

A PASSIONATE LIFE

DON BROPHY

DARTON · LONGMAN + TODD

Published in 2011 by
Darton, Longman and Todd Ltd
1 Spencer Court
140 – 142 Wandsworth High Street
London SW18 4JJ

First published in 2010 in the USA by
Bluebridge, an imprint of United Tribes Media Inc.

ISBN 978-0-232-52859-6

A catalogue record for this book is available from the British Library.

Jacket design by Stefan Killen Design
Cover art top: Fra Bartolommeo (Baccio della Porta) (1472–1517), St. Catherine of Siena,
Museo di S. Marco, Florence. Photo credit: Finsiel/Alinari / Art Resource, NY
Cover art bottom: Ambrogio Lorenzetti (d. c.1348), Effects of Good Government (1338).
Palazzo Pubblico, Siena. Photo credit: Erich Lessing / Art Resource, NY

Image on page ii: Andrea Vanni, St. Catherine of Siena, San Domenico, Siena.
Photo credit: Scala / Art Resource, NY

Text design by Cynthia Dunne

Map by Chris Erichsen

Printed and bound in Great Britain by CPI Antony Rowe, Chippenham

CONTENTS

ↄ⟨ↄ

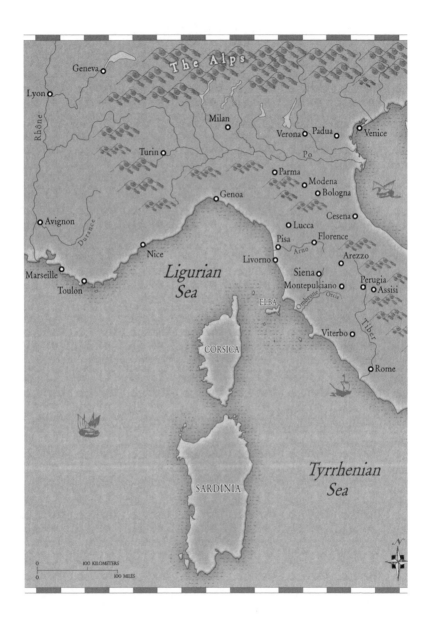

PART ONE

CHILD OF THE CITY

I

༄

THE DYER'S DAUGHTER

In the first light of day the rooftops of Siena gradually turned from black shapes into brown and then, as the sky lightened, began to glow a deep amber-red, strewn across three knobs of hills like a banked fire of coals. Viewed from the top of the soaring Torre del Mangia, nearly completed in the center of town, the contours of the walled city began to fall into place, a profile pierced by a multitude of towers, leaving pools of darkness where narrow valleys lay between the hilltops. Slowly the March light inched from roof tiles to the brick facades of dwellings whose shutters, one by one, winked open to the new day. Somewhere a rooster crowed, dogs barked. From scattered neighborhoods church bells proclaimed a time for prayer. Sequestered in convents around the city monks and nuns had been awake for hours, leaving their pallets while it was still dark to ask God's blessing on this day and on the world, their voices joined in a wavering chant:

> *A solis ortu usque ad occasum,*
> *laudabile nomen Domini.*
> [From sunrise to sunset,
> may the name of the Lord be praised.]

In front of the handsome Palazzo Pubblico, Siena's government building, night shadows pulled back to reveal the great fan-shaped Campo, newly paved with brick and stone, which served as the city's main square and civic center. Already men and women could be seen strolling into its wide open space from the warren of streets that bound it on all sides. Deliberately the people began their routine of setting up stalls and opening shops. In this medieval city, the day began early. Farther away, along the fringes of the encircling walls, gates creaked open to admit oxcarts laden with produce from the countryside, the fertile Sienese *contado*. Entering through the Camollia gate in the northern wall were a few pilgrims who had trekked from Lombardy or from countries beyond the Alps and who would make Siena a stopover on their way to Rome. This was a special day for pilgrims and city dwellers alike: March 25. It was the Feast of the Incarnation, when the faithful recalled how God had cast his lot with the human race, taking on the vulnerability of ordinary flesh. In this particular year, March 25 was also Palm Sunday, the beginning of Holy Week. Preparations were already under way to mark the day with great solemnity in the *duomo*, the magnificent cathedral built of white and black marble a short distance from the Campo. The day was special, too, because for Siena, as for the other city-states of Tuscany, March 25 marked the beginning of the new year: 1347.

This new year found Siena at peace with its neighbors and still close to the peak of its influence and wealth. Siena was one of the cities that—on the surface at least—were giving new shape to the possibilities of urban life in the late Middle Ages. The cities of northern Europe were mostly dirty, disease-ridden, and controlled either by hereditary monarchs or families of nobles who lived outside the walls on feudal estates. To the south, the great city of Rome was languishing, its public monuments crumbling. But in Tuscany nearly all of the cities were self-governing states whose lawmakers were elected and whose leadership was in the hands of the merchant class. Their economy was no longer founded on agriculture but on trade and finished goods—and one thing more, on money. Tuscan cities, especially Florence and to a lesser degree Siena, had become the bankers of Europe. The gold florin minted in Florence was Europe's most trusted currency. With a population of almost 50,000, Siena was nearly bursting at the seams. Six times during the Middle Ages—including twice in the last two dozen years—Siena's walls had to be extended to enclose larger areas. The increasing population did not come from a rising birthrate, however; due to the state of public health in the fourteenth century, sickness and death in cities always exceeded new births. Instead, Siena grew by attracting people from the region under its control, which included numerous villages and some larger towns to the south and west. Each of the Italian city-states tried to control its immediate region as a way of keeping itself supplied with food and labor, and the collision of cities bent on expanding their territories had given rise to a series of bloody little wars. Florence and Siena, abutting each other's territories, were hereditary rivals. After a Sienese alliance defeated the Florentines in the Battle of Montaperti in 1260, Siena was briefly the dominant power in the region. Unfortunately for Siena it was very briefly: Florence came back only nine years later and annihilated the Sienese at Colle di Val d'Elsa. By 1347 Siena had accepted Florentine hegemony but remained fiercely independent in spirit.

Urban life in Siena in the 1300s was vigilantly ordered. All of the streets were brick paved and, except for the droppings of draft animals, kept clean. One man in each *contrada*, or ward, was responsible for sweeping. Since 1310 it had been illegal to keep pigs or sheep inside the city or throw garbage into the street. Already in the fourteenth century, the proud citizens of Siena shared a civic ethos about the maintenance of their city where they lived so close together. And while a housewife might still dump water from a second-floor window, at least she would warn pedestrians by first calling, "*Guarda!*"

People and buildings were packed tight inside the walls. Via di Fonte-branda, a main thoroughfare, was only twenty-four feet wide. Many smaller streets leading to the right and left in a confusing tangle were much narrower. Sienese liked to joke that if invaders ever managed to break through the walls, they would soon get lost in the side streets. Simply getting sunlight for the houses standing so close to each other was a challenge. Many dwellings had wooden balconies projecting over the streets. The Siena commune tried to limit the number and size of balconies because they cut off sunlight to the street below, but on this issue homeowners paid little attention to the law.

The Fontebranda neighborhood, on the west side of the city, was tucked into a cleft between two hills—one to the north, dominated by the severe Gothic walls of San Domenico Church; the other, Castelvecchio hill, to the south, the oldest part of Siena where the duomo and the Palazzo Pubblico stood. Fontebranda was named for its spring-fed fountain—Fonte Branda—so well known in Tuscany that Dante had mentioned it in his *Inferno*. The fountain was located a short distance from the Porta Fontebranda, a city gate that faced westward, toward the fertile lowlands and the sea beyond, some forty miles away. Generally in Siena, the poor lived closer to the walls while the wealthy made their homes on the hilltops. Fontebranda was not the poorest neighborhood of the city. As a center for the leather and cloth trades, it had its share of stinking tanneries, but it also was home to a good number of prosperous weavers and dyers—guild members, most of them. One of its principal streets, leading uphill from the fountain, was Via dei Tintori, the Street of Dyers. There, in the ward known as the Contrada dell'Oca (Goose Ward), a dyer named Giacomo di Benincasa, in business with his sons, had rented a house the year previously from the wool guild.

The combined dwelling and workplace was large and most likely a step up in profession and social status for Giacomo. While certainly not a palazzo, it had ample space for a family with many children and a business to run. Built against the side of a hill, it had three floors. The lowest floor contained the dye shop, the *tintoria*, with its large vats for soaking wool and flax. The doors of the shop opened directly onto Via dei Tintori—convenient for tradesmen and for carting or carrying water from the fountain. Dyers needed generous quantities of water. In the rear of the dye shop was a stairwell leading down to a small wine cellar, and another going up to the family quarters that occupied the floors above. Because of the slope of the hill the middle floor was also on street level, facing out onto Vicolo del Tiratoio, just a few steps from the small parish church of Sant'Antonio Abate. The middle floor held the bedrooms and perhaps a small sitting room. While the building exists to this day, we can only guess the original layout of the rooms—the interior has been so modified that there is scant trace of the room arrangement of the fourteenth century. On the top floor was a large kitchen that served as a family space and a terrace laid out to hold a small garden.

The family of Giacomo did not belong to the nobility. Had they been nobles it might be possible to track their lineage back through successive generations and connect them to famous or powerful ancestors. The faint trail of Giacomo's antecedents includes a notary and several merchants in the thirteenth century. Giacomo himself was a full member of the wool guild, the *Arte della Lana*, which was no trivial thing at that time. It took years to attain guild membership and often required family connections. As a member of the guild he was a full citizen of the commune of Siena. He could vote in state elections or even hold public office if nominated by the party in power. When a guild member died, all the other members closed their shops to attend the funeral, which provided opportunities for enlisting support for the deceased's widow and children. Within the guild, Giacomo was a master dyer by profession. That could mean a highly skilled worker or even something more. As one writer close to the family put it, Giacomo's work involved the "mixing and manufacture of the colors used for dyeing." The business of mixing and making colors in the era before the introduction of chemical dyes suggests his tasks were more complex than simply coloring fabric. Indigo, for instance, had to be imported from the East, so the one who created dyes had to be an importer. Other colors in medieval times were concocted from native plants and insects. If Giacomo mixed and sold these dyes for use by other tradesmen, then he would be working as a wholesaler, in addition to being a dyer himself. While we don't know the full scope of his business, it is clear that he was a businessman of considerable status and prestige.

Giacomo di Benincasa's wife, Lapa, came from an established merchant family. Her father, Puccio di Piagenti, did business as a mattress maker and was a recognized man of culture in Tuscany, being a poet of some renown. No examples of his verse remain, but it is known he dedicated one of his poems to Guido Cavalcanti, a friend and colleague of Dante Alighieri in Florence. Puccio's aesthetic genes, however, may have died with his generation, since Lapa grew into a strong-willed woman not generously endowed with subtlety. Some have called her simplistic; if so, she made up for it by strength of character and devotion to her family. Giacomo married her soon after he had lost both of his parents, so he may have welcomed a woman with both feet on the ground. There was probably some disparity in their ages; she outlived him by several decades. Whatever their differences, Lapa and Giacomo made a good team: where she was impulsive, sometimes volatile, he was quiet and slow to judge but firm when a decision had to be made. Years later she told the story of a customer who sued Giacomo over an unpaid debt, almost bringing him to ruin. Lapa was furious at the man, but her husband refused to criticize him, insisting, "God will show him his mistake." Sure enough, circumstances proved that the customer was mistaken. The two men eventually were reconciled.

Together Giacomo and Lapa had twenty-five children—an enormous number by today's standards, and a lot even in that era. Most of their offspring died before adulthood. Available records put names to only ten of them. The eldest known son was given the name of Giacomo's father, Benincasa. The next son after him was Bartolomeo, and Sandro was the third. Sandro, however, had disappeared from the record—perhaps he died—by the time the family moved to Via dei Tintori, since by then Giacomo's business included only two sons, Benincasa and Bartolomeo.

Of the boys, Bartolomeo made the most notable marriage, taking as his wife Lisa Colombini, niece of Giovanni Colombini, one of the most colorful and controversial characters in Siena. Colombini was a wealthy merchant who in midlife underwent a religious conversion so sudden and shattering that he resolved to live his life differently from that moment on. His sin, as he saw it, was grasping, usurious moneymaking. In an effort to make amends he had himself scourged in front of the Palazzo Pubblico. He sold his goods for prices that were lower than cost and then gave away much of the wealth he had left. When his wife complained, Colombini reminded her that she had once begged God to teach him charity. According to the story, she answered, "I prayed for rain, not for the Flood." Wanting to do still more, Colombini settled his wife financially and then donned rags to serve the poor in the hospital. He preached in public places about the evils of money, which did not endear him to the bankers in Siena. When he began to attract followers, the city fathers had had enough. Colombini was exiled from the Sienese state for several years. He wandered through the cities and towns of Tuscany, preaching and practicing poverty. Eventually he was allowed to return. After his death in 1367, his followers, called the *Gésuati*, continued to remind people of the corruptions of wealth.

Giacomo and Lapa had daughters as well as sons. There was Maddalena, who married Bartolomeo di Vannino, and Nicholuccia (called Niccola), who married Palmiero di Nese dalla Fonte. Both sisters will disappear from our story. However, the son of Niccola and Palmiero—Tommaso dalla Fonte—will have an important part in all that follows.

After Niccola in birth order came Bonaventura, who married Niccolò de Giovanni Tegliacci. Then there was another sister, Lisa (not to be confused with Bartolomeo's wife of the same name). And after Lisa came another son, Stefano.

By this time Lapa was surely weary of childbearing, but nevertheless another pregnancy began in 1346—perhaps around the time the family moved into its new home. It reached full term on this twenty-fifth day of March in 1347. In a second-floor bedroom on Via dei Tintori, Lapa gave birth to twin girls who were promptly named Caterina (or Catherine, as we shall call her) and Giovanna.

The newborns were weak, and because Lapa could not nurse both she handed the more sickly Giovanna to a wet nurse while keeping Catherine for herself. It was a difficult decision no doubt, but more easily made in the fourteenth century than today. With infant mortality so high, parents invested their hopes in the strongest children. In Lapa's mind she wasn't depriving her weaker daughter, since all of her children had been wet-nursed during some part of their infancy. The pregnancies had come too fast and she never had sufficient milk for the ones already born. Catherine, coming toward the end of Lapa's childbearing years, would be different. Mother and daughter had a chance to bond in ways that Lapa never did with any of her other children. In this case Lapa—never the most intuitive one—made a wise choice. Catherine was nursed until it was time for weaning while Giovanna, tended by the wet nurse, died not long after birth.

As mentioned, the city Catherine was born into was at that time still close to the zenith of its power and influence. It was self-governing, a center for banking and cloth-making, and a favorite stopping place for pilgrims on the Via Francigena, the great route of pilgrimage from northern Europe down to Rome. It was also a city of dreamers. Dante found the Sienese ardent, vain, and given to grandiose statements. Even as Catherine lay in her crib, Siena was attempting another grandiose statement by reconstructing and extending its cathedral, aiming to make it the largest church in Christendom. Under the leadership of the ruling council known as the *Nove* (the Nine), the commune had just completed paving its expansive Campo, the great square, or piazza, in the center of town that was the setting for the magnificent new Palazzo Pubblico and the tall, graceful Torre del Mangia connected to it. The Gésuati might warn about the dangers of money and ostentation, but in 1347 Siena wore its prosperity with a certain amount of swagger.

Unknown as yet to anyone in Tuscany, that self-confidence would soon be tested. Something was happening in central Asia that would bring Siena's plans to a standstill and challenge its resiliency and faith. People in Asia were being struck down by a sickness, abruptly and in great numbers. Signs of the disease included headache, nausea, and fever, and sometimes swelling of the lymph glands in the groin, under the armpits, and on the neck behind the ears, creating distinctive "buboes," which gave the disease its name: bubonic plague. There was no known cure. In more than half of the cases it led inexorably to death. One frightening thing about the disease was that no one knew what caused it. While people realized clearly enough that it could be passed from person to person, they blamed the transmission on a theory of vapors, or even on planetary influences. Not until long after was the bacillus traced to fleas that infested black rats. The rats attached themselves to ships, especially those loaded with grain. They carried the deadly fleas to ports in the Crimea and from there to Europe. By October 1347 the plague had reached Messina, in Sicily. Before the end of the year it was in Genoa. In January people in Marseille were falling ill. From there the contagion spread like wildfire north into France.

The Black Death reached the cities of Tuscany in the spring of 1348. In March Florence was struck a terrible blow, especially in the poorer neighborhoods where people lived close together in unsanitary conditions. Giovanni Boccaccio described what happened next: "Being confined to their own parts of the city, they fell ill daily in their thousands, and since they had no one to assist them or attend to their needs, they inevitably perished almost without exception. Many dropped dead in the open streets, both by day and by night, whilst a great many others, though dying in their own houses, drew their neighbor's attention to the fact more by the smell of their rotting corpses than by any other means. Any what with these, and the others who were dying all over the city, bodies were here, there, and everywhere."

The cloud of plague reached Siena the following month. The city gates had been locked to keep out strangers who might be infected, but to no avail. As people fell sick, shops were closed. The municipal courts shut down, and also the wool industry, including the dyers. The Council of Nine appointed a three-man committee to oversee the handling of the dead. Plague-pits were dug in various parts of the city. To propitiate the Almighty, candlelit processions wound through the streets; the Gésuati went into the public squares proclaiming the need for penance. There was a surge of moral righteousness. A statue of Venus standing in the Campo was pulled down and broken by a mob because it smacked of dissolute living.

A picture of Siena during the plague has been left to us by Agnolo di Tura, a cobbler and diarist. He wrote, "There are not words to describe how horrible these events have been and, in fact, whoever can say that they have not lived in utterly horrid conditions can truly consider themselves lucky. The infected die almost immediately. They swell beneath the armpits and in the groin, and fall over while talking. Fathers abandon their sons, wives their husbands, and one brother the other. In the end everyone escapes and abandons anyone who might be infected. Moreover, it appears that this plague can be communicated through bad breath and even just by seeing one of the infected. In these ways they die and no one can be found who would want to bury them, not even for money or in the name of friendship. Those who get infected in their own house, they remove them the best way they can and they bury them without the supervision of a priest. No one controls anything and they do not even ring the church bells anymore. Throughout Siena, giant pits are being excavated for the multitudes of the dead and the hundreds that die every night. The bodies are thrown into those mass graves and are covered bit by bit. When those ditches are full, new ditches are dug. So many have died that new pits have to be made every day.

"And I, Agnolo di Tura, called the Fat, have buried five of my sons with my own hands . . . There is no one who weeps for any of the dead, for instead everyone awaits their own impending death. So many have died that everyone believes it is the end of the world."

It wasn't the end, but it was close. The plague lasted through the summer months, then slowly lessened in intensity when the weather turned cooler in September and October. People gradually returned to the city. Some shops reopened, while others did not. By Agnolo di Tura's estimate 52,000 died in Siena alone. That number, however, would equal roughly the total population of the city in 1347. Most historians believe Siena lost about 60 percent of its inhabitants. In Europe as a whole, an estimated one-third of the population died.

As one might judge from di Tura's account, children were particularly vulnerable to infection from the plague, and newborn children probably even more so. But as far as we know, no one in the household of Giacomo di Benincasa succumbed to the disease. Perhaps Catherine, being breast-fed, shared whatever immunity her mother possessed. Perhaps, like many citizens, the family fled from the city during the height of the infestation. They owned a small farm with a vineyard in San Rocco a Pilli, about five miles south of the city walls. It was part of the dowry brought into the family by Bartolomeo's wife, Lisa Colombini. The quarters would have been crowded with all of them living there, but for a short time in mild weather it would not have been impossible.

The biography of Catherine written by Raymond of Capua after her death fails to mention, even in passing, the plague year of 1348, and certainly does not speculate about the effect it may have had on her emotional development. Looking back from our perspective, the psychological impact of the pandemic is impossible to ignore. Historians have documented the waves of survivor guilt that swept across Europe in the wake of the "great mortality," as it was called. Bands of flagellants paraded through the towns of Germany and France, ritually whipping their bodies in an effort to expiate the sins that they believed had angered God and brought on the terrible punishment of the Black Death. The infant Catherine was then too young to feel guilt, but when the events of that year were disclosed to her as an older girl—as they surely would have been—she must have wondered at the ways of God and why she survived when so many others did not. Not only was she spared from the plague, she would also have learned that she had survived her twin sister. Her survival had been assured when her mother chose to nurse her instead of Giovanna. Being a "chosen one" is usually accepted as a blessing, but in some circumstances it can be a heavy burden.

Although the household got through the plague year intact, their city did not. Siena sustained an almost mortal wound from the plague and its aftereffects. Many businesses went under. Working men, now fewer in number, demanded—and got—higher wages for their labor. Prices skyrocketed. Peasants in the countryside, who had lived in servitude for generations, walked away from their estates, knowing they could find better-paying jobs elsewhere. The city of Siena never fully recovered from its population loss. Driven by a new determination to avoid disease-ridden cities, people from the countryside opted to stay where they were. Suddenly there was plenty of land available on farms and in smaller towns and money to buy it. Many of those who made it through the year found themselves beneficiaries of wealthier relatives who had passed away. Inside the city, Agnolo di Tura told how quickly the promises of personal repentance were forgotten once the danger was past: "[A]ll who survived gave themselves over to pleasures: monks, priests, nuns, and lay men and women all enjoyed themselves, and none worried about spending and gambling."

The Sienese commune, while not insolvent, lacked the means in the new economic climate to do everything it wanted or even to deliver basic services. The attempt to greatly enlarge the duomo had to be shelved. With a population not even half as large as it had been a few years earlier, shops and homes stood empty and decaying. The streets—once the city's pride, all of them paved and swept clean—fell into disrepair. By the end of the century the Via Francigena—the great pilgrim route that ran through the center of the city—was so potholed and muddy as to be unusable in bad weather.

Giacomo's family, too, suffered from the economic downturn in the wake of the Black Death. Some years or months before the plague year, the eldest son, Benincasa, with his father's support, had entered into a partnership with two other dyers. The business did not go well. When both of the partners died, presumably of the plague, Giacomo and his son were saddled with much of the debt. They were sued in Siena's Market Council by a creditor and lost their case. How much they had to pay is not recorded, but it was the first step in a series of financial misfortunes that would test the family in the years to come.

But within the household on Via dei Tintori, life continued. Catherine was weaned because Lapa had become pregnant yet again. Perhaps the pregnancy was a response by her and Giacomo to so much death in the city. When the baby came it was called Giovanna, after Catherine's dead twin sister. The family grew in another respect as well. Catherine's older sister Niccola had died of the plague along with her husband Palmiero. Suddenly parentless, their son Tommaso came to live with his grandparents and became like a brother to Catherine. He was ten years older than she—an earnest, devout young man who may already have been considering a vocation to religious life. Except for Catherine's favorite and adored older sister, Bonaventura, Tommaso became the family member closest to her heart. Unlike girls in the fourteenth century, boys often learned how to read and write at least in a rudimentary way so that, growing up, they would be able to decipher ledgers and invoices. In Tommaso's case, he was more interested in stories about the saints than commercial accounts. While not the smartest student, he learned enough to read the *Legenda Aurea* (*Golden Legend*), a collection of devotional stories written the previous century by the Italian Dominican Jacopo da Varazze that had become wildly popular by Catherine's time. Sitting at the kitchen table during the evening, Tommaso would struggle through the text, reading aloud, perhaps about Saint Agnes who was beheaded at the age of thirteen because she refused the advances of Roman soldiers. It is not difficult to imagine little Catherine listening, wide-eyed and silent.

From what is told about her, the girl Catherine was not usually silent. She grew into a happy, bubbly child who loved to talk, and was much petted by her older brothers and sisters. Judging from the bond that grew between them, Bonaventura may have been the one who watched Catherine while their mother was busy with the younger Giovanna. Neighbors on the street were so taken by little Catherine that they would invite her into their homes to feed her tidbits and listen to her chatter. Lapa had a hard time keeping track of her. Someone gave the girl the name Euphrosyne, one of the Graces in Greek mythology—the personification of joy—and it seemed to fit.

The city itself had a role in Catherine's formation. As a twentieth-century commentator has pointed out, "Medieval people lived as much in the streets as in their homes; open archways, balconies, and exterior staircases provided ready access between private and public places so that family life was scarcely separated from life in the extended family of their neighborhood. Like most Sienese, therefore, Catherine was a child of the city as much as of her family; the objective reality of the world around her was text and teacher to her observant and inquiring mind."

For chores the girls helped to clean the house and prepare food. Although Catherine was too small at first to carry anything heavy, one can imagine her going down the hill with an older sibling to fill pails of water at the fountain of Fontebranda. It was hard, physical work, and Catherine grew into a vigorous young girl. Stories recount the way the teenage Catherine lugged heavy packages up the stairs from the dye shop to the living quarters. This was offered as evidence that in the years before she undertook her fasts and became gradually more frail she was strong and healthy.

She was also pious. Where this came from is hard to know exactly. It is fair to say that most children growing up in medieval Siena were pious by nature. It was in the air they breathed, in the sound of the bells ringing out the hours of the day, continually reinforced by the church calendar with its parade of saints and martyrs. For most people in the Middle Ages churchgoing was serious business; praying was as common and omnipresent as eating. Years later, Catherine's first biographer would claim that a kind of holiness "showed in germ what afterwards grew up and came to full fruition"—intimating that she was singled out by God from her earliest years. As a faith statement it will serve, but it is a hagiographer's attempt to sacrilize ordinary history. In Catherine's case it should be noted that her father was a man of reserved and devout temperament who expected to find those same qualities in his children. Curse words were never permitted under his roof. Giacomo himself had grown up in a devout family. He was a Franciscan tertiary (a layman affiliated with the Franciscan order), and his sister—Catherine's aunt Agnes—joined the Dominican tertiaries after the death of her husband. Catherine's sisters served as models of behavior for her, as well as her sister-in-law Lisa—not to mention nephew Tommaso, on a track to become a Dominican friar. In addition, there were the experiences of her short life to date, above all the knowledge that she survived the calamity that took so many lives in her city. Is it any wonder that these influences insinuated themselves in her personality, deepening the colors of her naturally buoyant spirit? She accepted praying as an activity to be mastered, like setting the table or fetching water. She took delight in it, learning the child's game of going up the stairs and pausing on each step to kneel and say an *Ave*. Somewhere she must have heard—probably from Tommaso—about the desert hermits of the fourth century who lived in caves and gave their nights and days entirely to prayer. It must have struck her imagination as wonderfully romantic—not in any way depressing but grand and adventurous. Exploring silence and solitude for herself, initially in small ways, her extroverted spirit gradually encountered mystery. In this way the child Catherine came to experience the tides of desire.

At first, much of this development occurred as a kind of play. Catherine had places in the house where she hid herself and learned to be still. When she was about six or seven years old and friends visited her they would pretend they were in a convent. Sitting or kneeling primly, they would recite prayers like the nuns and sometimes beat their shoulders with improvised scourges. Catherine was always the prioress. It was a game they enjoyed enormously.

A child living in a home where so many siblings were older could not help but be aware of political events that were roiling the city at this time. Catherine's father and older brothers were involved in Siena's public life, both in the guild and the commune. She heard them talking about it, particularly her brother Bartolomeo. There was muttering about the Council of Nine, the oligarchy of bankers and merchants who had controlled Sienese affairs for over sixty years. Things had changed after the plague. The city was doing poorly and dissatisfaction was rising. The Nine were further embarrassed in 1353 when the mercenary army of Fra Moriale raided Sienese territory, burning estates, terrorizing and murdering people. Strong walls kept the mercenaries out of the city, but Siena's pitiful army could not chase them away. Finally Siena had to pay Moriale 13,000 gold florins to leave, suffering the added humiliation of having to reimburse him for the horses he had lost.

One day during that summer or fall, Lapa asked Stefano and Catherine to deliver an item to Bonaventura who lived with her husband in another part of the city. The two children set off, climbing up from the narrow valley where their house was located, cutting across the slope of Castelvecchio near the duomo toward the Porta Ansano neighborhood where Bonaventura lived. One expects young Catherine was thrilled to visit the sister she loved so much. Most likely she and Stefano spent several hours at Bonaventura's house and then, following the same route, headed home before evening. Stefano moved on ahead, Catherine trailed behind. They passed the ancient hospital of Santa Maria della Scala and the duomo and came at last to the steep stairway that led down to Fontebranda. One could see across the valley to the imposing church of San Domenico on the crest of the opposite hill. It was late afternoon and the light was changing. Suddenly Catherine stopped and looked up. There, floating in the sky above San Domenico, she could see a number of human figures, just like in the frescoes painted on the walls of Siena's churches. Enthroned in the center was Christ, wearing white papal robes and a tiara and holding a pastoral staff with his left hand. He was looking straight at her. Standing to one side of the throne were the Apostles Peter and Paul, and on the other side John the Evangelist. Grouped around them were other figures. Catherine stood, transfixed. It seemed as though Christ was smiling at her. He raised his right hand and made the sign of the cross over her. She was rooted to her place, lost in the vision. Stefano, glancing back, saw that she had stopped. He called to her but she did not answer. He called again. Still no answer. Finally he ran back and tugged her sleeve, demanding, "What are you doing here? Why don't you come?" She was forced to turn from the vision and look at her brother. She cried out, "Oh, if you could see what I see you wouldn't have disturbed me." She turned back to the vision, but it was gone. Disappointed, she burst into bitter tears.

Catherine made Stefano promise not to tell their parents about the vision. Neither did she speak of it, but in the days after it was always on her mind. The Son of God, the Savior of the world, was pleased with her. He had smiled at her and blessed her. She would carry that knowledge all of her life. Yet, as she related the event to her confessor years later, she reproached herself for looking away. The disappearance of the vision in that moment was a source of enormous sadness. She blamed herself for it. In the words of one early account, "From this moment, she was always tormented from inside, fearful, conscientious, and afraid of falling into sin, as much as was possible for a girl of her age." At home she began to hide herself away with more purpose and to discipline her body with more vigor.

We will come back to these disciplines later. For now it is fair to wonder what we're supposed to make of the vision itself. Was the girl Catherine delusional? Did she really believe she saw heavenly beings? There is no getting around the fact that Catherine believed that this vision and others she would have in the future were completely authentic: Christ and the saints appeared and interacted with her just as surely as human visitors did. Not only did Catherine believe this was so, but her spiritual advisors, her family, her followers, and almost everyone who came in contact with her or who knew her by reputation believed it as well. One might write this off as an example of the credulous era they lived in, and to be sure the late Middle Ages was a time of feverish religious enthusiasm. Catherine was not the only visionary in medieval Italy. There were dozens, and most of them were women. For example, Agnes of Montepulciano (1268–1317) was visited by the Virgin Mary, who allowed her to hold the baby Jesus. Margaret of Cortona (1247–1297) was visited by Jesus, who told her which priests were chaste and which were not, while Angela of Foligno (1248–1309) was invited by Jesus to drink blood that flowed from his side. Yet it would be a mistake to discount these stories as quaint examples of folk religion propagated during an uncritical age. Religious visions are not limited to Italy, or to women, or to the fourteenth century. There has been no age or faith without religious visionaries, including our own.

One way to distinguish between delusions and energizing visions is by weighing the effect they have on the visionary. Delusions arise from a distorted view of the world and lead a person to relate to his or her environment in bizarre and dysfunctional ways. Healthy visions, on the other hand, enlarge a person's innate capacities and provide motivation and direction for human growth. Rather than leading the visionary into a private world, they become vehicles for social engagement. They can become a source of energy for the one having the vision, and for others as well. A single person announcing "I have a dream" can enlarge the vision of a whole society. Therefore, one should not be too hasty in deciding whether a particular event, which may appear very odd on the surface, is delusional—or is a graphic representation of the soul's deepest purpose. If it turns out to be the latter, one will be able to tell from the fruit it bears.

However, it is essential to note that Catherine herself recognized the difference between her visions and physical reality. Although "real" on one level, the visions were gifts given only to *her*. Stefano had not seen Christ in the sky. Other people on the street could not see him. Even at the moment of awakening, when Stefano grabbed her sleeve, Catherine was conscious that she and her brother did not share the same experience. *If you could see what I see.* Years later Raymond of Capua wrote that Catherine's visions "for the most part took place in her imagination, but sometimes they were perceptible . . . by her bodily senses." There was complete agreement between Catherine and her spiritual mentor on that point: visions were products of her imagination, planted there by God. She "saw" them, and sometimes her other senses perceived them as well, but in all cases they arose in her own imagination.

One more aspect of the young girl's vision is worth mentioning. According to Raymond of Capua, the figure of Christ seen by Catherine in the sky was dressed in papal vestments. This may be the only instance in Christian iconography where Christ appeared wearing papal robes. One wonders what inspired it. Had the child Catherine seen a mural with a vested pope and confused that image with Jesus? Had she heard adults discussing the new pope, Innocent VI (elected only the previous year), and had the pope and Christ somehow blended together in her mind? The conflation of icons is interesting because it was Catherine's habit in later years to equate loyalty to the pope with loyalty to Christ. Curiously, a different account of the vision written years before Raymond's does not mention specific papal trappings. The *Miracoli* claims she saw Christ "dressed in totally white clothes" and holding a pastoral staff. There is no tiara.

Six-year-old Catherine went home in sadness, believing her inattentiveness had severed a connection with the other world and blaming herself for it. Such feelings are common among children as a first response to loss. But the larger experience of being connected, even momentarily, had been so powerful that it gave her a steely determination to recover it. Far from lapsing into lasting sadness and fear, Catherine resolved to eradicate all inattentiveness from her character through vigilance and self-discipline. She had no Zen master to slap her face and cry "Wake up!" so she whipped her own body. "Brother Ass," as Francis of Assisi had called the body—sometimes it needed whipping in order to move forward. Her attitude toward food also changed. The Fathers of the Desert believed gluttony was the font of all other sins, so she resolved to fast, thereby denying herself food's soporific comfort. Above all else, she sought solitude—hard to find in a house crowded with family. Her own room may have been shared with young

Giovanna, and probably also with her older sister Lisa. However, since Stefano was old enough to work but still too young to marry, his room was empty during the day. It and the family wine cellar became Catherine's prayer spaces.

She longed to be one of the desert hermits. Tommaso had told her about them. Now she reflected on the luxury of having one's own cave or hermitage to pray in without interruption or distraction. There would be no one to tug on her sleeve and ask, "What are you doing?" It was common knowledge that a few hermits, both men and women, lived outside Siena's Porta Ansano in their rude shelters. Catherine weighed going out to join them. Her mother wouldn't notice—Lapa didn't know where Catherine was half the time anyway. So one day she took a loaf of bread for herself and began the long walk up and over the hill in the direction of Bonaventura's house—but instead of stopping at the house she kept going, through the gate in the city wall and out into the countryside. The landscape there was broken, with narrow valleys and rock outcroppings. Finally she found a suitable place under a rock overhang. She settled herself and prayed. Time passed. One medieval account reported that during the prayer the Virgin Mary appeared to Catherine who, in turn, begged Mary to accept her as the spouse of Jesus. Raymond of Capua, on the other hand, omitted Mary's visit but claimed Catherine was lifted into the air as she prayed. Neither account mentioned whether she ate the bread. What we do know is that Catherine suddenly realized the light was failing. Being just a young girl, she thought it would be wise to go home. As expected, when she got there no one realized she had been away.

Catherine was not ready to leave home, but her short experience in solitude outside the city walls may have confirmed for her that she was different from everyone else in her family. She was unique. She was chosen. And she was coming to see that she would probably have to battle in order to maintain that difference.

2

⑥↷

THE MANTLE

wo years later the Nine fell from power in Siena. It would have happened eventually, anyway, given the fractious politics of Tuscany, but Siena's merchant class had emerged from the Black Death weakened in numbers and influence, and in 1355 the noble families saw an opportunity to regain their dominant position.

The Nine—their full title was the Nine Governors and Defenders of the Commune and the People of Siena—had first taken power in 1287, following a series of violent struggles between Siena's noble families on one side and the emerging merchant class on the other. After much travail and bloodshed the nobility was pushed aside and rich middle-class merchants prevailed. They formed a government run by an executive council of nine men, three from each of the three *terzi*, or districts, that make up the city to this day. But although "the people" held power, it was far from being a democracy. The rule of the Council of Nine turned out to be an oligarchy of a different sort—open to bankers, merchants, and a few wool guildsmen, but closed to everyone else: noblemen, doctors and lawyers, members of lesser guilds such as butchers, bakers, carpenters, and, of course, common laborers. It was government by a clique, a "distributed tyranny"—but very narrowly distributed. Because the nobles were continually feuding among themselves, they could never mount an effective challenge to the arrangement.

In spite of their narrow base of power, the Nine had turned out to be effective leaders. For more than sixty years they had presided over a government that improved the city's public works and its streets, paid its debts, and allowed its citizenry to live in relative peace. Only in the last years, since the Black Death, had its ingrained nepotism and genteel corruption become apparent. So when Charles of Luxembourg, king of Germany and Bohemia (and future Emperor Charles IV), made a state visit to Italy in 1354, Siena's noble families found a figure they could rally around. With the grudging consent of the Nine, an invitation to visit Siena was extended to Charles by two noble families that normally hated each other—the Salimbeni and the Tolomei. On March 23, 1355, on his way to Rome to be crowned emperor, Charles entered Siena accompanied by a thousand knights. Almost immediately people planted in the crowd began shouting, "Long live the emperor and death to the Nine!" Soon the whole city was in an uproar. Charles had promised not to intervene in Sienese politics, but after two days of increasing violence in the streets he went back on his word and quieted the mob by throwing his support behind the nobility.

The next day, frightened by the tumult, the emperor and his retinue fled while Siena set about forming another government, without the rich merchants. The noble families believed they would have a significant place in any new arrangement. At first they did, but soon a coalition of middle-class guild members—but excluding former members of the Nine—stepped into the leadership gap. Twelve counselors were chosen to serve as the executive, their members again split among the three terzi. And so the rule of the Twelve (the *Dodici*) began, while the nobles and the disenfranchised poor still watched from the sidelines. Siena had entered an era of political instability.

The family of Giacomo was not displeased with this outcome, since they were tied more closely to the new ruling elite than they had been to the old. Catherine's second-oldest brother, Bartolomeo, was deeply involved in political affairs. On two different occasions he served on the *Signoria*, the governing council of the commune, once in 1368 and again in 1370. Her oldest brother, Benincasa, and the youngest, Stefano, also held political office in 1368. It seemed that the family was at last taking a more prominent place in society.

Catherine, too, had been involved in cementing her relationship in a new order, but not the political kind. She was still dealing with the vision in the sky and its significance for her life. The more she reflected on it the more convinced she became that the one who had smiled and blessed her ought to be the focus of her attention. She wished to live in that gaze permanently. Being just eight years old, however, there was no way for her to act on her desire. Had she told others about it, they would have merely teased her and discounted her experience. Being used to solitude now, she decided to take action on her own and tell no one. So one day she went off to "a retired place," in the words of Raymond of Capua, and made a promise to God.

Raymond and nearly all the biographers who followed him have called it Catherine's "vow of virginity." If sometimes we have difficulty understanding Catherine, it may be due to the fact that most accounts of her life dating from that era were written by men. The words attributed to her in those biographies have been run through various male filters. Raymond, for instance, prefaces his account by noting Catherine's desire to live a "life of angelical and virginal purity," and he ends her spoken vow by having her promise to "keep my virginity for ever spotless." For the remainder of his biography he refers to her matter-of-factly as "the Virgin." Such is the language of traditional piety. Catherine herself didn't see it that way. While she may, indeed, have spoken of virginity, she did not see virginity as a way of holding herself aloof. She wished to be involved with God passionately, in body and soul. If one looks at the letters she crafted, the word "virginity" appears only infrequently, while "marriage"—a word that connotes commitment and union—is far more common, and "love" and "desire" are slathered on almost every page. The passive implications of "virginity" (the word Raymond prefers) fail to capture her spirit. Her so-called vow of virginity had little to do with sexuality and everything to do with commitment. It was less a denial of sex than an affirmation of passion. Catherine wished to give herself completely to the Christ of her vision; she wanted no person or cause to come between herself and him.

This is not to say she was blind to the everyday meaning of virginity. Although only eight, she lived in an age when girls were normally married at fifteen, so marriage was a reality looming on the horizon. In some way she knew already that she could never be married. The attention required by a husband and children would, of necessity, be taken from the one who demanded everything and promised everything in return—and she could not allow that to happen. Instead she pleaded with Mary to marry her to Jesus, "the one I long for from my inmost heart . . . and I promise him and promise you that to no other spouse will I ever give myself."

The notion of being married to Jesus was not Catherine's invention. She was surely acquainted with the ancient Christian legend of her great namesake, Catherine of Alexandria, who, it was said, had been taken into heaven and there married to Jesus in the presence of his mother. That earlier Catherine was one of the most popular saints of the Middle Ages. Her statue had an honored place in many, if not most, churches. Catherine of Alexandria was a patron of the Dominican order; Siena had a convent of Dominican nuns named for her, near the Porta Laterina.

Many other women in the later Middle Ages likewise aspired to mystical marriages with Jesus. The list is long and includes Hadewijch of Brabant in Flanders, Angela of Foligno in Umbria, Birgitta of Sweden (who lived in Rome after 1350), and Margery Kempe in England, who already had a husband. Marriage to the Son of God was just one of the ways medieval women had come to relate to Jesus. For them Jesus was no longer the cool, iconic figure idealized in the first millennium. In the eleventh century people had begun to envision him as a bloody, sweating, suffering, and intensely physical Christ who invited a strong human response in return. Because the image of him had evolved, the encounter between believer and Savior likewise evolved, shifting from a bloodless act of faith in a saving Lord to a personal and often intimate union with a flesh-and-blood male. For women there were obvious erotic overtones in such a union. The concept may have borrowed some of its energy from medieval traditions of courtly love in which lovers, although chaste, felt drawn to each other passionately. Margery Kempe, for one, had visions in which she snuggled in bed with the infant Jesus and sometimes caressed his toes. Catherine's marriage with Christ, while definitely enriched by fleshly qualities, did not lapse into the erotic beyond an imagined kiss or two as she got older. She was not shy about physical metaphors; in a few years hence, for instance, she would urge another woman to "join the mouth of our holy desire with God's desire and so [be] united [with him] in peace and tranquility." Yet her images always had theological grounding—even her claim that the real wedding ring that joined Jesus and humankind was his foreskin. However bizarre this may sound to us, the circumcision of Jesus was honored in medieval times (and still is by some modern Christians) as the first shedding of his blood, so the foreskin image had more to do with Jesus's suffering than his manhood. One commentator has noted that for Catherine the body of Christ was more often female than male, in the sense that she felt called to enter into it, nurse from it, and be fed by it. We will see these images over and over in her writing.

This popular concept of being "married" to Christ gave medieval women a distinct advantage over men. While males had a higher status in society, they could never aspire to marriage with Jesus. Men's religious experience was less intimate as a consequence. Many more women than men experienced ecstatic prayer and enjoyed the divine favors, visions, and charismatic gifts associated with it. As a group, women in the Middle Ages were universally recognized as being loci for the transcendent. Compared to men, they were hardwired for the supernatural.

Catherine would work out the full meaning of her mystical marriage as she went along. Now, at an early age, she knew only that her relationship with Christ who had appeared to her in a vision must be the central focus of her life. Her days were given to drawing closer to him with the help of devotions and penances. Food played a major part in this process. The church calendar in the Middle Ages entailed a great deal of fasting—Lent and Advent, vigils, and seasonal ember days—so that children growing up were acutely sensitive to the religious significance of food. Feasting and fasting had a central place in religious practice, and food preparation was the female domain. Catherine took her fasting further than what the church demanded. She decided at this young age to give up meat entirely, slipping her portion onto Stefano's plate when her parents weren't watching.

One may believe Catherine was very young to get involved in these forms of penance. Probably she was. Yet it was not unusual in Italy during this era for young children to adopt severe penitential practices. Historians have called them "penitent children." Pious stories circulated of boys and girls aged seven and younger spending long hours in prayer and punishing their bodies, sometimes whipping themselves until bloody. There was the case of the boy Giovanni da Matera in the twelfth century who, "from the age of reason," wanted to live in solitude as a hermit and while still very young fled from his parents to an island off the southern coast of Italy. He almost died in the process. Restored to health by a celestial voice, he subsequently went to Calabria where he lived a penitential life into adulthood. Then there was Bona of Pisa, a mystic and visionary who served as a spiritual guide to a group of men in her native city. Born in 1156, Bona began to practice austerities at the age of seven. She gave up meat, fasted on bread and water three days a week, and slept in a manger of straw in imitation of the baby Jesus. A popular story related how Jesus gave her money to buy a hair shirt when Bona was only ten. There seemed to be a concentration of these penitent children, most of them girls, in Tuscany and Umbria. Gerardesca of Pisa, born shortly after Bona died, gave up "family delights," also when she was seven. As an older girl she consented to be married to please her parents, but after the ceremony persuaded her husband to enter a monastery so that she could live a life of penance. A century later pious stories circulated about Chiara of Montefalco who developed an intense prayer life when she was four and who joined a local hermitage around the age of ten. Chiara was best known for combating heresies that flourished in her day. She took part in public disputations and became renowned for her grasp of theology even though she lacked formal schooling. In her later years Chiara became a peacemaker among the Italian states, settling disputes and freeing prisoners.

Like these children, Catherine from an early age had an intense prayer life and practiced private mortifications. Her way of life also embraced charitable activities. Giacomo and Lapa, like many families in the neighborhood, looked after the poor who came begging at their door. From her parents Catherine learned the value of sharing her family's prosperity—learned it so well that, in addition to food and coins, she freely gave away her father's clothing and some of her own. The story of the miraculous wine cask may date from this period even though Raymond of Capua places it later in his narrative. According to his account, Catherine gave beggars wine taken from the family's best wine cask, rather than from its second best. The family, too, was drawing wine from the better cask. This went on for weeks and months. Puzzled that the cask should be so bountiful, the family finally opened it—and found it to be bone dry.

Catherine strove to be a dutiful child in her household chores and when running errands. One day her mother asked her to take some money to the church and request that a mass be said for a family intention. In Raymond's account she went off to the "parish church," probably Sant'Antonio Abate across the street, although it could have been San Domenico on the hill overlooking the neighborhood. Her family was going to San Domenico more frequently now that Tommaso dalla Fonte was preparing for the priesthood there. The walk to the Dominican church and back would have taken more time. Either way, Catherine returned late from her errand and Lapa laced into her, using language Catherine didn't like. According to Raymond, she stopped her mother and said, "Beat me as you think fit . . . But I beg you never . . . lose control of your own tongue as to curse anyone, good or bad. That, for you, is a thing unbecoming your venerable age, and as for me it wounds me to the heart." Catherine then explained that after requesting the mass, she remained in church while the mass was celebrated, then came straight home. Lapa listened to this in wonderment. Later she mentioned the incident to Giacomo, declaring, "Do you know what your daughter just said to me?"

Running errands was fine for a young girl, but at the age of twelve all that changed. By then girls were approaching marriageable age and weren't allowed in the streets unchaperoned. Some did their mending while sitting at a window where they could be surreptitiously inspected by young men passing by. Others primped for Sunday mass or trips to the market where they paraded with their families. For most girls it was exciting to be on display. Giacomo and Lapa, with a number of daughters, had been through the process plenty of times. Marrying off daughters was time-consuming and expensive, considering the dowries involved. Yet marriages were valuable for cementing alliances between families, so in the end they felt their money was well spent. Bonaventura and the other girls had made useful connections for the family of Giacomo. If Catherine was not the most beautiful of daughters, she was developing into a handsome young woman and would do well. Her parents probably didn't say so, but they could see that Catherine was blessed with her father's kindness and her mother's strong will.

Naturally Catherine hated the whole process. Not only hated—she feared it. She hadn't told anyone of her promise to Christ, but the time was coming when she would have to say something. She hid herself away as much as possible. If one of her father's apprentices came up from the dye shop, she would flee to another room. Her mother tried to dress her up for appearances in public, but Catherine adamantly refused to go along with it. Finally Lapa threw up her hands and asked Bonaventura to help, believing the older sister could surely talk the recalcitrant younger one into cooperating. Bonaventura spoke to Catherine in loving tones until finally she consented to wear something new. She also agreed to bleach her hair to give it the high yellow color so much admired in society. As things developed she began to relax and enjoy herself, happy to be with her big sister. It was like a game they were playing. For a period of time—a few months or even a year or more—her commitment to Jesus, while not forgotten, faded into the background.

For years afterward Catherine would blame herself for weakness during this time. When she reflected back on it she would weep and accuse herself of wickedness. Confessors would argue with her, pointing out that she had not gone back on her promise and that no harm had been caused by it. Yet Catherine would not be consoled. She did not blame herself for being "worldly" as much as blame herself for loving Bonaventura more than God. It was another instance of turning her gaze away from Christ. Sin can occur in an instant. She had allowed it to happen twice already and regretted it deeply. She told her confessors that it was her fault—hers alone!

Then something happened to change things dramatically. In the summer of 1362, when Catherine was fifteen, her sister entered into a difficult labor. History doesn't give us the details of her problem. We know only that on August 10, Bonaventura and her baby died in childbirth.

One can imagine Catherine's distress—her beloved sister dead. Did she ask herself whether death was the inevitable consequence of earthly marriage and childbirth? It's unlikely she did, since her own mother had borne so many children safely. Grimly Catherine returned to her penances, grieving for her sister and for her own momentary softening of purpose. Around this time she began to compare herself to Mary Magdalen, who was redeemed by Jesus from an alleged life of sin. There was a popular medieval legend that Mary Magdalen came to Toulon in France after the resurrection of Jesus, where she lived and fasted in solitude for thirty-three years. For Catherine, Magdalen seemed like a suitable saint on which to model her own life.

While Catherine was grieving, her family was trying to move on. Giacomo and Lapa had lost a daughter, but they still had three unmarried girls—Lisa, Catherine, and Giovanna. One would expect their attention would turn next to Lisa, but that didn't happen. Perhaps there was a reason why Lisa could not marry. Instead, talk continued to center on Catherine. Raymond of Capua and other contemporary sources don't mention prospective bridegrooms by name, but more recent speculation suggests that she was being matched with Bonaventura's widowed husband, Niccolò de Giovanni Tegliacci. Any husband at all would have worried Catherine, but Niccolò especially so. In the early years of his marriage to Bonaventura Niccolò's use of coarse language had greatly distressed his wife. Catherine may have feared that she was being pushed into a sinner's bed.

Whether or not Niccolò was the prospective husband, Catherine knew she had to do something. According to Raymond of Capua she sought counsel from Tommaso dalla Fonte who was now a priest. Catherine knew Tommaso would respect her vow to Christ. Another account suggests

Catherine's meeting with Tommaso was arranged by the family. Whichever way it happened, she sat down with him and opened her heart for the first time. She told him about the vision of Christ in the sky, about her vow, and the difficulty she faced at home. Tommaso listened gravely. Together they considered her options. Finally Tommaso offered a suggestion. He reminded her of her childhood nickname, Euphrosyne, one of the mythical Graces. But there had also been a saint by that name in long-ago Christian Egypt. According to legend, when St. Euphrosyne's wealthy father arranged a marriage for her, she secretly chopped off her hair, dressed in the clothing of a young man, and ran off to become a monk. Tommaso suggested that Catherine, too, could cut her long hair that was the mark and the treasure of an unmarried girl. Catherine immediately went home, took some shears (readily available in the dye shop) and cut her hair down to a stubble. She put a white veil over her head to hide the result, and waited.

It didn't take long. Soon enough, Lapa asked Catherine why she persisted in wearing a veil and snatched it off her head. Seeing the ruin of her daughter's hair, Lapa screamed, the family came running, and a general *tumulto* ensued. Catherine was assailed by her parents who demanded to know how she could do such a thing. Even her brothers joined in. After all, their sister's marriage offered them the possibility of an alliance with yet another influential family. Their future and the future of the family business could depend on it. It was not up to Catherine, they argued, to make such a decision by herself.

How long this went on is not clear. It could have been hours, days, or even weeks. Through it all, Catherine tried to remain unperturbed, probably not without moments of private satisfaction. One would expect the family's unhappiness reached the ears of Tommaso, since he was one of the family as well as being Catherine's mentor. While bound by the confidentiality of the confessional, Tommaso probably blunted the family's anger by refusing to join in their condemnation.

Still, the resentment was deep and tangible. Lapa let it be known that Catherine's mangled hair signified nothing in the long run; once it had grown back they would still arrange for her marriage. To underscore this, they continued to look for suitable husbands. While that was going on, Lapa also proclaimed that Catherine would live among them as a servant girl, without a room of her own, and obliged to do all the dirty work in the kitchen. Catherine set out to do this without complaint, cheerfully even, enduring the bitter looks of her mother and the barbed comments of her brothers. When asked later how she got through this difficult time, Catherine said she used to imagine she was employed at the house of the Holy Family in Bethlehem—that Giacomo and Lapa were Joseph and Mary, parents of her future husband, Jesus. In addition, she said, now that she was denied a private place to pray she tried to find a place inside herself that no one could take from her. It was the hard-won fruit of months and years of solitary prayer. Raymond of Capua would recall years later that when he complained to her of being burdened by duties and obligations, Catherine would tell him, "Build yourself a cell within your heart, and never put a foot outside it."

Once the deed was done and digested, her willing demeanor around the house took the edge from their complaining. Hostile comments were replaced first by dark looks, and then by grudging acceptance. She was proving that she was stronger than they. Her father noticed it first. He happened to see Catherine in an unguarded moment, obviously praying. The stillness of her posture and her rapt attention stopped him. In pious accounts it was said later that Giacomo beheld a white dove hovering over her head. He didn't need the dove, however. He knew what he was seeing. He reflected on it thoughtfully.

Catherine must have sensed that her family's feelings toward her were softening and concluded that it was time for her to speak up. As Raymond of Capua tells it, she gathered them together and gave a speech explaining her motivations and intentions. Whether these are her precise words we'll never know; they rather sound like Raymond has worked them over. Yet there is a forceful ring to the speech that is pure Catherine:

"It is now a long time since you first took counsel, and began negotiations, as you said, to have me married off as the bride of some mere mortal man. The very thought of this filled me with loathing, as I made plain to you in many silent ways, whose meaning, however was unmistakable. But God has commanded us to honor our father and mother, and for the reverence due to them I have never bluntly spoken out my mind until now. But the time has come when I can be silent no longer. I will lay bare my heart to you and say out plain and straight what I am resolved to do. It is no new-found purpose that I speak of, but one that has been clearly known to me, and firmly willed, from childhood.

"Already, when I was a child in years I made a vow of virginity, not, however, in the way a child would do, but after long consideration and acting on solid grounds. I made this vow to my Lord and Savior Jesus Christ, and to his glorious mother. I promised them that never would I take another spouse but him alone. And now in course of time, as the Lord himself had willed it, I have arrived at mature age and mature knowledge. Take notice, then, that my resolution is so firm in this regard that it would be easier to soften the very rock than to move my heart a hairsbreadth from its holy purpose. The more you try to do so, the more you will discover that you are only wasting your time. Be advised by me, and put a stop once and for all to any matchmaking in my regard. This is a matter in which I have not the slightest intention of yielding to your will. I must obey God rather than man. If you are willing to keep me in your house on this condition—even as a servant-maid if you so desire—I for my part am willing to serve you with pleasure, to the best of my knowledge and ability. But if you decide that I must, because of my resolve, be banished from your home, then rest assured that my heart will not deviate one jot from its resolution. I have a spouse of boundless wealth and power who will never let me lack for anything, but will unfailingly supply my every need."

At the end of this, it was said, several in her family were weeping. They must also have been struck by wonder. Here was Catherine, their daughter, their little sister, making an adamant statement of independence. It would have been unusual for a male child to make such a declaration to his parents in the fourteenth century. For a female child it was almost unheard of. Young women, in a sense, were family possessions, to be married off in a manner that served the family good. Girls were generally more obliging to their parents than boys. Literature from the period suggests that daughters aspiring to religious life met more parental opposition than did sons seeking to be priests. A woman entering a convent had to bring a dowry with her and did not gain the prestige of office associated with the priesthood. In Catherine's case her family could not even rejoice in her connection with a prestigious convent. They were being asked simply to bow before her inner conviction.

Giacomo found his voice first. As the head of the family it was his authority that was being challenged. It speaks well of the man that in that moment he announced he would accept Catherine's vow. Indeed, he urged her to be faithful to it, promising that the family would give up its attempts to arrange a marriage for her. Then he instructed the family to leave her to her prayers and to the husband she wished to serve.

And so Catherine prevailed. From that moment on she was restored to her family's good favor. One suspects, too, that from that moment her parents and siblings began to look at her with a degree of awe. She was standing among them now with her inner life revealed, or at least partially revealed. They began to realize that while she was still their daughter, their sister, she was also someone who had already gone beyond the family in ways they could not yet grasp. As time went on that sense of awe in connection with Catherine would spread beyond her family, then beyond Siena, then beyond Tuscany. Stories began to coalesce around her—of the vision in the sky, the white dove over her head—and people passing her on the street would look twice, three times. She was beginning to be seen as someone special.

But most of that was still in the future. For now Catherine was considering a way to ratify her inner commitment through a further alliance. She had fallen in love with the idea of becoming a Dominican, the religious order of men and women founded by the Spaniard Dominic de Guzmán in the early thirteenth century. She used to watch Dominican friars pass her house dressed in their dramatic black and white habits; on one occasion, she ran outside after they were gone to kiss the stones touched by their sandals. To a girl of Catherine's age, the Dominicans had romantic cachet and other attractions as well. They were an alternative family in the service of God—which must have seemed a much grander calling than her own family of dyers. They were the Order of Preachers, dedicated to teaching and proclaiming the word of God, a mission that required moving about in the world. As such, they must have evoked images of freedom from the expectations of her family.

It would have been natural to discuss these feelings with Tommaso, since he was a Dominican. He most likely asked whether she wanted to be a nun. Catherine, who as a young girl liked to wander all over the neighborhood, may have shuddered at the prospect of being cloistered—as all nuns of that era were. A century earlier Clare of Assisi had hoped to become a wandering mendicant like her cousin Francis, but church authorities found it inappropriate for a woman to be loose in the world and so forced her into a convent. Catherine did not want to be trapped like that. Luckily for women in her time there was another option: she could become a tertiary, a third-order member of a religious community who was not under vows, not cloistered or even living in community, but who wore a religious habit and who could find nurture within a supportive group of women. Both the

Franciscans and the Dominicans had male and female tertiaries. In Siena the Dominican women were called *Mantellate* for the large black mantles they wore as outer garments.

Catherine thought about this. She knew of the Mantellate. She had seen them on the streets. Her aunt Agnes was a Mantellata. But that raised another issue—all of the Mantellate she knew were widows, or at least married women, and she was an unmarried young woman of fifteen or sixteen. Tommaso acknowledged that the Sienese Mantellate were mostly widows, but he thought Catherine's admittance might not pose an insurmountable problem. They would pray over it.

The Mantellate of Siena were just one small part of a great movement that brought new groups and classes of laypeople into religious life during the late Middle Ages. The evolution of cities and the development of the middle class had opened new fields of ministry for a church that until then had been organized along feudal and predominantly rural models. Traditional forms of religious life had stressed the value of stability—the monk being bound to his monastery and the canon to his cathedral. However, the thirteenth century had witnessed the emergence of mendicant friars who moved from town to town preaching, teaching, and witnessing to a simple way of life. The Dominicans and the Franciscans (founded by Francis of Assisi) represented flexible responses to the needs of the day. In addition, they tended to draw their members less from the aristocracy, as the great monasteries did, than from the tradesmen and lower nobility residing in towns and cities.

In northern Europe another new phenomenon had arisen—informal groups of independent women called Beguines who lived quasi-religious lives, either as individuals or together in common dwellings. Beguines existed outside the authority of churchmen who, for that reason, grew suspicious of the movement and accused some women of heresy. The French Beguine Marguerite Porete was burned at the stake in Paris in 1310. Beguines had no official rule of life, nor were they bound by irrevocable vows. Their communities usually consisted of widows or unmarried women, some of whom did not have the dowries to marry or enter convents. Their alliances with other women provided them with social and spiritual support and directed them into human services such as nursing or teaching. Thus new and creative opportunities of ministry were opened to women who enjoyed a way of life that combined active and contemplative elements. Beguine communities proliferated in the Rhineland and the Low Countries; it is estimated that in 1320, 15 percent of the adult female women in Cologne lived as Beguines.

In Italy the movement took a slightly different form. Men and women could become friars or nuns in one of the mendicant orders, or choose the path of a tertiary. Female tertiaries were called *pinzochere* (penitent women), and their prayers and charitable works were accepted as contributions to the church's great work of redemption. In Catherine's time each group of tertiaries or penitents was independent and free to frame its own association. Like the Beguines of northern Europe, the penitents of Italy represented something new, never before seen in the church. They were ordinary believers who preferred to remain that way, women and men who lived an apostolic life in a manner that placed them midway between the monastic and the lay state. In future years the church would spare no effort to bring these informal lay groups back under ecclesiastical control. Many Beguine groups were suppressed by church edict. Dominican tertiaries eventually were gathered into formal religious communities and placed under vows of obedience. However, Catherine's era was a window in time when Beguines and penitents operated quite freely.

There is some question as to when Catherine first became interested in the Mantellate. According to Raymond of Capua she was already thinking about it *before* the frank meeting with her family. He recounts a dream in which St. Dominic appeared to her, holding in his hands the habit worn by the tertiaries and saying, "Dearest daughter, be of good courage; do not lose heart, no matter what the odds against you. Be assured that you will one day wear this habit which you long for." Raymond says the dream encouraged Catherine, but when she mentioned her desire to Lapa much later, her mother opposed it, believing she was too young. Besides, Lapa reminded her, the Mantellate were widows.

The dating and sequence of all these events—the dream of St. Dominic, the haircutting, the confrontation with the family—are points of debate among scholars. For one event, however, we know the date with certainty: on April 18, 1363, Catherine's younger sister, Giovanna, died at the age of fourteen. The cause of death is not recorded. In his biography, Raymond of Capua does not even mention Giovanna's passing. For Catherine and her mother, however, it must have been an event of real sadness that bound the two women more closely together. The struggles and disagreements they had over the years faded in the face of this new tragedy. Once more Catherine was the youngest in the family and her mother's dearest child.

Their renewed closeness was immediately put to a test. As the fruit of her reconciliation with her family, Catherine had been given a small room of her own in the family home, and there she began to practice austerities with renewed—even shocking—energy. She had already reduced her food intake. Now she arranged a few boards just off the floor to serve as her bed, with a stone as her pillow. She had acquired a hair shirt—a garment of legendary discomfort—that she wore next to her skin. Not completely satisfied by that, she obtained a thin chain that she wrapped around her body so that it chafed her waist and left it raw. For years she had already practiced self-flagellation. Where previously she used a rope, now she turned to an iron chain. Much later she told Raymond that she would whip herself with the chain for ninety minutes at a time, at the end of which there would be blood on her back and running down her legs. Hearing the sound of the chain, Lapa would stand outside the door crying out and pleading for her daughter to stop. Even the neighbors heard the commotion.

Catherine's sleeping habits were another issue between them. Not only did she sleep on wooden boards, she spent much of the night awake and in prayer. When Lapa found this out, she dragged Catherine into her own bed. Outwardly compliant, Catherine would wait until her mother was asleep, then slip out and go back to her own small room. Her mother berated her for it afterward, so Catherine changed her tactics: she placed some boards under the sheets in her mother's bed so she could sleep the way she wanted. At last, discovering the boards, Lapa resigned herself to the inevitable. She admitted that it was a waste of time trying to change her daughter, so she sent Catherine back to her room to sleep in whatever way she wanted.

Yet Lapa worried. Perhaps if she could get Catherine away from the house the fearful austerities might diminish in intensity. She proposed a trip to the famous hot springs in Vignoni (today's Bagno Vignoni), about thirty miles south of Siena in the Orcia Valley. Surprisingly, Catherine had no objection, so the two of them set off on the road. When they arrived, and as Lapa prepared to enter the hot, natural pool, Catherine announced she would find her own bathing spot and went off by herself. This incident may have prompted the later charge that Catherine practiced "pious abstinence" when it came to bathing. If so, the charge has scant foundation. Several persons testified that Catherine was most particular about keeping clean. In this case she might have preferred privacy in order to hide the lash marks on her body. And there was another reason: Lapa found her later soaking in the hottest pool, her body red from the scalding, sulfurous water. Years later Lapa related the incident to Raymond in Catherine's presence. When Raymond asked Catherine how she had endured the steaming water, she replied "with dovelike simplicity" that she had contemplated the fires of hell in the pool and begged God to accept this earthly pain as payment for her sins.

Back home from Vignoni, Catherine began to pester her mother once more about arranging her admission into the Mantellate. Lapa resisted, but when the entreaties continued she finally relented and agreed to visit the prioress of the convent at San Domenico, the church where the penitential women held their regular meetings. She explained to the prioress her daughter's avid desire to be a Mantellata, but all of Lapa's pleading came to naught. The prioress responded firmly that the Mantellate never accepted maidens, either old ones or young ones, but only "widows of mature age and unblemished reputation." Such precautions were necessary, she said, because Mantellate did not live in a convent but at home where they were subject to the temptations of society. It was essential, she said, that members be persons of "utmost respectability."

Catherine was disappointed when this news was relayed to her, but not crushed. After all, she believed her invitation to join the Mantellate had come from St. Dominic himself. She renewed her prayers to God and, as the days passed, continued to implore her mother to do something about it. According to Raymond, Lapa tried a second time, perhaps this time with Aunt Agnes in tow to give her appeal added weight. The answer of the prioress, however, was the same: there was no way Catherine could be accepted as a Mantellata.

At this critical moment Catherine became ill, her face covered with "pimples." Raymond speculates that it was an ailment brought on by the burning waters of Vignoni, but in the same breath he says it was an illness "which often attacks young people," so most likely it was chicken pox. Whatever the cause, Catherine was feverish and sick. Lapa hovered over her, wanting to help in some way. Seizing the moral advantage that all sick people enjoy, Catherine said to her, "If you want me . . . to get well and strong, you must satisfy my longing for the habit of the Sisters of Penance of St. Dominic." If not that, she added, it might be the death shroud.

Off went her mother to the prioress, this time with fire in her eyes! Lapa di Puccio di Piagenti was not a woman to be trifled with when the health of her chosen one was at stake. This time she explained more forcefully her daughter's determination to give herself to Christ and about the illness that, even as they spoke, was threatening her life.

The prioress listened to the outburst thoughtfully. At the end, she asked, "Is she pretty or attractive? In light of her great enthusiasm—and yours—perhaps we could accept her. But if she is very pretty, then there could be a scandal—people being what they are—in which case, we could not give our consent."

"Come and see for yourself," Lapa suggested.

A few Dominican sisters respected for their good judgment accompanied Lapa back to Via dei Tintori. They found Catherine in bed, her face covered with pox. She was magnificently unattractive. Next the sisters questioned her about her desires. As she responded to their questions they at first were charmed, then edified, then profoundly impressed. Nodding to each other, they went back to report to the prioress.

A few days passed while the application was being considered. The process required the consent of the prioress and of other Mantellate as well. With these at last secured, Catherine received the joyful news that she had been accepted.

History has not recorded the date of her clothing ceremony. It was on a Sunday, most likely in late 1364 or early 1365. Catherine was joined by her Mantellate sisters in the delle Volte Chapel of San Domenico Church, almost certainly with her family and Tommaso dalla Fonte in attendance. The garments were blessed with prayers and holy water. With Catherine kneeling on the bottom step of the altar, the assembled community sang *Veni Sancti Spiritus*. Then the other Mantellate helped her don her clothing: first the white wool tunic cinched with a belt and a long white scapular over it. A wimple was wrapped under her chin and then over her head, covering the brow. That was topped by a white veil. Over her shoulders was placed the voluminous black mantle that was the mark and pride of her sisterhood.

It was hers now. Catherine would wear the Dominican habit for the rest of her life.

3

THE ROOM

When Catherine was given the freedom to pursue a life of prayer, she also received from her parents, as mentioned, a small room for herself in the house on Via dei Tintori. At last she had what she longed for—a place of solitude and silence where she could grow closer to God. For a middle-class family in the fourteenth century, when privacy did not have the same value it has today, a room of one's own was a great luxury. In large families girls shared bedrooms and often the same bed. Adult women spent every minute of their day at work in the public gaze, preparing food, shopping, minding children, doing laundry, cleaning, and, when they had a quiet moment, making and mending clothes. There is little wonder that some felt called to be anchorites, living behind closed doors. In such places they could be autonomous and insulated against male authority. The later Middle Ages were remarkable for the number of female anchorites, such as Julian of Norwich in fourteenth-century England, whose solitude gave them space to discover their uniqueness and reflect on their connection to a male divinity.

Space was limited at the family house because Catherine's two oldest brothers also lived in the house, along with their wives and children. But by shifting things around a place was found for her—a small room on the middle floor under the stairs that led up to the kitchen. It was a space of only about nine by five feet and had but a single small window facing out onto Vicolo del Tiratoio, where across the street was the little church of Sant'Antonio Abate—St. Anthony of the Desert, the patron of solitary ascetics. Catherine's furniture consisted of one trunk and her bed of boards that also served as a bench and, when she needed one, a table. On the wall she hung a crucifix and pictures of saints. There was nothing else. In this place Catherine would spend the most important formative period of her life—a time of roughly three years in the 1360s during which she slowly came to understand herself and her calling.

To most of us today the space would seem constricted, even claustrophobic. For Catherine it was room enough to grow in, a place where her focus could be concentrated, without distractions. It was all she needed. She had moments when, alone there, the walls fell away and she found herself in a land where time ceased to exist and where Jesus and the saints would visit her and talk. In Siena today one can still go to the house—now called Casa di Santa Caterina—and peer into (but not enter) the room where Catherine prayed and struggled with herself out of a desire to live totally for God.

Tommaso dalla Fonte stated that once Catherine moved into her room—probably even before her acceptance as a Mantellata—she never left it except to attend mass each morning at San Domenico and never spoke to anyone besides him during confession. His statement cannot be true, however, because we know that other male Dominicans entered her room, invited there by Tommaso, and spoke with her. By virtue of attending mass with them she also became friendly with other Mantellate. Some of these, too, visited her room where they would weave garlands of flowers and discuss spiritual subjects. Finally, a certain amount of conversation was required to maintain living arrangements in the house. Catherine could neither read nor write at this time in her life; she had to communicate by speaking. She did not eat with the family but she had to fix her food in the kitchen and carry it downstairs, and while she was out of her room there were nieces and nephews running through the house who could not be avoided. Finally, we know that in the evening she liked to walk in the garden attached to the kitchen. No doubt she strove to maintain her prayerful composure on these occasions, and no doubt the family strove to respect it, yet her commitment to enclosure was surely more elastic than Tommaso described it.

There is purpose in solitude. Catherine still harbored a powerful desire to grow nearer to the one who had blessed her. This was difficult to do with other people around but easier when sitting behind closed doors. It is astonishing what rises up in the consciousness if one sits long enough in a quiet, swept-out place. Dark spirits as well as friendly ones emerge, and not infrequently dark spirits disguised as friendly ones. Discerning the difference between them is not always easy. There are inevitable temptations for people seeking enlightenment to fashion a message of their own and then hail it as a revelation from God. The only way to avoid this kind of self-deception is to chip away slowly at the calcified human ego so that one waits, not merely in silence, but humbly in silence, indifferent to the outcome. Catherine had won a struggle with her family by being more willful and determined than they. Now, in solitude, her very strength became a weakness. For her to approach her beloved, willfulness was an impediment. The process required nothing less than warfare against herself. Her years as a recluse were the very opposite of leisure time; they were hard, hard work.

Tommaso di Antonio Caffarini, a Dominican friar who became friends with Catherine and who later prepared documents for her canonization, related a vision she described to him around this time. She saw a tree with large and delicious fruit whose base was surrounded by a hedge of spiny thorns. In her vision many people came to the tree and tried to reach it, but, seeing the thorns, settled instead for unwholesome grain growing nearby. Others managed to get through the hedge but when they got to the tree found the fruit out of reach and the trunk too smooth to climb. They, too, went away. A third group fought through the hedge, and managed to climb the tree. These alone endured to enjoy the fruit of the tree. This vision suggests that Catherine was fully aware, even in the beginning, that her way to fulfillment would be painful, requiring courage and perseverance.

As a hermit Catherine was committed to a life of penance and struggle. The Mantellate were supposed to be penitential women. They accepted suffering as a vocation—not in a masochistic way but as a means of uniting themselves with a savior who made suffering purposeful. It was a woman's work. Males, who had the social tasks of teaching and governing, were identified in the popular mind with the divinity of Christ, whereas females, who menstruated, bore children, and produced milk, more closely represented his humanity. They identified with the godhead through their bodies. To us, many centuries later, it is essential to keep this social context in mind. Catherine beat her body with a metal chain, deprived herself of sleep and food, and shunned normal human contact—all of which may seem bizarre, self-indulgent, and possibly unbalanced today. Medieval people, and Catherine in particular, did not see it that way. They believed that voluntary suffering had a wider context. Suffering was a way to restore peace to humankind.

If sin can invade the body of society, then so can virtue. Since the time of Francis of Assisi in the thirteenth century, the notion of freely accepted suffering, in the words of one commentator, "bore the mark of exquisite social concern." Such suffering was no longer the price of human sinfulness. Suffering embraced was the provenance of love.

Catherine did not come to her most mature understanding of the penitential life until she was older. By then she had given up the zestful pursuit of suffering to focus on its inner significance. In her *Dialogue* (*Dialogo*), written when she was about thirty-one, she acknowledged that physical penances done simply for their own sake breed pride. Rather than disciplining the body, one needs to discipline the will. The mature Catherine put her teaching in the voice of God: "There are two sorts of perfect souls [God declares] . . . The first are those who give themselves perfectly to punishing their bodies by performing severe and enormous penances . . . These have all set their object more in mortifying their bodies than in slaying their selfish wills. They feed at the table of penance, and they are good and perfect if their penance has its root in me and is guided by the light of discernment. In other words, they must truly know themselves and me, be very humble, and be wholly subject to the judgment of my will rather than to those of other people. But if they are not thus truly and humbly clothed in my will, they may often sin against their very perfection by setting themselves up as judges over those whose way is not the same as theirs."

Catherine was not completely free from Augustinian dualism that saw the "world" and heaven in violent opposition. The belief that the spirit warred endlessly with the flesh was too ingrained in the medieval temperament for her to avoid it. She once referred to the human body as a "dung heap" and always believed that fleshly desires obstructed spiritual progress. What saved her and other medieval Christians from becoming body-hating, world-hating spiritualists was reliance on the saving presence of Christ's body freely shared with his followers—on the cross and in the eucharist. Indeed, as the believer progressed in the way to God, his or her body merged with the body of Christ. As we will see, Catherine herself had a mystical experience in which it seemed that she and Christ exchanged hearts. One of her fondest images was the body of Christ whose wounds offer access to humans. One enters his body by the wounds of the feet and moves upward, as though on a staircase. Once inside, the seeker becomes immersed in Christ, ascending all the time and at last reaching the center of

Christ's being where the seeker's own body and disordered will disappears, being wholly absorbed into God. Compared to Augustine, medieval people saw corporality as a good thing: Christ's body was the venue of salvation, and human bodies were a means for encountering him.

Catherine frequently spoke of having "holy hatred" for oneself, but this was not hatred for the flesh as such. The phrase signified the dissatisfaction that properly arises from placing one's ego ahead of God. As she would write to one of her disciples years later, "I long to see you with perfect light and with discernment . . . But you cannot have this light perfectly unless you use hatred to rid yourself of the cloud of self-centeredness. Try first earnestly, then, to let go of yourself so that you may gain the light. Let your own view of things be entirely submerged in the will of God."

Catherine was given to extreme figures of speech such as "dung heap" and "holy hatred" because she had set herself upon a radical path with the goal of being "entirely submerged" in divinity. She was determined to rid herself of self-centeredness. Once she was in her small room, she set out to do it in a systematic way.

The Mantellate rule of life prescribed spiritual practices that were supposed to carry its members along a path to God. Received at the same time as the habit, the rule of the sisterhood described how members would be selected, the times of coming together, the manner of their prayer, and the charitable services they would perform. Basically the rule required them to stay close to home, avoid "worldly celebrations and useless shows," pray the canonical hours, attend worship services together, and visit the sick or poor in hospitals or at home. It was a detailed program and more than enough for most persons. It soon became clear, however, that Catherine had no intention of following parts of it—which must have come as a surprise to the other tertiaries. For one thing, because she was living as a recluse she could not undertake charitable work in the city. Later, when she did leave her confinement, she went about town by herself in direct violation of the rule and also mixed freely with men.

One may wonder why Catherine sought admission to the penitential society if she didn't plan to follow its regimen in every particular. The age she lived in explains part of it. Society in her era was highly stratified and required everyone to have a place. The Mantellate served in a middle ground—not quite nuns, not quite married women—yet provided her with a recognizable and accepted status. It has also been suggested that her profession was less a commitment to a specific way of life than a means of securing victory over her family, putting her beyond their reach—unmarried but honorable. For Catherine it suited her needs. Although she didn't follow the rule in every respect, she was extremely devoted to the Dominicans. She loved her habit, relished the company of her sisters, and had a great attachment to St. Dominic, the order's founder.

In adopting a way of life that was different from other Mantellate, she depended on the support of influential friars at San Domenico. First Tommaso dalla Fonte and then others became her ardent defenders. She needed defense, since not all of the friars at the church held her in high esteem. A few of the older friars and some of the nuns at the convent were critical of her behavior. One of the things that annoyed them was her habit of bursting into tears when she received communion at mass—not discreet little tears but loud sobbing. After communion she would often lie on the floor in an ecstatic swoon. Some unfriendly friars were so annoyed by it that they "accidentally" kicked her as they passed by. In response to Tommaso's plea to get a handle on her emotions, Catherine said she couldn't help it—after she received communion, overwhelming feelings of gratitude and love cascaded over her. She entered into God as naturally as a fish enters water and was unable to control her reactions. A few priests even refused to give her communion because they didn't like what followed. On one occasion when she was denied, it seemed to her that Jesus approached her as she knelt by herself and let her drink from his wounded side as a baby would drink from her mother's breast. If the story sounds odd to us, it was not unique to Catherine. Similar legends circulated about other women in the late Middle Ages receiving "miraculous" communion. This was an era when the practice of frequent communion was in decline. Since the late thirteenth century laypeople had been forbidden to drink from the chalice of consecrated wine. Suddenly stricken with feelings of unworthiness, believers everywhere partook of the consecrated bread less frequently. They seemed content merely to gaze at a host as it was lifted up by the priest at mass. Some of the more misogynist preachers discouraged daily reception of the eucharist by women. Miraculous accounts such as Catherine's suggested that when male clerics denied women communion, God himself would intervene to ensure they were fed.

On another occasion at San Domenico, Catherine had been instructed by Tommaso to stay at the back of the assembly and not approach the altar at communion time because her presence annoyed the priest presiding. Years later in *The Dialogue* she described what happened. "When the priest came to break the host for his own communion . . . a tiny piece fell off. By [God's] permission and power this tiny bit of host left the altar and went [i.e., flew] to the other end of the church where [I] was standing." There she received communion.

After communion Catherine would often fall into an ecstatic state, sometimes for lengthy periods. She would lose all sense of where she was. Her skin would turn pale. Her arms and legs would become rigid. Frequently mass would end and other worshipers would get up and depart, leaving Catherine in the shadow of a pillar, rigid and unseeing. The lay brother waiting to lock up the church would come by, jangling his keys as a hint to leave. On one occasion, two lay brothers, after calling into her ears and pinching her arms in an unsuccessful effort to wake her, picked her up and deposited her outside the front door of San Domenico. She came to her senses lying on the ground in the noon sunlight.

In addition to attending mass at San Domenico, Mantellate were required to pray the canonical hours at set times during the day. Since many of them couldn't read, the rule permitted the women to recite a certain number of *Paters* and *Aves* in place of the Latin psalms. Catherine wanted to fulfill the rule but she quickly grew tired of the repetition. Her personal style of prayer tended to be free-form and meditative; she found rote prayers tedious. She dearly wished she could read the psalter and pray the hours as the friars did. This desire eventually brought her into contact with another Mantellata, Alessa dei Saracini, who, as the daughter of one of Siena's noble families, had been educated and could read. Catherine may have seen Alessa with a prayerbook in San Domenico's delle Volte Chapel and perhaps voiced her own longing to be able to read the sacred texts. Alessa, a cheerful, heavyset widow, volunteered to teach her. For weeks or even months afterward she came to Catherine's room and took her through the alphabet, then introduced her to simple words. Catherine found it very frustrating. Her intuitive nature rebelled against learning letters; she wanted to read the *psalms*! So Alessa chose a book and together they began going through it—Alessa pointing to the words and sounding them out. Suddenly, it seemed, Catherine was reading, slowly at first, and often in need of help, but she was reading. In his biography of Catherine, Raymond of Capua made it sound miraculous. As he told the story, Catherine prayed and was "taught by God himself. She rose up, and could ever after read any written words with the speed and accuracy of the most accomplished scholar." Surely he overstated the case. Catherine never did learn to spell and could not write until years later, probably with others spelling out the words for her. While she may have been able to recognize some Latin words, most likely she never actually read either the Latin psalter or the Latin bible; those parts of them she knew (and they were many) were committed to memory from repeated hearings at worship services. It is quite certain she never learned conversational Latin because translators were needed during her visits to the Holy See where business was conducted in that language. Her reading abilities were probably limited to her native Tuscan, the language she used for her letters and *The Dialogue*. There is evidence she read the devotional works of Domenico Cavalca (1270–1342), written in Tuscan, since lengthy fragments from his works appear in her own writing.

These years of seclusion, which fed Catherine spiritually, were also instrumental in her intellectual development. Reading and reflecting on the texts proclaimed during services opened new doors for her. She was particularly drawn to the epistles of Paul and the central place he gave in his writings to Christ, her mystical groom. She also reveled in Paul's role as an apostle, preaching the word to unbelievers. As time went on, she saw herself more and more following in Paul's footsteps.

Two other teachers supported her intellectual development during this period. One was the Dominican already mentioned, Tommaso di Antonio Caffarini, a colleague of Tommaso dalla Fonte at San Domenico friary. Caffarini became acquainted with Catherine even before she took the habit and was closely associated with her for the rest of her life. After her death he played a major role in promoting her canonization. More important still was another Dominican, Bartolomeo Dominici, a novitiate classmate of Tommaso dalla Fonte and only four years older than Catherine herself. People warmed easily to Fra Bartolomeo, who had a gentle manner and a speech impediment, probably a stutter. Unlike dalla Fonte, who was not gifted intellectually, Dominici was a scholar. After ordination he had gone on for further studies, so he didn't meet Catherine until 1367 or 1368, around the end of her time in solitude.

For Dominici their encounter was exhilarating in a platonic way. "When first I began to visit her," he recalled, "she was young and her countenance was always serene and joyful. I was also young; yet far from experiencing in her presence the embarrassment which I might have felt in the company of other women of her age, the longer I conversed with her, the more utterly were all earthly passions extinguished in my breast. I have known many—both laity and religious—who experienced the same thing; there was something in her whole appearance so redolent of purity as to be far more angelic than human."

Dominici brought Catherine friendship, learning, and books. He also planted in her a desire for social reform—a passion she also inherited from her politically active brothers. Dominici was deeply involved in a movement to reform the Dominican order and would talk to her about the need for religious communities—and the entire church—to return to the purity of ancient traditions. Through him and Tommaso Caffarini, Catherine, although unschooled in a formal way, began to develop theological sensitivity that came to flower later in her letters and her mature writing.

While during this period she attended church and made a few friends, most of Catherine's time was still spent in solitude, shut away in her small room. She kept her own schedule, reading or just sitting before her crucifix. She tried to stay hidden during the daylight hours when the rest of her family was about, leaving her room at night, when they were in bed, to fix herself a few bites of food or to walk in the kitchen garden under the night sky. She liked to think of the starry heavens as God's own garment. As she put it, "The garment of yours is covered with stars, all the different virtues, for we can have no patience without the stars of all the virtues along with the night of self-knowledge, which is a sort of moonlight." The words were written years later yet sum up the objectives of her shut-in years. In her understanding, self-knowledge was something more than just psychological insight. It was a matter of knowing oneself in the eyes of God, as a creature, as fallen and redeemed. It was knowing one's place. The medieval mind was absorbed by the need for order and strove to understand human existence as part of a larger and more elaborate pattern. It focused less on the individual person than on that person in relationship to others. Being oriented to God allowed one to move ahead confidently. As Catherine explained it in a letter some years later, "You know that a person who walks with a lamp at night doesn't stumble. Souls who have God as their lamp cannot stumble either. They open the eye of their understanding and reason to see which road this gentle Master took. And once they have seen it, because of their will and desire to follow their Master, they run attentively and eagerly. They don't stop to look back—at themselves, I mean. They see themselves well enough where knowledge of their sins and failings is concerned, and admit of themselves that they are nothing. And at the same time, they recognize in themselves the immeasurable goodness of God, who has given them whatever being they have."

Catherine struggled to understand her place in this pattern early in her years of solitude. Raymond of Capua tells us of an interior dialogue she had with God, during which God told her, "You are she who is not, and I am he who is." It was a foundational theological insight. From sermons at San Domenico, she was probably familiar with the description of God proposed by the Dominican Thomas Aquinas a century earlier: God is Pure Being—God simply Is. All the rest of creation takes its being from God but does not possess being in the same way God does. Everything and everyone else "is not" until God intervenes. The unenlightened do not recognize their dependency. Like infants, they imagine themselves at the center of the universe. Those who carry this illusion into adulthood and through life are actually claiming Godlike status for themselves, worshipping at their own altar, a juggling act that no human can sustain forever (although at some point everyone tries). This fundamental orientation to God and the human unwillingness to acknowledge it lay at the heart of what Catherine meant by self-knowledge. *She* knew her place. She would need that knowledge in years to come when she became a celebrity—when people gawked at her in the street as though she were some kind of living saint or when disciples bent down to kiss her hand. She allowed such things to go on but she claimed she paid them no mind, and probably didn't.

There were days in her hermitage at home when she really struggled. There were times when the walls seemed to close in and the room was filled with buzzing, as though with a swarm of insects. Then she would flee from her room to San Domenico to escape her demons, yet as often as not when she returned to her room the buzzing was still there. There were nights when she would pray for strength against temptations and the prayer was dry as dust—just words in her mouth, with not a drop of consolation in them. On those nights her fertile imagination was visited by handsome young men who beckoned her to stroll with them outside the city walls where they could be alone. All sorts of images flashed through her head. She understood that this sort of thing happens in solitude. Yet that didn't make it any easier. At last, if the lash applied to her back didn't help, she would pray, even to the point of welcoming the challenge, saying, "It is no hardship for me, but rather a delight, to endure for my Savior's name all you have been inflicting on me."

One night when she prayed in that manner the demons that pursued her were stilled. Then it seemed that Christ called down to her from the bloody crucifix on the wall: "My daughter Catherine, look at what I have suffered for your sake. Do not take it hard then, when you too must suffer for my sake."

On that night the room was at peace and Catherine rested in it happily. It was the first time in a vision that she had been called by name.

Nights were the hardest time. Catherine slept very little. She claimed she was able to reduce her sleeping time to one half hour every two days. Perhaps she believed that was the case, but it's unlikely she slept that little. Often our nights of wakefulness are punctuated by unnoticed periods of sleep. She did take pains, however, to stay awake in the hours after compline, or night prayer, when the friars at San Domenico were sleeping. It was her way of ensuring that an unbroken stream of prayer was maintained. She officially retired only when she heard the bell ring matins and knew the friars were back in their chapel.

Her bed was hard, with a stone as headrest and a red blanket to cover her body. The comforts may have been primitive, but Catherine relished them. She celebrated the feeling in a letter she wrote some years later to a Sienese nun: "First you find your cell, and you see that inside is a bed. It is clear that you need your cell, but your cell isn't all that you need. No, you turn your glance and your longing to the bed, where you'll find your rest. And this is what you have to do: go into the dwelling, the cell of self-knowledge. There I want you to open the eye of your understanding with loving desire. Walk across the cell and get into bed, the bed in which is God's tender goodness, which you find within this cell, yourself. (Surely you can see that your existence has been given you as a favor and not because it was your due.) Notice, daughter, that this bed is covered with a scarlet blanket dyed in the blood of the spotless Lamb. Rest here then, and never leave."

As the months passed, the dyer's daughter became more comfortable in her "cell of self-knowledge" until she reached a point where the room became a part of her and she could escape its security while at the same time never leaving. Her time stopped. She didn't need to sleep; she didn't need to eat. Or so she thought.

By this time her fasting had reached extreme proportions. She had already given up eating meat and drinking wine when she was a girl. During the years spent in her small room she confined herself to bread and water and uncooked vegetables, which she chewed for their juices and then spat out the fibrous residue. That was on an ordinary day. On those days designated as official church fast days, Catherine took nothing but water. Raymond of Capua claimed that one year, "from [Lent] until the feast of the Ascension of our Lord," a stretch of about eighty days, "she kept a complete fast, taking all that time no bodily food or drink whatever." On Ascension Day, he said, she consented to take some wheat bread and oil along with vegetables.

This kind of self-denial sounds incredible centuries later. Indeed, Raymond may have exaggerated its severity. People have questioned the motivation for Catherine's fasts and wondered about their effect on her health. She tired easily as she got older and was often laid up with exhaustion and depressed spirits. There were days when only her fierce will made it possible for her to rise up and move about. Fortunately for her, she had will in abundance.

The decision to fast was Catherine's alone. Like most medieval people, she believed fasting and other bodily penances were a way of atoning for her own sins and the sins of others. The fasting impulse was particularly strong in the decades following the Black Death, which people regarded as a manifestation of divine punishment. In addition to atoning for sins, fasting served other purposes for believers. It was an intentional distraction that helped them stay focused on the spiritual path—pain has a powerful capacity for awakening the mind. Benedict of Nursia, according to legend, threw himself on a thorn bush when assailed by erotic temptations. In Catherine's case, she dreaded the possibility that she would lose her focus on Christ even for a moment. Still vivid in her memory was the moment when she looked away from the vision in the sky to talk to Stefano, or when she worked to make herself attractive at Bonaventura's urging. Raymond of Capua mentioned still another example that, in a small way, reveals her secret fear. She was in San Domenico Church with Bartolomeo Dominici. The two of them were sitting in a pew together, discussing some point in the spiritual life, chatting quietly. Suddenly Catherine's brother Bartolomeo appeared, strolling down the aisle. Distracted, Catherine glanced up and turned to watch as he disappeared. She turned back to Dominici only to realize she had not been listening. This shocked her and she burst into tears. It was the same thing all over again! She was determined that in future situations such as these, the discomfort of fasting, like a tight string around a finger or an iron belt around her waist, would keep her focused.

Fasting can also be an instrument of control. For medieval women, who had little control over their destinies or even over their own bodies, fasting was an accessible way of asserting independence. Catherine, when she sat at the family table as a girl, used fasting as a way of proclaiming her singularity. The others at the table could see her plate and its contents. Perhaps they also noticed the way she slipped pieces of meat onto her brother's plate. Her eating behavior was a way of announcing, "I am not the same as you." In particular it was a way of claiming independence from her mother, who was charged with the responsibility of feeding her family. Catherine let it be known that she, and she alone, would decide what food went into her body.

Extreme fasting also has the effect of suppressing menstruation in most women, which makes for still another kind of control. Most likely Catherine did not know about this when she began to fast, but one has to believe the eventual discovery did not displease her, since she was so utterly opposed to marriage for herself. It is interesting to note that her practice of fasting became more intense as she entered the age of puberty.

She was not the first in her family to use fasting as a means of control. Everyone in the family knew the story of Bonaventura who early in her marriage had been appalled by the crude language of her husband, Niccolò. The daughter of Giacomo hadn't been used to that kind of talk while growing up, yet she chose to say nothing to her husband. Instead she began to fast and continued until she was pale and thin. Finally, Niccolò noticed the change in her and asked if anything was wrong. Only then did she tell him how disturbed she was by his manner of speech. Niccolò promised to change his behavior, and apparently did.

As Catherine's reputation grew and the extent of her fasting became general knowledge, her influence broadened, in Siena and beyond. It set her apart. She became a curiosity. More than that, her fasting made her powerful, since her very survival in the face of such radical fasting came to be seen by believers as a miracle and an act of God. In her writings she never laid claim to it as a source of power. Only in one letter did she ever mention her fasting at all. Yet other people did call attention to it, especially the anonymous author of the *Miracoli* and Raymond of Capua in his biography, so that in time her fasts became a central part of her legend. Of course it must be noted that both Raymond's *Life* and the *Miracoli* were exercises in mythmaking. During an age that equated fasting with holiness, these accounts aimed to enhance the belief that Catherine was very holy. There is reason to believe that she did not fast quite as radically as legend would have it. Testimony at her canonization proceedings maintained that in the late 1370s, when she was supposed to have given up bread, Catherine would occasionally eat raw and cooked greens seasoned with oil, along with bread, moldy cheese, and pieces of eel. Only toward the end of her life did her fasting become truly extreme.

However, some people were disturbed by reports of her eating habits. Contrary to what one may assume, fasting was not invariably praised during the Middle Ages. There had been so many fraudulent claims that people grew suspicious of reports about "miracle fasts." Some believed that excessive fasts were the work of the devil; not a few suspected that Catherine herself was a witch. Tommaso dalla Fonte, as her confessor, was concerned for her health and sufficiently alarmed by these reports that he commanded Catherine to cease her fasting. She tried to do it. At his orders she sat down to at least one meal each day, but her digestive system had become so unused to food that she experienced agonizing pain when she ate. According to Raymond of Capua the food "that had been violently forced down was violently forced back again." Catherine would wind up exhausted and still unfed. Yet, because Tommaso would not relent, she continued to force herself to eat. It got so bad, said Raymond, that Catherine was "brought . . . to the death's door." At this point she posed a question to Tommaso: if a fast ever threatened her life, would he forbid her to do it on the grounds that it would be suicide?

"Of course I would," he answered.

Well then, she said, since it seemed that *eating food* was threatening her life, he should forbid her to eat for the same reason.

Outflanked, Tommaso could only say, "Act, then, as the Holy Spirit shall instruct you."

So Catherine went back to her fasting, and rumors continued to circulate about her. When Raymond became her spiritual director some years later, he, too, was suspicious of her eating. He watched for a time as she struggled to eat—watched as her body went into cramps and spasms, and watched as she put bitter herbs down her throat to induce vomiting and thereby get some relief. Raymond was more sophisticated and flexible than

Tommaso and refrained from commanding Catherine to change her eating habits. Instead, he tried to support her way of life, which he eventually came to believe was a holy one.

Seven centuries later we have a more precise name for Catherine's condition. Most people looking at her case today would agree Catherine suffered from an eating disorder. It has been charged that she and other medieval women who undertook extreme fasts suffered from a form of anorexia nervosa. It was not today's form of anorexia observable in individuals with poor body images and an obsessive desire to be thin. Catherine did not have a poor body image, and she didn't care how she looked. The medieval version was more like "holy anorexia" and began with extreme fasting adopted as a penitential practice. Most medieval women, including Catherine, did not indulge in binge eating, although some did. Once the disorder took over, however, the results were the same as regular anorexia: cycles of eating and vomiting, giving rise to depression and frequently a physical inability to eat. In many cases it ended in death. Some researchers believe that long-term starvation such as Catherine's produces lesions in the hypothalamus that, in turn, creates an aversion to food. Whatever happens organically, it is clear that established cases of anorexia nervosa are extremely difficult to overcome.

One argument put forth by a modern scholar to explain the onset of Catherine's disorder focuses on the period of her life when she was weaned. According to this theory, the child Catherine was so disturbed at being denied her mother's milk that she became fixated on food and fantasized for the remainder of her life about being breast-fed.

While it is highly probable that Catherine suffered from some degree of anorexia, giving it a clinical label does not adequately explain her fasting in its full moral, religious, cultural, and psychological dimensions. Her eating habits, initially undertaken for religious reasons, gradually took on their own momentum and escaped her control. She knew it was so. In spite of this, her fasting had the capacity to forge her spirit and character. And it continued to have sign value in her dealings with the public.

Catherine herself never romanticized her fasting or held it up as an example for others to imitate. Quite the opposite, toward the end of her life she wrote to another Mantellata, urging her to fast only moderately and guard her health. The one time she did comment on her fasts was in a letter to a Florentine priest who had heard about them and written her, warning her to beware of demonic influences. Catherine's reply is instructive:

"Dearest father," she wrote, "I sincerely thank you for your zealous concern for my soul . . . You wrote to ask me whether I thought I could be deluded—or rather thought I could *not* be deluded—and said that such a belief is itself a trick of the devil. Here is my answer: Not only in this matter, which is beyond the powers of human nature, but in all my other actions as well, I am always fearful because of my own weakness and the devil's cleverness. I do indeed believe I can be deluded. For I realize that though the devil lost beatitude he did not lose his intelligence, and with that intelligence—or better, cleverness—I know, as I said, that he could deceive me. But then I turn to the tree of the most holy cross of Christ crucified; there I lean; there I want to nail myself fast. I have no doubt that if I am nailed fast with him in love and in deep humility, the devils will have no power over me. And this is not because of my own power but because of the power of Christ crucified.

"You wrote especially that I ask God for the ability to eat. I tell you, father—and I say it in the sight of God—that in every way I have been able to manage I have forced myself to take food once or twice a day. Over and over I have prayed and do pray and will continue to pray to God for the grace to live as other people do in this matter of eating—if it is his will, for it certainly is mine. When I have done as much as I can, I enter within myself to get to know my own weakness and God, and I realize that he has given me a very special grace to overcome the vice of gluttony. But I tell you, it very often makes me sad that I have not overcome it simply for love. I for my part don't know what else to do about it, except to beg you to ask supreme eternal Truth to grant me the grace of being able to eat—if it pleases him and is for his greater honor and my soul's good. And I'm sure that God's goodness will not make light of your prayers."

Here we see that, rather than taking credit for her fasts, Catherine confessed them to be a "weakness" and wished to be rid of them. Some translations have used "infirmity" or "malady" in place of "weakness," suggesting that Catherine saw her condition as a form of illness. If so, it was an illness that resisted cure. Her fasts only got more severe over the years. While there would be periods of respite, her fasts compromised her health and threatened her life in ways that her mentors were powerless to change. Perhaps she sensed that her time would be short. In that case, she was determined to spend herself lavishly.

As the months in her hermitage at home passed Catherine fasted and prayed, prayed and fasted. She hadn't laid down a fixed duration for her solitude. Most likely, when she began she thought she would remain an anchorite for the rest of her life. Yet as time went on and as she reflected more intensely, her worldview inevitably widened until gradually it brought her to look beyond the walls of her room. The many conversations she had with Tommaso Caffarini and Bartolomeo Dominici about reform in the church opened her eyes to the need for broad-scale institutional conversion. Her afternoons listening to other Mantellate tell stories of their service to the sick and poor made her more aware of unfortunate and needy people in her city. Her family tradition of service to the community weighed on her as well; during the years 1367 and 1368, when she was moving away from solitude, her brothers were most deeply engaged in communal affairs. But more than all of the above, her return from the cell into the world waited on the fulfillment of that promise she had made when she was eight. She had vowed then that she would have no other husband than Christ. But what did that mean, exactly? Even Catherine was not sure. She had been a child when the vow was made. Now, in 1367, she was a young woman, anchored in prayer, disciplined in spiritual practice, secure in her abilities. And for years now she was of marriageable age.

The turning point came—as so many turning points did come to Catherine—in the form of a vision. It was the last day of carnival in the year 1367. All over the city people were celebrating. Feasting was in progress in the house of Giacomo. The family assembled upstairs around the table while downstairs Catherine sat alone in her room with the intention of making reparation to God for the dissolute behavior that characterized Siena during carnival. As her biographer later described it, God's voice spoke to Catherine as she prayed in her cell. Suddenly she perceived the Virgin Mary holding the child Jesus, accompanied by John the Evangelist, Paul the Apostle, St. Dominic, and the prophet David. Mary took Catherine's hand in her own and held it out toward her son who placed on Catherine's finger a ring with pearls and a diamond. According to Raymond, Jesus said: "Behold, I espouse you to me in faith. That faith will be kept untarnished until the day when you will celebrate with me the everlasting wedding-feast in heaven. From now on you must never falter about accepting any task my providence may lay upon your shoulders."

This "mystical espousal" with Jesus marked a turning point in her life. She didn't recognize it immediately, being still attracted to life in her hermitage.

She wanted to continue in that comfortable place. Yet she was like a woman who, before her nuptials, has eyes only for her groom, but once fortified in marriage turns her face to the needs of her work, her family, and her world. In a sense, her spirituality had become too broad for her to be content any longer with a one-to-one relationship—Catherine and Jesus, side by side. From this point on it was going to be Catherine and Jesus and everyone else. She found the change painful to contemplate. When Jesus suggested in another vision a short time later that she join her family for dinner, Catherine protested bitterly: if union with God is the highest good, why is she being sent away to eat common food? She even dared to quote scripture back to Jesus—"One does not live by bread alone"—all to no avail. She later recalled that every time she was obliged to leave her room and socialize it was so painful she thought her heart would break. Still, the voice that rose from a deep place within her sounded authentic, so she listened to it. It said: "On two feet you must walk my way; on two wings you must fly to heaven."

It was time to move on. The emphasis on two feet and two wings underscores the dual obligations recognized in most world religions between the "inner way" of prayer and contemplation and the "outer way" of compassionate service to humankind. Thus far Catherine had concentrated on the first and had been content and happy in her cell. Now she was coming to see that in order to move ahead she must use all of her self—both feet and wings—and plunge once more into the life of her city.

Reluctantly she took the advice. She began again to do chores around the house as she had done when she was younger. She labored in the kitchen, turned the spit at the hearth, worked in the garden. Frequently now she would join her family for meals around the table in the kitchen, no longer the recluse. In the course of her days no doubt she lifted her face to the towered skyline of Siena, the walled-in city, and beyond, out of sight, to the verdant hills of Tuscany rolling down to the sea. It was all waiting for her, calling her.

She was twenty years old.

4

THE CITY

ommaso dalla Fonte was worried. Catherine kept complaining to him about temptations that assailed her during prayer, and he didn't know what to tell her. It was a difficult task she had taken upon herself—to keep her eyes always on God and let nothing come between herself and her beloved. It strained human capacity. The temptations she experienced were not unusual in themselves. Most people might accept them as normal daydreaming. Into her mind floated unsought invitations to relax her austerities, to ease up her life of prayer, and take more pleasure in people and surroundings. There seemed to be nothing evil in any of them, except she knew that if she submitted to them, even for a moment, more invitations would follow: suggestions to reorder her priorities, to reevaluate her relationships, and to become—well, like everyone else. So she would shake herself out of her fantasies and cry, "No!" She would *not* put any pleasure or person ahead of her divine spouse! She knew that if she gave in to these temptations—which presented themselves in sweet and natural ways—they would rob her of her treasure. She sometimes referred to the Devil as "the old pickpocket"—someone who would sidle up in a friendly way but then, before one knew what was happening, disappear with one's purse. Before that could happen to her she would fall on her knees before the cross, or beat herself with the lash, or run off to Tommaso to weep and accuse herself of near surrender and demand to know *when* it would ever end!

Poor Tommaso, who knew all about ordinary holiness, had never encountered someone who desired to live completely and absolutely for God. He spoke with his friend Bartolomeo Dominici about it. Bartolomeo made suggestions about approaches to take with the young mystic, but in a confessional setting Tommaso lacked Bartolomeo's manner. Rather than trying to understand her, he tried to direct her by laying down firm prescriptions. For instance, Tommaso thought he could get Catherine to eat simply by commanding it, not realizing that her eating habits had passed beyond the control of simple willpower and become a physical condition. After a time Tommaso acknowledged he was in over his head as Catherine's confessor and asked Bartolomeo to take over those duties, which Bartolomeo did sometime in 1368.

Tommaso would always remain close to Catherine, and she continued to confide in him. However, their relationship subtly altered as more and more she became the senior partner and he accepted the role of disciple. All of that was still in the future. In 1367, when he was still her principal advisor, Tommaso sought a way to ease her struggles with temptations. At an Augustinian monastery outside Siena's walls lived a hermit who was considered to be an expert on the subject. Tommaso was determined to bring him and Catherine together. So one summer day that year the two of them left the city and walked about four miles due west to the monastery of Lecceto to meet William Flete. He was to have an enormous influence on her life and development.

Flete was one of the more remarkable men in Siena. He was an Englishman who had completed his studies to become a master in theology at Cambridge but for some reason never took his degree. Instead he turned his back on the English branch of the Augustinians and came to Italy where there was a movement afoot to live the Rule of St. Augustine in its original purity. Lecceto, hidden in a forest of ilex trees near a lake outside Siena, was a center for the reform movement in the order. There Flete lived mostly as a hermit—called *il baccelliere* (the bachelor) by his brother monks because of his theological training—delving into his books and offering counsel to clergy and laypeople who came out from the city to see him. Flete was in his early forties when he first encountered Catherine.

We don't know what they spoke about that day, but we do know it was the beginning of a friendship that would last for the rest of Catherine's life. She and Flete were the same sort of people—gifted intellectuals who relied on experience more than book learning. Both were contemplatives drawn to prayer and solitude. Flete was probably the first trained theologian

Catherine had ever met. Through him she encountered the ideas of Augustine of Hippo, the great theologian of the early church whose worldview helped to balance the philosophy of Thomas Aquinas that she absorbed from the Dominican friars. It was through the thoughts of Augustine and Flete that Catherine elaborated her ideas about knowledge of self and knowledge of God, which had a central place in her subsequent preaching and writing. From about 1367 to 1374, Flete had the single greatest influence on her personal and intellectual development. Under his tutelage she changed from being an uncertain young woman, just beginning to feel her way in the world, to a confident apostle who did not shy from preaching to popes and government leaders. Even after Raymond became her mentor, Catherine did not hesitate to put one of her followers under Flete's supervision: "I . . . commend to your kindness this young man whose name is Matteo Forestani," she wrote him in 1375. "Do all you can to help him become truly and solidly virtuous, especially in disciplining his own will and his attitude toward the world."

Catherine's own attitude toward the world was being reshaped in these first months out of solitude. For one thing, she was beginning to visit the sick in their homes and in hospitals as Mantellate were supposed to do. Sometimes she was accompanied by Alessa Saracini or another Mantellata she had become friendly with, Francesca di Clemente Gori, called Cecca. But at other times she went out by herself, making her way up and down the steep, narrow streets of the medieval city to enter dim, fetid rooms of the bedridden. Medicine was a primitive science in the fourteenth century. There were no real cures for serious illnesses. The main service Catherine and her Dominican sisters could provide was to clean and rebandage the suppurating wounds, wash and feed the patients, and pray for them. Given the contrariness of sick people, then and now, these good works were not always appreciated. Raymond tells of one elderly woman at the leper hospital outside Porta Romana. Catherine went regularly to care for her, but the more she helped the more the woman demanded, sometimes heaping scorn on her, announcing her as "the queen of Fontebranda!" when Catherine walked in. Catherine showed no annoyance, but Lapa was furious when she heard what her daughter was doing. "You'll get leprosy, too!" she cried. In fact, says Raymond, Catherine did develop a strange rash on her hands, but ignored it. Finally the poor woman became critically ill. Catherine watched her until the end, then

washed and clothed her dead body and buried her "with her own hands."
The mysterious rash disappeared.

On another occasion Catherine was assigned to a Mantellata named
Andrea, abandoned by her family and dying of breast cancer. Catherine's
cheerful demeanor grated on her bitter patient, who took pleasure in casting doubt on Catherine's reputed chastity. Catherine insisted she was still
virginal, but the woman's malicious stories spread to the other Mantellate
and even got back to Lapa, who railed at Catherine for agreeing to help
"that stinking woman." Discouraged, Catherine appealed to God in prayer.
It seemed to her that Jesus appeared holding two crowns, one of gold and
one of thorns. He asked her, "Would you prefer to suffer in this life or the
next?" She reached up and pulled the crown of thorns down on her head.

Andrea eventually softened, stopped her rumor-mongering, and accepted
Catherine's ministrations. It made the job somewhat easier. However, Catherine couldn't help feeling disgust when she had to clean the woman's ooz-
ing, infected breast. In principle she dearly wished to embrace suffering in
whatever form it appeared, but this nauseated her. One day after she cared
for the woman, she gazed down at the small bowl containing foul water
mixed with pus and effluent from the wound. Holding it in her hand, she
considered a way of overcoming her disgust. Suddenly she raised the bowl
to her lips, tipped it, and drained its contents. Years later she told Raymond
she never tasted anything so sweet.

It was the sort of gesture that legends are made of: the one who found
it impossible to eat food was nourished by the dregs of suffering and found
them sweet. It was a communion of sorts. She who drank from the side of
Christ also partook of humanity at its most repulsive. They were joined in
her person. It is astonishing in retrospect to see how often Catherine used
food images and the act of eating and drinking in a positive way, given the
fact that eating was such a problem for her. It may relate to the medieval
fascination with the eucharist. By the late Middle Ages the eucharist had
become powerful in the public imagination because of the way it simultaneously embraced the physical and the spiritual. It was a lens through
which Catherine and other medieval mystics beheld the social order. One
of Catherine's favorite metaphors was the image of "eating souls," which
for her meant absorption rather than destruction—taking others into one's
own self and being joined to them. The food of the soul, she liked to say, is
other souls. Writing to Bartolomeo Dominici in 1372, she remarked, "Souls

are a food so sweet and mild that they will make us fat, till we can enjoy no other food. I tell you, your teeth will be so strengthened that you will be able to eat big mouthfuls as well as small."

She was devouring her city and its people in big mouthfuls in 1367 and 1368. She was renewing her acquaintance with its streets and squares, meeting new people, becoming a familiar figure at the hospitals of Misericordia and Santa Maria della Scala. Twenty years after the first onslaught of the Black Death, Siena was still struggling to get back on its feet, hampered by a reduced population, weak business prospects, and political instability. On the surface things were peaceful, but there was a feeling of unease in the air. As a group, the citizens of Siena prided themselves in the art of governing. Shortly before Catherine's birth, Ambrogio Lorenzetti had painted on the walls of Siena's council chamber in the Palazzo Pubblico allegorical frescoes celebrating Good Government and its effects. It portrayed peasants toiling happily in the fields, merchants transporting goods to and fro, laborers working together to construct new buildings while human figures representing the Virtues gazed down on them with benevolence. The frescoes represented Siena's public myth. In reality, society in fourteenth-century Siena was almost hopelessly fractured. The original city had evolved out of small Etruscan, Roman, and early medieval settlements built on three adjoining hills. Although the narrow valleys between them eventually filled in with dwellings to make a single community, Siena's tripartite origin had been imprinted on its population. The area within the medieval walls was divided into three terzi, or districts—the terzo of Camollia where Catherine grew up, of San Martino, and of Città. Citizens had a fundamental loyalty to their terzi. The three competed against each other in games, challenged each other in the annual *palio* horse race (held in those days outside the walls), and sometimes tangled in street fights. In an effort to bring these factions together, the city fathers in the first half of the fourteenth century erected a central government building, the Palazzo Pubblico with its magnificent Mangia tower, right where the three terzi abutted. The palazzo faced the expansive Campo, adorned with a fountain. The Campo was a place where citizens from all three terzi could meet, forget their differences, do their shopping, and gossip. During times of political unrest it was an ideal place to riot.

But the divisions among citizens created by the terzi and their subdivisions, the contrade, paled before the far more insidious divisions resulting from class and wealth. In 1368 the greatest part of the workforce was still poor and without the right to vote. The fall of the Council of Nine thirteen years earlier had done little to change their condition. Leadership of the commune had been passed to the Twelve but was still firmly in the control of the merchant class. The twelve individuals who actually made decisions were drawn from the General Council (*Consiglio Generale*), or legislature, each individual serving just two weeks and then stepping down while another took his place. In theory it meant no one person or clique could take over the government, but with the General Council under tight control and the pool of potential members so limited, it continued to be rule by a few. The nominal head of government, serving at the will of the Council of Twelve, was the *podestà*, whose duties were administrative rather than policy making. Most Italian city-states at the time had a podestà— generally a nobleman hired from a distant city and therefore not beholden to any local faction.

The nobility represented another and still more dangerous fault line in society. Nobles were allowed to hold public office—in the *Biccherna*, for instance, Siena's treasury, or the *Gabella*, the tax office. However, they were forbidden to sit among the Twelve, which meant they were barred from real political power. Historically the nobility were excluded from governing because they squabbled so constantly among themselves—riven by ancient feuds and resentments—that they could not be depended upon to serve the interests of the commune. In the thirteenth century most of the great families had been engaged in banking. Siena had been one of the banking centers of Europe, maintaining agents in various parts of Europe, but a hundred years later financial dominance had passed to Florence. Pushed out of banking, Siena's noble families transformed themselves into real estate moguls, hungrily grabbing up properties in the city and in the Sienese contado, the countryside. Even before the plague, four families controlled 20 percent of all landed wealth in the city-state; fully one-third of all urban and rural property was owned by 2 percent of the citizens. However, these enormous landholdings proved not enough to keep the younger *signori* occupied. With no banks to run and no crusades in progress, the sons of noble families spent their time plotting against each other and sometimes battling in public places. In 1315 the vendetta between the Tolomei and Salimbeni had become so violent that it boiled over into street warfare. Shakespeare's feuding Montagues and Capulets from Verona would have felt right at home in Siena.

As she made her way around the city to visit the sick or engage in apostolic work, Catherine would have passed the mansions of the nobility—the Salimbeni and the Tolomei, the Malavolti, Piccolomini, Gallerani, and Saracini families. The mansions were politely referred to as palazzos but really were fortresses. Their grim exteriors were topped by tall towers for defensive purposes, allowing the ever-suspicious families to peer down on surrounding streets. Seen from afar in old drawings and prints, the tower-marked city crouched on its hilltop site like an animal with bared fangs. Most of the towers were eventually dismantled by Spanish forces in the sixteenth century, from which Siena would emerge defanged and docile.

Catherine had friends among the nobility. She may have been repelled by the lifestyle of its more dissolute members, but she had no objection to noblemen and noblewomen in principle. Alessa dei Saracini, a daughter of one of Siena's most distinguished families, was one of her closest companions. Francesca "Cecca" Gori, the Mantellata who served as Catherine's scribe for many years, likewise came from nobility. She was a widow with three sons, all of whom became Dominican friars, and a daughter, Giustina, who eventually entered the convent. Among the other Mantellate, noblewomen numbered prominently. One of them was Agnesa Malavolti, the widow of Orso Malavolti. Another of Catherine's scribes was a male member of the Malavolti clan, Francesco di Messer Vanni Malavolti. He became a monk after the death of his wife and children and later testified during Catherine's canonization process.

In addition to personal friendships with members of Siena's ranking families, Catherine was aligned with them politically. She was never engaged in party politics herself. However, her brothers served in the government during the years of the Council of Twelve, and the Twelve maintained discreet but friendly contacts with the Salimbeni, a family that had already made several naked grabs for power and would again in the future. As we will see, Catherine's continued friendly relations with the Salimbeni would disturb reformist elements in Siena as time went on.

The factional nature of Sienese society—the ongoing jealousies, infighting, arguing, and plotting, coupled with the control of wealth and property by a few—left Siena with political instability no matter how carefully the government was put together. Economic issues added to the uncertainty in the second half of the fourteenth century. After the collapse of its banking business, Siena depended mainly on agriculture for income. Little besides

grapes for winemaking could be grown on the mountainsides, but its flat-
lands closer to the sea produced grain and livestock. There was also ore to
be mined in the hills to the south. But several factors made reliance on
agriculture and mining problematic. For one thing, there was no reliable
seaport for exporting grain, ore, and trade goods. An attempt to develop
a port at Talamone, some forty miles away on the Ligurian coast, never
really worked out. The other nearby ports of Pisa and Livorno were outside Sienese control. Farming depended upon good weather, but during
the fourteenth century Tuscany had endured a series of droughts. Europe
as a whole was experiencing a Little Ice Age—the Baltic Sea had frozen
over twice, in 1303 and again in 1307. Lack of rain had devastated crops
in northern Europe, where famine was even more serious than in Tuscany.
On top of all this, during periods of truce in the Hundred Years War, Siena's
outlying farms were threatened by unemployed mercenaries. Without a war
to engage them, foreign soldiers would band together to loot the farms and
villages of Italy. The pillagers, led by bandit chiefs called *condottieri*, were
unable to break into walled cities like Siena but had a deadly effect on the
countryside. To save its dependent towns, the cities had to bribe the mercenaries to go away.

Some of Siena's income derived from manufactured trade goods such
as wool, cotton, and silk cloth. Unfortunately the processing of these, especially the wool, required water, which was a limited resource in a hilltop
city. Florence, with the Arno river at its doorstep, produced four times the
number of wool cloths as Siena. To ease the water problem Siena in the early
fourteenth century had built an ingenious system of underground water
mains called *bottini*, supplying fountains in different parts of town. When
those didn't prove sufficient, the Nine instituted a search for a rumored
underground river, called the Diana, said to flow beneath the city. Alas, after
tearing up the city to sink test wells, no river was ever discovered.

The search for the Diana elicited amused comments from the Florentines, including Dante. Popular opinion in Florence tended to view the
Sienese as a dreamy, impractical people prone to flights of nostalgia and
excess. Siena's failed plan to turn its duomo into the grandest church in
Christendom was one example. The two cities of Florence and Siena, only
some forty miles apart, were rivals in everything from business to athletics
to outright war. Florence had been a Guelph town, which meant that in
the long struggle between the popes and Holy Roman emperors for influ-

ence in central Italy, Florence took the papal side. And because Florence was Guelph, naturally Siena was Ghibelline, throwing its weight behind the emperor. In the old days one could tell Guelph and Ghibelline cities apart because Guelphs tended to put square towers on their public buildings, while the towers of Ghibellines were round or oval. After the battle of Colle di Val d'Elsa in 1269, Siena fell under Florence's influence, although not outright control. The Council of Nine that ruled Siena so successfully between 1287 and 1355 came to embrace the Guelph way of doing things—the magnificent Mangia tower overlooking the Campo is perfectly square.

By Catherine's day the old distinctions between Guelphs and Ghibellines had largely lost their meaning. Siena's government of the Twelve tilted in a Ghibelline direction, although by this time even the Twelve accepted the principle of equality among citizens that was a bedrock tenet of Guelph politics. In a similar manner, Florence—the city once famous for its Guelph, or pro-papal, leanings—was becoming more and more distrustful of Pope Urban V for his attempts to enlarge the size of the papal states in Italy. When papal armies in 1370 moved into Perugia, some seventy miles to the south, Florence became truly alarmed. In an effort to counter the perceived threat to its own territory, Florence made friendly overtures to Bernabò Visconti, the absolute ruler of Milan, who at the time was engaged in a bloody war with the pope. Factionalism, it seemed, was prevalent not only in Siena but wherever one looked in northern and central Italy. The entire region was torn apart by competing interests.

One of the sorriest fractures of fourteenth-century society existed within the church itself. The papacy had abandoned Rome and relocated in Avignon, in southeast France. How this came about is a long story. Briefly, it was the end result of a long struggle between the popes and the French kings over church–state issues such as the selection of bishops, the taxation of church property, and whether civil law would prevail over church law. These were delicate questions being asked at a historical moment when church and state were just starting to break from each other and begin their continental drift. Lacking any precedents, the questions had to be settled by the principals involved—and King Philip the Fair and Pope Boniface VIII were two of the most bellicose and intransigent principals of their day. When Philip brought trumped-up charges against a French bishop, Boniface issued the bull *Unam Sanctam*, asserting that the spiritual and temporal authority of the pope superseded any royal authority. From there, things deteriorated. Philip whipped up hostility against Boniface among the French clergy and people. Secretly he sent a company of Frenchmen to abduct the pope, then at his summer estate in Anagni, south of Rome. Boniface narrowly escaped and fled, shaken, back to Rome where a short time later he died. The college of cardinals at this time was almost evenly divided between French and Italian churchmen. They elected an Italian (Benedict XI) to replace Boniface, but he ruled for less than a year. In June 1305, the cardinals, meeting in Perugia, elected a French archbishop who took the name Clement V. Fearing for his safety, he declined to go to Rome for his coronation and instead was crowned in Lyon that November. Subsequently he settled in Avignon on the lower Rhône. For the next seventy years a succession of seven popes (all of them French) would make their residence in Avignon—a city that was technically not French territory but was certainly under the eye (and thumb) of the French monarch.

The "Babylonian captivity" of the popes in Avignon weighed heavily on Italians, who without the pope could no longer boast of being the center of Christendom. The city of Rome suffered economically from the absence of the papal court and the business it generated. The absence was felt in other ways, too. The papal states on the Italian peninsula lacked a resident pope to watch over them. They were governed instead by legates who were often French and unsympathetic to the local population. The arrogance and callousness of these appointees offended the Italians in the extreme. Francesco Petrarch described the sad state of Rome in one of his letters: "In [the pope's] absence . . . peace is exiled; civil and external warfare rages; dwellings are prostrate; walls are toppling; churches are falling; sacred things are perishing; laws are trodden underfoot; justice is abused; the unhappy people mourn and wail, calling with loud cries upon your [the pope's] name. Do you not hear them? . . . Must the Queen of Cities be forever widowed? . . . How can you sleep, under your gilded beams, on the bank of the Rhône, while the Lateran, the Mother of all churches, ruined and roofless, is open to the wind and rain, and the most holy shrines of Peter and Paul are quaking, and what was once the Church of the Apostles is but a ruin and a shapeless heap of stones?"

At this point in her life, Catherine was not yet writing letters, but surely she and her circle—Tommaso dalla Fonte, Tommaso Caffarini, Bartolomeo Dominici, William Flete—shared Petrarch's sentiments. In addition to the political fallout from the papal exile in Avignon, they were offended by reports of the licentious behavior of the Avignon curia. Cardinals and other clerics lived in ostentatious splendor on large estates in the Rhône valley, with companies of servants, ornate carriages, and mistresses to care for their every need. In Rome, Birgitta of Sweden complained bitterly that "priests and ordained clerks keep mistresses, go out with them when they are in a state of advanced pregnancy, and as happy fathers they receive the jesting congratulations of their colleagues—'is it to be a boy or a girl?'" The Avignon popes themselves—decent men on the whole—deplored the excesses but seemed unable to stop them. They permitted the buying and selling of papal offices because, frankly, they needed the money and had no other means of getting it.

This, then, was the city of Siena and the larger world that Catherine, fresh out of her hermitage, found herself in—and where she would exercise her ministry. She came, armed with optimism and the fire of her convictions, into a society where cynicism was endemic. A few idealists like Bartolomeo Dominici and William Flete, for whom the problems of society and the church may have seemed intractable, contented themselves by reforming their religious communities, thereby creating safe havens outside civil society. Catherine, however, who as a girl wanted to be a hermit, was coming to a vision larger than theirs. Her involvement in the city itself was founded on a passionate belief that intimacy with the divine was available to *all* persons and that her "marriage" was a commission to bring everyone into its embrace. In this regard she was surely an innocent, and probably naïve, but she was no idealist. Already at her young age she had come face-to-face with sinfulness in the world and in herself and refused to shrink from it. She accepted the fact of sin and was not surprised or put off by it, believing that the other face of sin and corruption was opportunity. She was not in the least squeamish. These convictions allowed her to wade into difficult situations with the confidence that her energy and God's support would ultimately win out. Setbacks would daunt her, but never for long. She had steeled herself since childhood to accept them and move on.

Two major events struck blows at Catherine's family in the summer of 1368. First Giacomo's health failed. That was followed soon after by the collapse of Siena's government.

We don't know the cause of Giacomo's illness. Raymond of Capua only says that Giacomo took to his bed and it soon became clear to everyone that he was nearing the end. Catherine rushed to his side. Her father had been her great defender in confrontations with the family, and now she was determined to protect him from suffering that she believed awaited him in purgatory. She pleaded with God to release him from that obligation. In his biography, Raymond makes her dialogue with God sound like a judicial process, with God arguing for justice and Catherine begging for mercy. Finally accepting the demands of justice, Catherine struck a plea deal. She begged God to lay Giacomo's obligatory punishment on her rather than on him. Immediately, says Raymond, she experienced a pain in her side that remained with her for the rest of her life. She welcomed it with joy and announced to her father that he was free to go. Giacomo died on August 22, and was laid to rest that same evening after a funeral in San Domenico Church.

Two weeks later the rule of the Twelve was toppled by an unlikely coalition of noble families and the *popolo minuto*—poor workers and lowly artisans. These groups at both ends of Siena's socioeconomic spectrum came together to take power from the middle class. Theirs, however, was a shaky coalition, and before the month was over it was overthrown by yet another group, led by the Salimbeni family and former leaders of the Twelve. It was an unstable time in Siena's history as various factions vied to find the right balance of political muscle and popular support. It would take another three years for the popolo minuto—who previously did not have the right to vote—to consolidate their power and to find themselves the dominant force in Siena's government. The ruling party that now came to the fore was known as the reformers—the *Riformatori*.

With Giacomo di Benincasa gone, the business he started and then left in the care of his three sons began to fail. Why this happened is not clear. Perhaps Giacomo experienced failing powers in the last years of his life and did not provide adequate supervision of the dye shop. Perhaps Bartolomeo and Stefano were so engaged in politics that they let the business decline. The scarcity of water that was hurting Siena's wool business might also partly explain the decline in the family fortunes. It may also have been the reason why Giacomo's eldest son, Benincasa, left his native city in 1369 and settled in Florence with his wife and children, presumably to set up a satellite dye business there. But before he left—and most likely before Giacomo died— the family purchased the rented house they had all been living in on Via dei Tintori. However, Catherine did not reside there all the time anymore.

She was beginning to stay more frequently with her sister Mantellata Alessa Saracini at one of the Saracini dwellings in the center of Siena.

There was one other family development that occurred around this time. Catherine's sister-in-law Lisa, the wife of Bartolomeo, became a Mantellata and began to spend time on a regular basis with Catherine and her friends. Lisa's uncle Giovanni Colombini, the merchant-turned-preacher, had died just the year before, having become a saintly presence to the people of Siena. The four women—Catherine, Alessa, Cecca, and Lisa—lived and worked in close association for the rest of Catherine's life. The death of her father must have been a watershed moment for Catherine. She was slipping the bonds of her birth family and beginning to create a new family of friends and disciples, one that would become even more remarkable than Giacomo's family or the Mantellate.

PART TWO

MAMMA OF TUSCANY

5

"OUR MOST KIND MAMMA"

atherine was twenty-two years old in 1369, in the full bloom of her womanhood. Yet when we try to imagine what she looked like we sense her energy more clearly than her face. Raymond of Capua never described Catherine's appearance except to say that her beauty "was not excessive." Neither did any other contemporaries describe her, and no portraits were painted from life, so we are left to speculate about her looks. People in the fourteenth century were only slightly shorter than moderns, so we could begin by guessing Catherine was moderately petite, perhaps five feet two inches, and thin from all her fasting. Her hair, once called lovely by her mother, was probably light brown—light hair being both common and prized in Tuscany; consider the golden-haired women in Botticelli's paintings a century later. As a Mantellata, no one could see Catherine's hair, since the voluminous Dominican habit of white and black covered most of her body, revealing only her face and hands. Were there pockmarks left from childhood disease? If so, no one mentions them. Most paintings of Catherine were done long after her death and are not to be trusted as true likenesses. There is, however, one fresco in Siena's San Domenico Church that was done shortly after her death by someone who actually knew her—Andrea Vanni. He was fourteen years older than Catherine and a member of her circle. His full-length portrait shows her standing, holding a lily (the symbol of virgins) in her left hand while the other is kissed by a female devotee kneeling at her feet. Catherine, her head cocked to the left, gazes soulfully at the disciple. A white coif cradles her chin, wraps over the ears and around her head, covering most of her brow. The coif is topped by a long white veil that hangs down and disappears under her black mantle. Her eyes are wide set, her nose long, and her mouth small. She seems to have a dimple or a cleft in her chin. The pose is formal and rather cool, in keeping with the Byzantine style favored by Vanni. His likeness of Catherine is probably accurate. X-rays of her skull done in 1947 revealed a woman with a small but elongated face, a strong nose, and a fine but prominent chin.

If she was not beautiful there was still something about her looks and manner that attracted people. It was not so much her features but her liveliness and spirit that seemed to captivate those who met her. As an adult she still had the vivacity that had charmed neighbors when she was a child. One of the first things people noticed was her smile. Bartolomeo Dominici was struck by her joyfulness. Two other disciples recalled her as "always kind, always full of clemency . . . ever joyful and smiling." For someone so hard on herself, she was remarkably tender and accepting with others. She had a sense of humor. Occasional droll remarks crop up in her letters. She liked to laugh, enjoyed singing, and she loved to talk—which she did sometimes at great length. There is a story about her and Raymond of Capua early in their relationship. Catherine had launched into one of her monologues that went on for so long Raymond fell asleep. Suddenly noticing him, Catherine interjected, "I might as well be talking to a wall as to you about the things of God." One hopes that the noble Raymond, jarred awake by the words of the artisan's daughter, had the grace to laugh along with her.

She had a capacity for attracting people. Her reputation for holiness certainly helped to draw people in, but it was her unaffected manner more than her piety that they responded to. She was not shy. She could communicate with street people and magistrates with equal aplomb and with the same blend of kindness and candor. And while she never minced her words, people came away from encounters remembering not her frankness but her tenderness and openhearted acceptance of them as individuals. She was approachable by people of all factions. These qualities made her a perfect intermediary when there was a need to reconcile differences between antagonists or warring families—of which Siena had more than its share. Throughout her life she was called upon to serve as a peacemaker. For instance, Catherine's friend Alessa Saracini worried about her elderly father and his disaffection from the church because of an old argument with a local priest. She wished her father would avail himself of Catherine's help but knew he would never seek her out. So Alessa did the next best thing: she invited Catherine to live with her at one of the Saracini residences in the center of the city. The timing was opportune because the house on Via dei Tintori had become the property of Catherine's brothers and their growing families after the death of Giacomo. Catherine did not fit in there anymore, nor did Lapa. Catherine had stayed with Alessa several times in the past. This would be a more permanent relocation. So sometime in the summer or fall of 1369, Catherine, and probably also Lapa (who had herself become a Mantellata after Giacomo's death), moved in with Alessa at her family residence near the Piazza del Mercato, behind the Palazzo Pubblico.

The move to the Saracinis' placed Catherine in the heart of the city, close to the Campo. Symbolically she was moving to center stage. This was underscored a short time later when a commotion in the street outside drew Alessa's and Catherine's attention to two convicted prisoners tied to posts in a cart and being publicly tortured on their way to the place of execution. According to the story recorded in Raymond's *Life*, Catherine immediately prayed for their souls, arguing with God that Jesus had died even for criminals. The legend goes on to claim that Christ appeared to the condemned men, who repented their sins and died in the state of grace. It is one of those unverifiable stories, but it serves to remind us that Catherine was coming into a place where faith was forced to contend with violence and brutality.

Things were getting difficult in Siena, for the city as a whole and the family of Giacomo in particular. Back in 1368 all three of Catherine's brothers had been elected *Defensores* (magistrates) of the commune. One suspects that the time they gave to politics came at the expense of the family dye business. As mentioned, in 1369 Benincasa went to Florence to open a dye shop. Late in 1370 all three brothers applied for Florentine citizenship, a necessary condition for doing business in that city. The two younger brothers, Bartolomeo and Stefano, continued to make their home in Siena, but their economic fortunes in the future hinged on their success in politics.

Conditions were even more ominous for the city itself. For thirty years marauding mercenary bands had been raiding the Sienese countryside, destroying farms and crops the urban center needed to sustain itself. As if these depredations were not enough, in 1370 Siena and all of Tuscany experienced widespread crop failures brought on by drought. The consequences were bad for the city, where people rioted over the absence of flour, and even worse for the countryside. The Maremma, Siena's grain-growing region close to the sea, lost most of its population to starvation and abandonment. Grosseto, its largest town, saw its population shrink from 1,200 people to 100. Rural folk fled into the city where at least some food was available. The commune was forced to buy emergency supplies of grain at ruinous prices.

It was probably around this time that Catherine performed her "miraculous multiplication of the loaves." When new supplies of flour were just coming into the market, Alessa decided to throw out the old, moldy flour kept in a storage bin in her basement. Catherine protested the waste, pointing to the number of people in need. She said she would turn the old flour into small loaves and give them away. This she proceeded to do. Those coming to her kitchen door not only thanked her for the free bread but praised its fragrance and taste. The bread, everyone agreed, contained not a hint of mold. Not only that but, according to the legend, the supply of flour in the basement never diminished, even though many loaves were made from it.

Her largesse with bread for others occurred at a time when Catherine was further denying it for herself. Beginning in the summer of 1370 she gave up bread in her diet and subsisted entirely on raw greens.

By this time Catherine had been working in the city for about three years. Her experiences with people had given her a deeper appreciation of political and social realities, but there was still a part of her that yearned for solitude. She missed her little room and the opportunities it offered to be alone with God, without other people around, watching and measuring her. That was especially true in this summer of 1370 when mystical experiences seemed to bombard her, one after another. They would sweep over her at unpredictable moments. Without the privacy of a cell her ecstasies became public events. Stories about her spread through the city, and people—both the curious and the devout—came by to witness the phenomenon of Catherine at prayer. What they saw was a young woman sometimes kneeling and sometimes lying on the floor in a trancelike state. She heard and saw nothing, oblivious to friends and strangers alike. Her limbs became rigid and unyielding. Visitors who tried to flex her arms or hands found it impossible. On occasion she seemed to cease breathing altogether.

From Catherine's point of view these "trances" were moments of intense intimacy with God. She attempted to describe them to Tommaso dalla Fonte. Once, while reflecting on the words from Psalm 51, "create a clean heart in me," she begged God to take her heart and will away from her and make them his own. It seemed to her then that Jesus appeared and removed her heart. Tommaso laughed. He said it was impossible, pointing out that a person couldn't live without a heart. But Catherine was adamant. "It is a fact, Father," she said. "As far as I can judge from what I feel in my body, I seem no longer to have a heart in it. Our Lord appeared to me, opened my left side, took out my heart and went away with it." Some time later she was alone in San Domenico Church after a Mantellate service. She had ended her prayers and was fully conscious when it seemed a light enveloped her and Jesus appeared, holding a bright red heart in his hands. Once more he opened her side and placed the heart inside her body, telling her that he was giving her his own heart. Catherine was overjoyed. She exclaimed to Tommaso, "Don't you notice . . . that I am no longer the same person but have become totally transformed?" Tommaso was not sure he saw it. Yet there was no mistaking Catherine's elation.

The summer passed this way with repeated mystical experiences. According to Catherine, Jesus appeared to her at different times alone or accompanied by the Virgin Mary, the Apostle Paul, St. Dominic, and Mary Magdalen. The parade of visitors gave her a sense of having one foot in another realm—a world that was so real and present to her that she wanted to leave her own world and live in that one. It was a death wish of sorts, at least in the sense that she yearned to be totally united with God.

Once, in this state of mind, she reflected on the passion of Christ and felt the pain of his suffering in her own body. She retreated to her bed while her friends watched anxiously. As she described it later to Raymond, "[Christ] who had enkindled in my heart this fire of love kept fanning it day by day to a more consuming flame; my heart of flesh could bear no more; love had grown strong as death; my heart was rent in two [and] my soul was set free from this flesh of mine."

Where this particular event took place—whether at the Saracini residence, or back in her room at the family house—is not clear. Her sister-in-law Lisa was present when it happened, along with Alessa Saracini and several other Mantellate. Convinced that Catherine was dying, they sent word to Tommaso dalla Fonte to come and administer the last rites. He arrived with several other friars just in time to see Catherine take her last breath, or what they thought was her last breath. There was weeping and lamenting among her friends. Tommaso prepared to anoint her body with the sacred oils. Four minutes later Catherine began to breathe again. A short time after that she returned to consciousness.

It was her deepest and most intense prayer experience yet. In Catherinian lore it has been called her "mystical death." Indeed, it has many similarities to what today is called a near-death experience, when persons on the cusp of death recall entering another dimension where they are surrounded by light and loving acceptance. Catherine's mystical death was something like that. She told Tommaso and later Raymond that while she was "dead" she beheld the Divine Essence, an experience so profound and transcendent she could find no words to describe it. Like Dante in the *Inferno*, she also glimpsed the torments of the damned, after which Christ, her bridegroom, appeared to her and told her she must return to life and warn people against behavior that could bring them to such an end.

There was more, according to Raymond's account. Christ also demanded "a radical change in the way of life that has been yours up to this. Your cell will no longer be your dwelling-place. For the salvation of souls you will even have to leave your own city. But I will be with you always. I will lead you forth, and will lead you back again, and you will carry with you the honor of my name. You will give proofs of the Spirit that is in you before small and great, before layfolk and clergy and religious, for I will give you a mouth and a wisdom which none shall be able to resist. I will bring you before pontiffs and the rulers of churches and of the Christian people in order that I may do as is my way, and use what is weak to put to shame the pride of the strong."

These words in Raymond's *Life* give the impression of having been composed after the fact, as though he wanted to list her subsequent achievements. They resemble commissions given in the Hebrew Bible to patriarchs and prophets such as Abraham, Moses, and Jeremiah. Still, no matter how much Raymond fashioned the words to suit his purposes or leaned on scriptural models to compose them, there is no reason to doubt that Catherine received a new sense of mission at this critical moment in her life. Somewhere in her subconscious she probably knew she must let go of her nostalgic attachment to the solitary life. The urgencies of Siena were drawing her into new ways of engagement and a new sense of herself. During prayer experiences such as the "mystical death" her psychic defenses were lowered and intuitive knowledge swept into her consciousness. This brush with her deep unconscious was for Catherine a kind of mountaintop moment, and like most mountaintop moments she quickly discerned upon reaching the top that there was no place to go but down—back to the city and its challenges, turning the fruits of prayer into compassion for other people and their needs.

Initially Catherine believed this revelation was meant for her alone. Gradually, as time passed, it began to inform more and more of her social vision and subtly affect her theology. She came to see that if she could find nourishment outside of her small room by connecting with men and women in the world ("eating souls," to use her phrase), then it followed that God was present in neighborhoods and urban spaces as well as in hermits' cells. Years hence she would criticize William Flete for remaining in his hermitage when in her mind great events required him to leave the safety of his room.

She knew people were depending on her. For instance there was Alessa's father, the aged Francesco Saracini. Aware of her status as a guest in the old man's house, Catherine never raised the subject of his enmity with his parish priest. In Francesco's presence she and Alessa would discuss their work as Mantellate in a way that evidenced their faith in a merciful God. Listening from a corner of the room while the women talked, the old man's heart was softened. After a time, he began to join their conversations, until one day he turned to Catherine and blurted, "Tell me what to do!" She told him he must go to confession and be reconciled with his enemy. This he proceeded to do. And not only would he be reconciled with his enemy, he decided to make him a special gift—his favorite falcon. A few days later an old *signore* with a falcon on his fist strode into church and approached his longtime enemy. The priest nearly fled in terror when he saw them. It took him a few minutes to understand this was a gesture of friendship, and the two men at last were reconciled.

In a small city like Siena the conversion of a prominent citizen, particularly a nobleman, could not be kept secret. The news of Francesco Saracini's change of heart and Catherine's part in it got around. Before long Catherine was being petitioned by other families to bring lost sheep back into the fold. The son and daughter of Francesco dei Tolomei had embarrassed the family through licentious living and, in the son's case, by murder. Their mother Rabe (short for Onorabile) appealed to Catherine for help. Catherine had several talks with Ghinocca, the daughter. So moved was the young woman that she gave up her lifestyle, even to the point of taking the habit of a Mantellata. This enraged her brother Giacomo, who vowed to avenge her. At the pleading of his mother the son agreed to do nothing until he talked to the Dominican Bartolomeo Dominici. Between Bartolomeo's arguments and Catherine's prayers Giacomo, too, in time had a change of heart. According to Raymond, Giacomo later married, "never looked back on his former, wicked ways, and showed himself the most peaceable and kindliest of men towards everybody." His younger brother Matteo joined the Dominicans and became a follower of Catherine.

Catherine was beginning to attract many followers now. In some cases they literally followed her through the city. Disciples would trail after her on the streets and gather around her at home to hear her speak and catch fire from her words. A few of them began to call her *mamma*—the way nuns would refer to a beloved prioress or abbess—and others soon picked up the practice, even though Catherine was still a young woman. The core group surrounding her was made up of Mantellate—the women who shared her vocation and ministry—particularly Alessa Saracini, Cecca Gori, Caterina di Ghetto (a niece of Tommaso dalla Fonte), Catherine's sister-in-law Lisa Colombini, and a few others. Then came the Dominican friars Tommaso dalla Fonte, Bartolomeo Dominici, and Tommaso Caffarini. William Flete also began to address her as mamma when she visited his hermitage at Lecceto. Eventually the band of disciples—her *famiglia*—was enlarged by laypeople: politicians, noblemen, artisans, and men of the world.

One of the first laymen drawn into her orbit was Neri di Landoccio Pagliaresi, a rising young politician from one of Siena's lesser noble families. In 1370 Neri (short for Rinieri) had just been elected to the General Council yet still wavered between possible careers in politics, poetry, or religious life. Neri was a bundle of anxieties. He was excessively concerned about his imagined sins and prone to fits of depression. He had become friendly with the Dominican friars at San Domenico Church, especially with Bartolomeo Dominici, who most likely introduced him to Catherine. Little by little she calmed Neri down and gave direction to his life. Eventually he opted to end his political career and devote himself entirely to her, joining her entourage on trips to Pisa, Florence, Avignon, and Rome. Being a literary man, Neri proved to be an ideal scribe. Catherine dictated letters to him and used him as a courier when she needed to send messages to important persons. After her death, he became a hermit in a hut outside the walls of Siena where he continued to serve her cause. Neri assembled one of the earliest collections of her letters. He also published several poetic *laude* praising Catherine and lamenting her loss, to him personally and to the world.

Neri was the recipient of one of the earliest of Catherine's letters. In 1372, he was accompanying two friars on a preaching mission to nearby Asciano when he wrote to Catherine, asking her to accept him as her spiritual son. In her reply she declared, "I have already received you and do receive you warmly. I pledge myself always in the sight of God to be answerable for all your sins." Perhaps sensing that Neri was torn between a political career and a religious one, Catherine urged him to detach himself from conformity with "the world" and its empty honors and instead seek to serve others in humility.

In the end Neri accepted her advice. In the meantime, though, he helped Catherine immensely by serving as a conduit between her and influential figures in Siena's political establishment. Chief among these was Cristofano di Gano Guidini, a member of the ruling Riformatori party. Many Riformatori were wary of Catherine for the way she maintained friendly relations with their political opponents. Cristofano did not share their caution. He quickly became a member of her inner circle. He looked to her for spiritual guidance, even asking her advice on which one of three women he ought to marry. (She told him her choice, but he didn't follow it and chose the wife he preferred.) While not himself a member of the nobility, Cristofano had close ties to Siena's most distinguished families and institutions. After Catherine's death he became notary (i.e., attorney) for Santa Maria della Scala Hospital, Siena's wealthiest and most powerful charity. Even more important for posterity, after her death he assisted in the translation of her *Dialogue*, what she called her "book," from Tuscan into Latin, thereby making it accessible to readers all over Europe.

Another layman who came to Catherine through Neri was Stefano di Corrado Maconi, a young nobleman the same age as she. Stefano sought Catherine's help because the Maconi family was threatened with a vendetta by two larger and more powerful families and desperately needed someone to intercede. Somehow Catherine was able to bring peace to the warring factions and in the process inspired a profound religious conversion in Stefano that utterly changed his life. While he continued to hold political offices at different times, Stefano became an important member of her *famiglia*. He was one of her principal scribes and in that role accompanied her to Florence and Avignon. His association with Catherine served him particularly well on one occasion when he was traveling and was captured by a band of mercenary soldiers. They were going to rough him up until they heard he was in Catherine's service. Apologizing profusely, they let him go.

Several years later Neri brought Catherine a different sort of man: Francesco Malavolti. Malavolti was a member of one of Siena's leading families and by his own testimony had lived a life that was "bold and hot-headed, lascivious and unrestrained." He had resisted Neri's frequent invitations to accompany him on a visit to Catherine until finally, grudgingly, he agreed. As Francesco described the encounter, "when we came into her gracious presence I had no sooner beheld her face than there came upon me such fear and trembling I almost fainted . . . I went at once to confession and became the very opposite of what I was before."

Francesco's experience says a great deal about the effect Catherine's presence seemed to have on people. Encountering her for the first time— just being near her—would sometimes leave newcomers shaken. Men and women in the fourteenth century sinned as regularly as we do today, yet people then believed the world of the numinous was close at hand. In the presence of a holy person that thin boundary would disappear and they would find themselves at least momentarily in a different realm. Two of Francesco's friends had experiences similar to his. When Francesco told them about his encounter with Catherine, Neri Urgughieri and Niccolò Ughelli laughed and announced they were immune to her influence. Yet when they joined him in a visit to Catherine and heard her talk about God they found themselves suddenly unable to speak and went away shaking their heads.

Some years later the same thing happened to a public figure who was notorious in Siena for instigating feuds. A man of many enemies, Nanni di Ser Vanni Savini did have one friend in William Flete, who pleaded with him to end his incessant feuding before it corroded his soul. When Nanni refused to budge, Flete made him promise at least to see Catherine. Nanni appeared at her residence one day when Catherine was away and only Raymond was home. Nanni was about to leave again when suddenly Catherine arrived, breathless from walking up the hill. Raymond reported that Nanni's "face fell" at the sight of her. When she urged him to end his constant fighting, Nanni refused, announcing that he had four grudges he was very attached to. Unsuccessful with arguments, Catherine retreated into silent prayer while Nanni watched uneasily. After a few minutes of this he spoke up to say he might drop one of his four. A few minutes more and he burst into tears, declaring that he felt so relieved by dropping one feud that he had decided to end them all. He fell on his knees before Catherine and begged her to give direction to his life. Catherine awoke from her prayer and sent Nanni into the next room with Raymond, who heard the man's confession.

And so her famiglia, her spiritual family, grew. Some of its members came to her after significant religious conversions, while others simply gravitated into her orbit. They were men and women from all walks of life—widows, politicians, tradesmen, artists, clerics. A significant percentage came from wealthy or noble families. The people that gathered around her were drawn by her words and her passion, which seemed to ignite something in them. She was the pole star around which they arranged themselves. Catherine's magnetism had almost a messianic quality. Some years hence Stefano Maconi would write to Neri: "About what you have written about our venerable and sweet Mamma, I am not amazed at this, nor do I doubt it, since I believe of her many greater things than what you have written. For I truly believe and proclaim that our most kind Mamma *is* Mamma, and I have a firm hope that every day I will believe with clearer illumination and proclaim with greater effect that [Catherine] is Mamma!"

Catherine nurtured her growing family by constant encouragement and attention. Her disciples would go to mass, and usually confession, together once a week. At other times they would gather to listen as she talked (and talked, and talked) about giving one's life totally to God. Now and then she took individuals aside to make suggestions about their practice of prayer and ways of overcoming temptation. Frequently her followers were content just to sit with her as she fell into prayer, watching as she became rapt, imagining her inner conversations with Jesus and the saints, then slipping into prayer themselves—grateful to be so close to authentic holiness. It was the School of Catherine, and its members, by sharing a devotion to their young teacher, grew close to one another, forging alliances that bridged social status and political inclination.

When she couldn't be with them personally, Catherine guided her followers through the medium of letters and notes. The earliest of Catherine's letters—those that have come down to us—were composed in the early 1370s and were directed to her spiritual family. Actually she may have started corresponding before then, perhaps as early as 1368, but those who received the earliest letters did not keep them or make copies. It is difficult to date Catherine's letters with precision because either she herself did not date them, or dates were deleted in the copying process. Scholars have attempted to arrange them chronologically from their provenance—for instance, by references to other events that can be pinpointed in time, or persons whose whereabouts were known, or by language analysis. Nevertheless, while we may not know their sequence with absolute precision, we have today 382 letters that can be accurately attributed to Catherine of Siena. It is remarkable that so many letters by an uneducated woman have been preserved for more than six centuries. Their survival is an indication of the value that people in her time and succeeding generations placed on them.

It is worthwhile to take time and consider these letters. Catherine's correspondence is one of the great documentary treasures of the fourteenth century. Compared to other correspondences from medieval Italy, only the letters of Petrarch (whose life overlapped Catherine's) are accorded greater value by historians. Petrarch, though, wrote in the elegant Latin of the educated class while Catherine's letters are composed in a vigorous Tuscan—the language of the streets and the people.

For that very reason Catherine's letters have been devalued as literature—particularly in her own country—by scholars who have argued that because Catherine was illiterate she could not have produced literary works. In Italy (and as a result, in the rest of the world as well) she has been excluded from the canon of great authors on the grounds that her works were dictated rather than written. But her so-called "illiteracy" is itself a topic of controversy. As noted, in Raymond of Capua's account Catherine learned to read in an almost miraculous manner as a young woman. Whether she could read Latin is open to question; Raymond claimed she could, but other scholars think it unlikely. It seems quite certain she could read the Tuscan language that was evolving into modern Italian. However, the notion of literacy embraces writing as well as reading, and her writing is a more problematic issue. Everyone agrees that Catherine, at the time she began her letters, could not write. Raymond said she had no sense of spelling. All of her correspondence was dictated to scribes—all of it, that is, until she reached the age of thirty when there appears a letter to Raymond that Catherine claimed she wrote in her own hand. The curious thing about the letter is that Raymond, in his *Life*, never mentions receiving it, nor does he comment on the news that Catherine could write. This silence from Raymond has prompted charges that the letter is a clever forgery placed into the collected letters after Raymond's death in an attempt to prove that Catherine was literate after all.

Such debates are best left to scholars. Whether Catherine's letters are traditional literature is not an issue here. That these letters originated with her, that her spirit breathes in them, that they capture both her mind and her voice, is beyond dispute. And we immediately see that her letters are different from usual letters. She didn't write to her friends the way most of us write to each other, as a means of conveying news and good wishes. Communicating information was not her primary objective. Catherine was concerned with the *formation* of her followers and others she corresponded with. Her letters took the form of reflections on spiritual themes, exactly like the discourses to her assembled companions. Most of them are more like sermons than newsy letters.

Catherine's intentions have often not been well understood or respected. Formalists and those who do not share her religious sensibilities have not warmed to her free-flowing Tuscan, her pieties, and her prolific and colorful metaphors. One recent commentator criticized Catherine's letters for their "excessively mannered, non-literary style" and "devotional clichés." Fortunately such opinions are losing weight as more historians are turning to popular culture to limn the temper of an age. Today there is a new appreciation of her letters as great vernacular texts. As one twentieth-century commentator observed, "Catherine's language is the purest Tuscan of the golden age of the Italian vernacular, as far as possible removed from Petrarch's Ciceronian Latin; her eloquence is spontaneous and unsought; at times, in her letters . . . the richness of the writer's ideas is such that the rapidity and ardor of her thought outleaps the bounds of speech—metaphor follows close upon metaphor, one image has hardly been formed when another takes its place until logic and grammar are swept away in the flood and torrent of impassioned words."

Catherine's letter-writing was an extension of her talking. In fact it *was* talking. Being unable to write, she dictated her letters to a scribe who would slowly record the words while Catherine waited, impatient to say what was next on her mind. With so many words bottled up, she grew restless with the process. She found relief by keeping several letters going at once: as one scribe labored to record a passage just dictated, another would read back to her the last sentence in a different letter so Catherine could pick up her previous thread and continue that one. Francesco Malavolti told the story of one occasion when she was dictating three letters to three scribes. She spoke a sentence without saying which letter it was meant for, and all three scribes took it down. Realizing her mistake, Catherine began to laugh. Strangely enough, said Malavolti, it fit perfectly in all three.

Her scribes in the early days were fellow Mantellate such as Cecca Gori or Lisa Colombini. As time went on most of the work was taken over by male disciples. Neri di Landoccio Pagliaresi and Stefano Maconi were two of the principals. When writing to people they knew, her scribes occasionally took the opportunity to append personal messages to the end of a letter. In one to Bartolomeo Dominici, Cecca added: "Fat Alessa says that you are praying for her and asks that you please ... keep praying for her. Pray for me too, Cecca the time-waster. And pray for Lisa." Sadly, most of these personal notes were deleted by redactors who copied the letters and assembled them in collections. Very few of the letter manuscripts we have today are indeed written by the original scribes.

Her letters went out to all sorts of people. They began as notes directed to her disciples but soon reached a much broader audience. As her fame as a spiritual director spread, nuns and monks would appeal for a good word and receive in return a long letter of encouragement. Then, as Catherine became involved in church and domestic politics, letters were written to popes, princes, dictators, bishops, and papal legates. Mixed among these were letters to a leather worker, a parish priest, a flax dresser, a group of prisoners, and a prostitute in Perugia (whom she advised to take the Virgin Mary as a model, for "she will lead you into her Son's presence, showing him for your sake the breast by which she nursed him, and so persuade him to be merciful to you").

Whether for a prince or commoner, Catherine's letters follow a regular formula. The first page has a heading that serves as a blessing, usually "In the name of Jesus Christ crucified and of gentle Mary." Below this is a salutation, then Catherine launches into her spiritual theme, usually beginning with the phrase "I Catherine ..." (in Tuscan, "*Io Caterina ...*"). For instance, her letter to the Sienese wool worker Sano di Maco, written most likely in the spring of 1375, opens as follows: "I Caterina, servant and slave of the servants of Jesus Christ, encourage you in the precious blood of God's Son. I long to see you a true knight, strong in your fight against the devil's every trick as long as you are on this battlefield, surrounded by enemies who are constantly fighting against us."

Then she goes on to develop her theme at considerable length using metaphors and insights from liturgical texts and scripture, yet always tailored to the reader's state in life. To a king or a ruler she may stress the need to be just and compassionate, yet resolute. To nuns she emphasizes the virtues of humility and obedience. Priests are urged to be zealous for souls while placing their trust in God rather than themselves. There are certain spiritual themes that run through all of her correspondence. One of these is self-knowledge, which amounts to seeing ourselves as God sees us. Writing to a Florentine nun in 1375, Catherine insists that "the sword of divine charity" must be "hidden in the house of our soul of true knowledge of ourselves. For when we know that we are not, and that we are constantly producing nothingness, we at once become humble before God and before everyone else for God's sake."

This exposition of spiritual themes, almost like a homily, may go on for several pages. Only when the spiritual reflection is complete does Catherine get to the news part of her letter—either a request or a piece of information treated in a short paragraph. The news is generally followed by a farewell, a final blessing, and then an evocation such as "Gentle Jesus! Jesus, love!"

Both the formation of Catherine's spiritual family and the beginning of her correspondence were taking place at a time when major events were shaking her church and her city. On December 19, 1370, Pope Urban V passed away in Avignon. Three years earlier, Urban had attempted to return the papacy from Avignon to Rome, arriving there in the fall of 1367. He had hoped his presence would help to rebuild the papal states in Italy, but when that did not happen he grew discouraged and returned to the city on the river Rhône in September 1370. Birgitta of Sweden had warned that he would die if he went back to Avignon. Sure enough, three months later her prediction came true. Elected as the new pope was another Frenchman, Pierre Roger de Beaufort, who had been made a cardinal when he was still a teenager by his uncle, the Avignon pope Clement VI. Now about forty years old, the new pontiff was rumored to be an honest man. He had some familiarity with Italy, having studied canon law in Perugia. He took the name Gregory XI.

What Catherine felt about Gregory's election is unknown. Just a few months later, though, it was not possible for her to ignore an uprising in

Siena that jeopardized the lives of her brothers and led indirectly to the collapse of the family's business. The uprising was touched off in the Contrada del Bruco (Caterpillar Ward) by wool carders, the poorest and least skilled members of the industry. These were the workers who had rioted the year before over the lack of flour. Now they became embroiled in a dispute with the wealthy artisans who controlled the wool trade. Enraged by the way they were treated, the Bruco workers stormed through the city seeking to harm guild members associated with the old, discredited party of the Twelve. Numbered among their targets were Catherine's brothers Bartolomeo and Stefano.

The story of what happened is recorded in the anonymous book of *Miracoli*. The account is sketchy. It describes mobs roaming through the city in search of the two brothers and their political associates, "wanting to kill them or hurt them." The brothers fled to the family house in Fontebranda but realized it offered no security. A friend advised them to seek sanctuary in the neighborhood church of Sant'Antonio Abate across the street. They were preparing to go there when Catherine interceded. She insisted she knew a better place than Sant'Antonio; it was the great hospital of Santa Maria della Scala across from the duomo. Catherine had nursed there as a Mantellata and knew the governor.

The hospital would clearly be safer than the church, but there was one problem: to get there Bartolomeo and Stefano would have to traverse the center of the city where mobs were out looking for them. Catherine had an answer for that. Wrapped in her Dominican mantle, she told the brothers to follow her. She would guide them there and guarantee safe passage.

According to the *Miracoli*, Catherine "took them directly through the *contrada* of their enemies. As they walked through, people bowed respectfully to her, and they passed safely through." She gave Bartolomeo and Stefano to the safekeeping of the hospital's governor, advising them to stay until things cooled down. Three days later the riots were over and they returned home.

However, Siena's political troubles were far from over. Opposition leaders were so shaken by the Bruco revolt that the Salimbeni family and remnants of the Twelve hatched a plot to overthrow the Riformatori government that was protecting the impoverished rioters. Their plan was detected just before the city gates were opened to the forces secretly assembled outside. A major struggle was averted. Still, some Salimbeni henchmen got into the city from another quarter and began to slaughter the Bruco leaders. Sporadic fighting quickly spread to the heart of the city and continued for two days before the rebels were overcome. Although the Riformatori government and its allies triumphed, it had been a close call. Several plotters were executed when the fighting was finally over. The Salimbeni and leaders of the Twelve, along with their descendants, were barred from ever holding political office. Among those proscribed were Catherine's brothers.

The rescue of her brothers is a telling reflection on the public status Catherine had achieved in Siena by 1371. Her religious habit provided some protection, but more than anything it was her personal presence that allowed her to walk past angry rioters with her brothers in tow and be greeted respectfully. These same rioters had not hesitated to break into churches to haul away and kill persons seeking sanctuary, but Catherine was left untouched. Her fame had obviously spread beyond a handful of devotees. Soon it would spread even beyond Siena.

The turmoil of 1371 also serves to highlight the political leanings of her family members. It is clear from the historical record that Catherine's brothers were associated with a guild oligarchy that resisted movements of the lower classes, the popolo minuto, to enlarge their political and economic rights. Whether or not Bartolomeo and Stefano took part in the attempted coup of the Salimbeni, they were surely allied in the public mind with the party of the Twelve that, over the years, had been sympathetic to the nobility and antagonistic to the poorer classes. These political views were shared not only by Catherine's brothers but by members of her spiritual familigia as well; indeed, one of those executed in the wake of the failed coup was Niccolò d'Ambruogio di Nese, a nephew of Tommaso dalla Fonte.

There is no evidence, however, that Catherine herself favored the coup or took sides in Siena's partisan struggles. She was opposed to mob violence and surely was appalled by the bloody reprisals aimed at Bruco leaders. In fact her principal fault, in the eyes of many, was her unwillingness to take sides. She ministered to the poor and campaigned on their behalf with the city fathers. On the other hand she refused to turn her back on the Salimbeni—surely no friends of the poor—after they were proscribed and virtually exiled by Sienese authorities. She was—and wanted to remain—outside partisan politics.

While Bartolomeo and Stefano had not been formally exiled, it was increasingly difficult for them to operate their business in Siena. Probably sometime late in 1371 they sold the equipment from the dye shop and joined their brother Benincasa in Florence. Catherine, her older sister Lisa, and Lapa were now the only members of their large family left in Siena. One senses their loneliness in a letter Catherine wrote, probably during the following year. The brothers must have had a hard time starting their Florentine business because the letter cautions them against longing for "transitory things" such as gold and silver and urges them to put their trust in God. She begs them to maintain family ties: "I ask you, Benincasa, you who are the eldest, to be willing to be the least of all. You, Bartolomeo, be willing to be less than your younger brother. And you, Stefano, I ask you to be submissive to God and to your brothers . . . Keep yourselves in perfect charity."

Things went poorly for the brothers in Florence; business was slow. Then sometime in 1373 Stefano died; the exact date and the cause of death are unknown. Some believe he went to Rome and died there. That same year the two remaining brothers liquidated the rest of their Sienese property. They were bankrupt. Catherine sent them a rather chiding letter reminding them of their obligation to Lapa—an obligation that was familial, but also, it seems, legal. According to law, the dowry that a woman carried into a marriage was placed under her husband's control but was still technically hers. As a consequence Lapa and Bartolomeo's wife, Lisa, had first claim to their dowries in any bankruptcy settlement. The two women had to sue in a Sienese court to claim their portions, which apparently included the house in Fontebranda.

And so in the end Catherine's birth family was scattered. But in the meantime she had established a new family that was just coming into its own.

6

ᔥᔣ

A Time of Testing

vents were moving in Florence's direction during those years. While Catherine's brothers struggled to set up shop in Florence, the wool business in general as well as the principal banking houses had rooted themselves in the city on the river Arno and were making money hand over fist. In 1374 Florence had not yet blossomed into its Renaissance glory, but signs of it were already in place. The walls of the duomo, Santa Maria del Fiore, had been raised and the nave covered, awaiting Filippo Brunelleschi who would crown it with his astonishing dome. Already completed in the center of town was the Palazzo della Signoria (today's Palazzo Vecchio), the fortified government building topped with crenellated battlements and the imposing square tower in which Savonarola would one day be imprisoned. Two centuries hence, Michelangelo's heroic statue of David would stand outside the palazzo's doors, with his sling casually thrown over one shoulder—a visible reminder to the great powers of Europe that the city of Florence, while modest in size, could be a lethal opponent.

Right at the moment Florence was carefully constructing its opposition to the new pope, Gregory XI. It was a strange turnabout for Florence, the city of Guelphs, which had stood with the popes when they struggled against the Holy Roman emperors. But now the city fathers found themselves on the other side. The Avignon popes were attempting to reconstitute the papal states that had fallen on hard times in the years after the papacy had abandoned Rome. It was a ticklish business—not only because local princes had taken advantage of the pope's absence to usurp his authority, but because the territory of the reconstituted papal states would wrap around the independent city-states of Tuscany on almost all sides. During the time when the popes' attention had been directed elsewhere, Florence had been free to maneuver pretty much as it wished. Now the city was being boxed in by an aggressive and unpredictable power. Florence's rulers cast about for possible allies in case the confrontation escalated into armed conflict. Bernabò Visconti in Milan, whom the Florentines in fact despised, was a bitter enemy of the pope and therefore a person of interest to the men now sitting in the Palazzo della Signoria. Additional allies were sought among the neighboring city-states of Tuscany, including Siena and Pisa. Finally, Florence rather hoped that citizens in some of the city-states the pope had already subdued, including Viterbo and Bologna, might rise up and reclaim their independence. The men in the palazzo gave their full energies to assembling their alliance.

Underlining its status as a center of commerce, Florence was becoming a destination for many sorts of visitors. Traders from Turkey were in evidence. Thanks to Marco Polo's travels the previous century, silk as well as wool were available in shops along the Ponte Vecchio. Geoffrey Chaucer had come in 1373 to arrange a loan for Edward III of England. Not to be outdone, the Dominican order had scheduled a general chapter in Florence for the spring of 1374 to review its mission and staffing. Bartolomeo Dominici and Tommaso dalla Fonte planned to attend.

In neighboring Siena, Catherine was throwing herself into a variety of activities with her usual energy. These included tending the sick, daily devotions, nurturing her family of disciples, and dictating a growing volume of correspondence. Few of the letters written during this period have survived. At the time they were not considered important enough to save. Nevertheless an increasing number of people sought her out for advice, some in person and others by letter. A physician in nearby Asciano wrote to ask if she thought he and a companion ought to go to Jerusalem to visit the Holy Sepulcher. She encouraged the idea but urged the pilgrims to first go to confession and "unburden your consciences as thoroughly as if you were at the very point of death," since the holy trip would also expose them to temptations.

Jerusalem was very much on Catherine's mind—so much so that she had written the new pope, Gregory XI, asking his permission to allow her and a group of companions to visit the Holy Land. Gregory was apparently intrigued by the letter. He had already heard stories about Catherine. Unlike his predecessor, Gregory was not threatened by prophetic women. He had been deeply impressed by Birgitta of Sweden and grieved over her death in Rome the previous July. Now he wondered if this young woman from Siena could be the new Birgitta.

There was one way to find out. Residing then in Avignon was Alfonso Pecha de Vadaterra, a Spaniard who had been Birgitta's confessor. Gregory dispatched him to Siena to take the measure of his young correspondent. It's not clear how the visit in March 1374 was arranged; most likely Vadaterra went first to San Domenico Church and was taken by a friar (probably Tommaso dalla Fonte) to Alessa Saracini's home that she shared with Catherine. We can imagine the papal envoy and the young woman sitting down face-to-face—Vadaterra proposing delicate questions and nodding at her replies. Catherine would have treated him with great respect. He was, after all, an archbishop.

Afterward she exulted in a letter to Bartolomeo Dominici: "The pope sent his representative here, the one who was spiritual father to that countess who died in Rome. He is the one who for love of virtue renounced the episcopate, and he came to me in the holy father's name to say that I should offer special prayer[s] for him and for the holy Church, in token of which he brought me the holy indulgence. Be glad and rejoice, for the holy father has begun to turn his attention to God's honor and that of the holy Church."

As things transpired, Vadaterra must have carried a favorable report back to Avignon because from that point forward Pope Gregory demonstrated growing confidence in Catherine. His confidence, though, was not shared by everyone. In fact, Catherine was coming under increasing scrutiny and criticism during this period when her fame was spreading across Tuscany and beyond. Catherine was neither surprised nor put off by the negative attention. Since childhood she had to deal with opposition in her family, so she wasn't shocked to encounter the same sort of reaction from people who barely knew her. When challenged openly, she disarmed antagonists by thanking them for their charitable correction that, she said, benefited her immensely. At the same time she vigorously defended herself against allegations of pridefulness that were implicit in most of the attacks. She proclaimed over and over that pride was not in her makeup because she placed her whole trust in the crucified Christ. Years later Raymond of Capua described Catherine as being "devoid of self-esteem" (i.e., inordinate pride). He added, "she allowed her reputation to be trampled underfoot by others, judging as unworthy of notice any ill opinion [opponents] might have of her. In a life directed by such principles pride was indeed ruled out, self-love cleverly outwitted, love of her neighbor, which is the fulfillment of the law, was practiced in its perfection."

Although she was defended by friends like Raymond, Catherine's genuineness was repeatedly questioned during her formative years and for the rest of her life. Nor was the criticism always founded on ignorance or envy. Some raised serious questions about her fitness to expound the Christian faith. Giovanni Tantucci was a theologian and a monk of Lecceto where William Flete lived. Catherine's friendship with Flete was not enough to forestall an anti-Catherine faction from developing in the monastery, and Tantucci (called "Giovanni Terzo" because there were two other Giovannis living at Lecceto) appeared to be part of it. He had a Franciscan friend, Gabriele of Volterra, also a theologian and the superior of the Franciscans in Tuscany, who had denounced Catherine from a pulpit in Siena. Together they proposed to visit the young lady and challenge her right to offer spiritual direction to disciples. It was beyond their experience that an illiterate woman should serve as a guide for men. The two theologians found her at home surrounded by her disciples and at once began to question her. Rather than respond to their questions, Catherine turned on Friar Gabriele and demanded to know how *he* could offer spiritual advice when he did not honor the Franciscan ideal of poverty. "With all your wisdom you are of little use to your fellow men and positively hurtful to yourself because you seek the shell of Christ's teaching and not the kernel. For the love of Christ crucified, give up this life of yours!" Gabriele was caught off guard. It was common knowledge that his lodging in the friary was furnished with lavish hangings and fabrics, whereas Catherine's patched and worn mantle witnessed a simple way of life. Embarrassed, the friar produced his keys and invited male members of her famiglia to clean out his room and give its contents to the poor. They proceeded to do so, leaving him only his breviary. Friar Gabriele ended his attacks on Catherine from that day and eventually moved to Florence where he was said to live in apostolic poverty. Tantucci was so impressed by the encounter that he transferred his allegiance to Catherine and became one of her closest followers.

A similar kind of confrontation took place between Catherine and another

Franciscan named Lazzarino da Pisa, a popular preacher and an acquaintance of Bartolomeo Dominici. There was a subtle rivalry between Franciscans and Dominicans that dated back to the years when both Bonaventure and Aquinas were teaching at the University of Paris. Not only did the two orders compete for candidates and influence within the church, their philosophical formation was subtly different: Dominicans were influenced by the realism of Aristotle while Franciscans followed the more idealistic philosophy of Plato and Augustine. The rivalry between the mendicant orders may have prompted Lazzarino to voice reservations about the maiden of Siena. His Dominican friend Bartolomeo volunteered to introduce them so the Franciscan could test her for himself.

They came to her house in Fontebranda. Catherine seated herself on the floor of her cell while Lazzarino sat on the clothes chest and began to question her about the scriptures. She confessed she knew little about scripture and asked the Franciscan to enlighten her—which he did at some length, Catherine nodding all the while and asking questions. When the Angelus bell signaled that it was time to go, she escorted him to the door and knelt in the doorway for his blessing. Lazzarino returned to his friary reflecting that Catherine, while devout enough, was sadly lacking in scholarship.

The next morning, as the story goes, Friar Lazzarino awoke in an unsettled mood. He couldn't put his finger on the discontent that seeped into his soul and increased as the day wore on. A great sadness pervaded him. Canceling all his classes, he sat at his desk and wept, bereft without knowing why. The sound of the evening Angelus brought back the memory of his visit with Catherine. In his mind's eye he saw her sitting on the floor, calmly listening as he rattled on about the Bible. There was something about her—her posture, her face, her stillness—that made a powerful impression on him. As he reflected longer his sadness lessened, then disappeared altogether. He immediately resolved to see her again.

The next morning he came to her door once more. This time when she opened it the Franciscan knelt and asked for *her* blessing. She took him to her room where this time they sat side by side on the floor. Lazzarino asked her to adopt him as a son and guide him on the path to God. She answered that he knew the path better than she, being a scholar of the scriptures. The Franciscan demurred, insisting that he knew only the externals, while she knew the heart. So she spoke to him of Francis of Assisi and the meaning of the Franciscan habit with its belt made of rope with three knots. She urged, "Follow humbly in the footsteps of the crucified Christ and your Father Francis." The story of Friar Lazzarino concludes with them sitting in conversation. It was said of him that thereafter he took enormous pride in being called a disciple of Catherine.

Opposition to Catherine came from at least three quarters. As already mentioned there was the simmering hostility among some Sienese Mantellate who, along with a few friars at the church, bitterly resented her popularity and lifestyle. They scoffed at reports of her sanctity and professed themselves scandalized by her bold way of speaking to male authority, not to mention the freedom she exercised in moving about the city. They didn't like the way she accepted disciples, many of them men, who looked to her for guidance. Consumed by envy because of the attention she received, they complained to the Dominican superiors about her public persona and succeeded in having Catherine reprimanded. For a time she was excluded from Mantellate meetings and refused communion and confession at San Domenico.

The very success of the young mystic's teachings and ministries made her subject to attacks. Bianco da Siena, a Sienese poet who had been a disciple of Giovanni Colombini, put his warning in verse:

> Beware, Catherine my sister, lest everything disintegrate . . .
> Beware that, having tasted fame, you become hungry for it . . .
> Beware lest vanity leads you into lies and cowardice . . .
> Lay aside the fantasies of vain prophecy,
> for if you follow them, you'll find yourself ensnared . . .
> Beware, beware poor woman, lest you be overthrown.

While antagonistic Dominicans made up the smallest of the opposition groups, they caused Catherine the greatest pain because they were members of her religious community. Raymond lumped her birth family and religious community together by remarking that those who knew her when she was young often failed to notice her development. "Men or women, they all acted like unreasoning children, finding fault when the flashing rays of this bright star dazzled their dim sight. They took on to teach her whose teaching of themselves was so far above them; and from out of the darkness in which they were shrouded, they complained of the light for shining. Not barking much but biting silently, they disguised their backbiting as honest zeal for what was right. And it was at their instigation that her confessor, reluctant though he was, had taken it on himself to reprimand her."

Catherine dealt with critics in her community by patiently ignoring their jibes and meeting their resentment with kindness. When asked, she would say their chastisements were healthy for her spirit. Much later Raymond of Capua admitted that Catherine was more hurt by these criticisms than she let on. "But she bore them all victoriously by her courageous and ever-vigilant patience ... [T]hat patience of hers was a greater source of support to myself than any other thing I ever heard or saw in her way of living."

A second group of opponents was not so much envious as skeptical. These were people who, like Bianco da Siena, had listened to the gossip on the Campo and concluded that no human being could measure up to the stories being circulated about Catherine. They guessed she was a naïve young woman who may have been sincere at first but now was a slave to pride—or vainglory, as it was called. Numbered among these critics were many who knew her only by reputation. They feared that she was playing with mysticism and getting in over her head—like the priest from Florence who warned her that fasting might really be the work of the devil. Catherine met such skeptics head-on. Fortified by years of painful struggle in solitude, she flatly denied that pride had a grip on her. Knowledge of God, she said, goes hand in hand with knowledge of oneself, and one learns soon enough that the self is not God. In a letter to two Sienese nuns in 1374, Catherine wrote, "I don't think it is possible to have virtue or the fullness of grace without dwelling within the cell of our heart and soul, where we will gain the treasure that is life for us, I mean the holy abyss that is holy knowledge of ourselves and of God ... [W]e recognize that we ourselves are the basest of lies, agents of that which has no being." In the "abyss" of self-knowledge, she suggested, the only mark of distinction is union with God—which is never earned, but God-given.

Some opponents were unconvinced by her disavowals. They would scoff at her in public and physically poke her while she prayed to see if her spiritual raptures were just pretense. She always passed their tests. Gradually, as more people came to know her personally rather than by reputation, the number of skeptics diminished but never disappeared.

The third and largest group of critics could never accept Catherine because she was a woman—and, what was more, an uneducated woman. Their opposition was less virulent but more deeply ingrained and harder to overcome because it was based on prejudices of class and gender. Medieval people, both men and women, accepted the misogynistic belief passed on from antiquity that women were lesser human beings. Women were believed to represent the material, appetitive aspect of humanity, whereas men reflected the rational and spiritual part. It followed from this that women approached God predominantly through their bodies, by fasting and other disciplines, whereas men came to God mostly through their minds. No one doubted that female spirituality had a place—but that place, it was commonly believed, was the kitchen, the nursery, or the convent where women could attain salvation through their mortified flesh. The trouble with Catherine, in the eyes of these critics, was that she didn't know her place. Instead of retiring to a convent she went about the city expounding ideas in the marketplace. She claimed for herself the Dominican vocation of preaching, and these opponents didn't like it.

Her lack of education was something Catherine could do little about. While she trusted her inner light, she was keenly aware that she did not have the background enjoyed by established teachers. She recognized her shortcomings from the moment she felt God was calling her to public life. Describing the scene later, Raymond of Capua gave her words that were similar to Mary's at the Annunciation. Catherine said to God, "How shall this be done? . . . How can one like me, feeble and of no account, do any good for souls? My very sex, as I need not tell you, puts many obstacles in the way. The world has no use for women in such work as that, and properly forbids a woman to mix so freely in the company of men."

Catherine tried to make up for her lack of schooling by associating with scholars like Bartolomeo Dominici, William Flete, and Giovanni Tantucci who could instruct her and support her when attacked. In time she grew out of her adolescent belief that mixing with men was somehow "improper," just as she got over her shyness about teaching. Still, when confronted by authority, she would sometimes demur that she was, after all, "just a poor woman" who didn't know very much. Some men were naïve enough to believe it.

It is instructive to watch how she dealt with two scholars who were determined to trip her up when she visited Pisa in 1375. Giovanni Gutale-braccia was a physician and Pietro Albizzo a lawyer—professionals and university men. In order to test her they devised a question for Catherine. They asked: Since the Bible says God spoke aloud in creating the world, are we to suppose God has a mouth and tongue?

Catherine threw it back at them by turning their academic question into a religious one. She said: "I am amazed that you, who teach others, should come to seek instruction from a poor little woman like me, whose ignorance you should rather enlighten. However, since you desire me to speak, I will say that God may inspire. It would be of very little purpose for me to know *how* God, who is Spirit and not a body, spoke in creating the world. What does matter both to me and to you is to know that Jesus Christ, the Eternal Word of God, took flesh and suffered to redeem us. It is necessary for me to believe in him, and to meditate on him, that my heart may be full of his love, who died for the love of me."

In accounts of the event, the two scholars were so touched by her answer that they were brought to tears. A short time later Albizzo begged Catherine to sponsor his newborn daughter at her baptism, which she did.

By far the most crucial test for Catherine came in Florence during the spring of 1374, at the general chapter of the Dominican order. It is not entirely clear why Catherine went to Florence. Most nineteenth- and twentieth-century accounts of her life declare that she was "summoned" there, presumably by the master of the order, Élias of Toulouse. Some biographers maintain that Élias personally interviewed her in Florence in order to "satisfy himself as to her real spirit," but this scenario is unsupported by evidence. There are no letters directed to Catherine or any of her colleagues containing an official summons. None of her own letters hint that she received a summons. Certainly there is no proof to support rumors that she was called to Florence to be examined for her orthodoxy or that she was publicly interrogated at a session of the general chapter.

Yet we are sure Catherine was in Florence in May 1374 while the general chapter was meeting, and it is appropriate to wonder what she was doing there. Dominican tertiaries and professed Dominican nuns were excluded from chapter meetings, which were open to male friars only. Perhaps Catherine wanted to be there to immerse herself in the Dominican charism at its source or to support those Sienese Dominicans who were delegates. Both explanations are possible but unlikely. Catherine was not the tag-along type; she traveled to places where she believed she could do good. So we are thrown back on the possibility that her presence at the chapter was sought by leaders of the community who wanted to assess her qualities at close range. The attention given to her by Gregory XI would have been reason enough for the Dominicans to initiate their own scrutiny. Most likely there was no official summons. Such matters are better handled indirectly. A discreet word by Tommaso dalla Fonte would have let Catherine know that her presence in Florence would be welcomed. Nor should we suppose that, once in the city, she was interviewed by the master of the order or questioned by a board of inquisitors. One or two "chance" encounters arranged through a friendly intermediary, bringing Catherine together with respected members of the order, would have sufficed to reassure them that she was a person to be nurtured. One of these casual interrogators may have been Raymond of Capua, the former prior of a Dominican church in Rome and a rising figure in the reform wing of the order. Raymond was a theologian and considered an authority on religious women. He had spent four years as rector of a convent of nuns in Montepulciano, southeast of Siena, and had written a biography of its foundress, Agnes of Montepulciano.

Catherine surely knew what was going on. While not a participant in the chapter, she would have known she was being watched and evaluated and that the outcome of the informal vetting process could lead to radical changes to her life. It was not her orthodoxy that was being examined as much as her public persona. The Dominican leadership needed to know if she was stable and dependable. Could she adapt herself to the structured mission of the order, or was she unmanageable? The conclusion they came to after speaking to her and consulting among themselves supported the first view. Élias of Toulouse took steps to bind her more firmly to the order by appointing Raymond of Capua to be her mentor. It was more than just a change in confessors. By this new edict Catherine was longer subject to the local Sienese Dominicans, some of whom had caused her so much distress. From now on she would answer only to Raymond and through him to Élias. The master mentioned Raymond's commission in his report on the chapter that was sent to the pope, and Gregory XI confirmed it in a letter that August—making it clear that Catherine's new status reflected the highest wishes of the church.

Catherine had every reason to be pleased. She was, in fact, delighted and honored. She related that in a vision some years earlier the Virgin Mary had promised her a confessor who would bring her great consolation, so she welcomed this new mentor as a gift bestowed upon her "by sweet Mother Mary herself." In Raymond she found a companion who was sophisticated, politically adept, with connections that reached far beyond Siena or even Tuscany, and yet someone who trusted and respected her religious experience. Born around 1330, Raymond came from Neapolitan nobility, a member of the distinguished DellaVigne family, and had a brother, Luizi, serving as an officer in the army of the queen of Naples. Raymond had studied law at Bologna before deciding to enter the Dominicans. Within the order he was highly regarded, although, perhaps, not distinguished in appearance. A twentieth-century Dominican described Raymond as a "mousy little man" who "suffered from ill-health, was constitutionally timid, somewhat prim and sensitive to scandal." When placed beside Catherine with her penchant for boldness and extravagance, Raymond suffers from the comparison. Yet they complemented each other perfectly. Given her humble origin and educational deficiencies, a companion who was both a nobleman and a theologian was wonderfully reassuring. For Raymond, Catherine proved to be a life force whose passion and earthy religious sensibilities were a constant, energizing challenge.

In addition to her connection with Raymond, the visit to Florence was an opportunity for Catherine to make a host of new friends in that city. Among them were members of the old *Parte Guelfa*, who tended to gather at the Dominican church of Santa Maria Novella. These were respected citizens, many of them nobility, no longer in power but still influential in government. As a group they were supportive of the pope in his war of nerves with the present Florentine regime. Chief among those whom Catherine befriended was Niccolò Soderini, a wealthy Florentine merchant whom she referred to as her "dearest respected brother." Soderini became her confidant and advisor on Florentine affairs. She visited his home and family, even accepting their hospitality during a later visit to the city. With her brothers facing financial difficulties with their dye business in Florence, it was to the ever-generous Soderini that Catherine appealed for help.

Another Guelph supporter was Piero Canigiani, who was wealthy both in money and sons. Canigiani was one of those who helped finance a house for Catherine and her companions during a later visit. But the greater gifts were his sons Barduccio, an attorney, and the younger Ristoro, who both became enthusiastic recruits for Catherine's famiglia.

There were many other Florentines Catherine got to meet during this first, short visit to the city. Most likely one was Florence's bishop, Angelo Ricasoli—or, if she didn't meet him personally, they at least knew of each other. Catherine did not have a high opinion of Ricasoli, who found himself in an awkward position, caught between loyalty to the pope and the more radical views of his faithful. In the spring of 1374 the issue of loyalty had not become a divisive issue for the bishop, but in time it became one.

Among Catherine's new acquaintances in Florence was one whose name is unknown. This Florentine had become fascinated by her story and decided to write it down for public edification. Judging from the language of the text that was produced, the author was a layperson and possibly a woman, since the writer claims to have befriended Catherine through the female Mantellate who traveled with her. He or she asserts that Catherine "came a few times to my house" in Florence where they talked freely about her life and religious experiences. The stories were soon gathered together in a short work known as *I Miracoli di Caterina di Iacopo da Siena*, or, in shortened form, the *Miracoli* (the *Miracles*). As the title suggests, the narrative concentrates on the uncommon events of Catherine's life—her visions, ecstasies, healings and service to the poor, fasting, and penitential practices. It records her early years briefly, brings together stories of her ministry in no particular order, and comes to a close in the autumn of 1374, just a few months after Catherine went home to Siena.

Superficial though it was, the *Miracoli* further enhanced the public perception of Catherine during the years when her fame was spreading beyond Siena. Apparently it was not published in a formal way but rather copied and circulated among convents and religious houses, reinforcing the word-of-mouth accounts already being passed around in those places. For about twenty years, until Raymond of Capua's *Life of Catherine of Siena* appeared, the *Miracoli* was the only written account of her life available. Oddly enough, when assembling sources for his biography Raymond seems not to have known about the *Miracoli*—or perhaps he knew about it but disregarded it for being uncritical. There were significant differences between Raymond's account of her life and the *Miracoli*. Raymond took pains to make Catherine an exemplar of Dominican spirituality, while the author of the *Miracoli* did not. The time frame of the anonymous work was more vague. It claimed Catherine had become a Mantellate at the age of fifteen, after living in solitude for seven years. In Raymond's version she received the habit when she was younger and had lived alone only three years. Despite these differences, the *Miracoli* is a fascinating snapshot of the emerging Catherinian legend.

While it proved to be a watershed event for Catherine in many respects, her trip to Florence was soon over. On June 29, she set off again for Siena, accompanied on the road by Raymond, her Mantellate companions, and her brother Bartolomeo, who was going back to visit his children left in Lapa's care. When they came to the gates of her city a shock awaited them. They saw carts piled high with corpses and driven by muffled attendants. The plague had returned to Siena! Bartolomeo and his wife, Lisa, along with Catherine, hurried to Via dei Tintori to be with the children. Raymond checked in at San Domenico where he found some of the friars cowering in their cells, afraid to venture into the streets and possible contamination. The return of the dreaded disease in 1374 killed almost as many citizens as the initial outbreak nearly three decades earlier. The death toll included a high proportion of children. Despite Lapa's care she lost eight grandchildren staying in her house. Catherine's older sister Lisa also died, and finally Bartolomeo himself was taken by the disease. Catherine readied the bodies of her young nieces and nephews for burial, all the while thinking to herself, "These at least I shall not lose!"

It was not a time to sit at home. Catherine and most of her sister Mantellate trudged through the almost-deserted alleyways of Siena bringing food and comfort to the sick. It was hard and dangerous work, and especially so for priests summoned to hear last confessions and anoint feverish bodies, since the possibility of contagion was very real. Some priests fled from the responsibility, but many others responded courageously. Catherine's friend Cecca Gori, who had given her three sons to the Dominicans, lost all three to the Black Death that year. With urging from Catherine, Raymond of Capua likewise provided care for plague victims, sometimes alongside Catherine and sometimes by himself. During her trips through the city Catherine was frequently joined by one of more of her disciples, often by the hermit Santi da Termamo, whom everyone called Fra Santi. This former companion of Giovanni Colombini lived in a cell outside the city walls.

It was around this time that people began to relate stories about Catherine's miracle healings—or at least healings that appeared miraculous. One of these concerned Matteo di Fazio dei Cenni, a young man who had seen Catherine at prayer and been so impressed that he became her disciple. Matteo was the rector of Misericordia Hospital, a focal point in the battle against the plague. One evening at the hospital he felt faint and the next morning while in the chapel he collapsed, complaining of pain in his groin. It was a sure sign of infection. An examination of his urine seemed to confirm it. Raymond came to visit Matteo in his room and was genuinely distressed that a young man of such promise was stricken. When Catherine heard about it she hurried to the hospital, barged into the sickroom, and announced, "Get up, Don Matteo, get up! This is no time to be lying soft abed!" Matteo couldn't hold back a faint smile. He sat up in bed and was astonished to discover he felt much better—hungry in fact. Raymond, who was not there when it happened, returned to find the table being set for what turned out to be a jolly meal. Matteo recovered completely.

The same kind of thing happened to Fra Santi. There came a day when Santi did not have the strength to get out of bed. Catherine had him carried to Misericordia where she assured him he would not die. Santi, though, was terribly sick. His life seemed to be ebbing away. Once more she came to his bedside and told him he would live. Santi was only semiconscious and may not have heard. His friends, including Raymond, were keeping a death watch. Approaching the patient a third time, Catherine fell on her knees next to the bed and whispered in his ear, "I command you, in the name of our Lord Jesus Christ, not to die!" According to Raymond, "At once his spirit returned to his body." Santi blinked, sat up, and asked for something to eat. As it turned out, Fra Santi would live to be at Catherine's bedside when she died.

There were other reported cures as well—of Bartolomeo Dominici, for instance, and a Mantellata named Gemma who had a swollen and possibly infected throat. Last of all, there was Raymond himself, who developed symptoms of plague after going for days with little sleep. Experiencing pain and swelling in his groin, Raymond feared the worst and struggled across town to Catherine's house, where he collapsed. She found him in bed, terrified and feverish. As Raymond tells it, she placed her hand on his forehead and began to pray. She lapsed into ecstasy and stayed there—presumably in that frozen pose—for a half hour. At first poor Raymond thought he was dying, but then "I seemed to feel as if something were being drawn out from me, rather forcibly, through every extremity of my body. I began to feel better, and then a steady improvement set in. What more need I say? Before Catherine came back to her senses I was completely cured." Whether his condition was hypochondria, or exhaustion, or bubonic plague, we'll never know. Nor did Raymond. What he did know was that Catherine came to his aid and he felt better.

Whether or not these events count as miracles, that summer of the plague was terrible for everyone. No accounting of healings could fully compensate for the grief over loved ones lost or the exhaustion that seeped into the bones of caregivers. Disease reduced both the population and the moral conscience of the city. Many citizens fled to the countryside, leaving sick and dying family members to fend for themselves. Neighborhoods were abandoned. Raymond recalled the emptiness of the streets when he set out on missions of mercy. "I was practically alone in my task in this great city, and the sick calls came so thick and fast to fetch me from home that I was left with hardly time to eat or sleep, or snatch a few short moments' breathing-space." It was the same for Catherine and the other volunteers.

At last, toward the end of summer, the rate of infection declined and a few people trickled back from their hiding places outside the city. Those who had remained were almost too numb to notice. Catherine was exhausted. Raymond thought it would do them all good to get away for a few weeks. He proposed a trip to Montepulciano, a lovely hilltop town to the southeast, in Sienese territory. He had a special love for the place where he had spent four years as a rector. So, after they regained a little strength, Raymond, Catherine, and a group of Mantellate including Alessa Saracini, Giovanna Pazzi, Catherine's sister-in-law Lisa, and two of Lisa's daughters set out for Montepulciano.

Catherine was looking forward to the visit. Raymond had been telling her about Agnes of Montepulciano—Blessed Agnes who at the turn of the century had founded a Dominican convent where her exposed body still rested, incorrupt. So eager was Catherine that when they entered the town, instead of going to the arranged hospice, she and a few of her companions went directly to the convent outside the walls. They came into the room where the body of Agnes was preserved and, in accordance with custom, bent to reverence it where it rested on a low platform. As Catherine bent to kiss the slipper-clad toe, many in the room said they saw the leg and the toe lift in the air to receive her kiss. There was wonder and astonishment: the body of Agnes paid deference to Catherine! The visitors from Siena accepted it without comment, but several of the local sisters were shocked and insulted—*their* Agnes upstaged by a parvenu. The dissenting sisters hinted darkly that Catherine was some kind of trickster—possibly a devotee of Satan.

It was the same old story. However much she desired to do the good and holy thing, she became a sign of contradiction. Doubt, scorn, and skepticism followed her everywhere. It was the peril of trying to live an intensely devout life in public. This time, however, she had Raymond on her side. The next morning when the party from Siena returned to the convent

Raymond was with them. He had learned about the whispering campaign against Catherine and was determined to stop it before it gained momentum. Exercising his authority as a former rector of the convent, he assembled all the nuns in the chapter room and began to question them about what they had seen when Catherine reverenced the foot of Agnes. One sister from the convent was determined to put her own spin on the episode. It is true, she said, that the leg lifted up, but she was certain that Blessed Agnes had a different intention than the one people imagined. She implied that in reality Agnes was trying to kick Catherine.

Raymond cut her off. "Dearest Sister, we are not asking you anything about Agnes's intention; for as far as we know you are neither her counsellor nor her secretary. The only thing we are asking you is this: did you see that foot being miraculously lifted up?" Meekly, the sister confessed that she had seen it. The chapter was soon concluded and the matter put to rest.

The weeks in Montepulciano were a time of recovery for Raymond and Catherine. Both of them were worn out by their labors in plague-ridden Siena, and both went through periods of exhausted prostration. Catherine became very ill, her face pale with dark circles under her eyes. Raymond sat by her bed and listened while in a faint voice she recalled all those confidences she had shared with Tommaso dalla Fonte over the years—accounts of visions, dialogues with God, extraordinary religious experiences. One would think the recollections would bring her joy, but looking down at her shadowy face Raymond thought he saw the image of the suffering Christ. On another occasion Raymond wept bitterly over his sins, which he feared were never forgiven by God. She arose from her sickbed and spoke to him of God's forgiveness and blessings until his anxiety lifted. In this way they came to trust each other and grow closer. They would still go through periods of doubt—public doubt for Catherine, self-doubt for Raymond—but now at least they would not be alone.

7

"Sweet Holy Crusade"

ometime after she returned from Florence, Catherine received an invitation from the absolute ruler of Pisa to visit that city, sixty-odd miles to the northwest of Siena. Just how Piero Gambacorta came to hear of Catherine is not known, although two of her followers, Bartolomeo Dominici and Tommaso Caffarini, had been preaching in Pisa and may have spread stories about her. Gambacorta had a daughter, Tora, who was interested in joining the Dominicans. Naturally his daughter was eager to meet the young woman from Siena who was making such a name for herself.

As it turned out, Catherine could not make the trip—at least not at that moment. In her letter of response she said the invitation "warmed my heart" but confessed her health made it impossible to travel just then. In addition, she hinted mysteriously that a visit to Pisa at that time could be a "source of scandal," preferring to come when she could do so without stirring up gossip. The first excuse, regarding her health, was completely understandable. Catherine was worn out from weeks of caring for victims of the Black Death. Considering the small amount of nourishment she took in, she was capable of amazing bursts of activity when sufficiently inspired, but those bursts were often followed by periods of exhaustion when she barely got out of bed. The trip to Florence and her nursing during the plague in Siena had used up all of her strength.

The issue of scandal is a different matter. What sort of a scandal could be caused by a trip to Pisa? Perhaps some people in Siena—other Mantellate, for example—were whispering about Catherine's travels with an entourage and the way she was fawned over by powerful men. But since Catherine was never inclined to give much weight to that kind of gossip, it is far more likely the scandal she spoke of was political. The city-states of Siena and Pisa were longstanding rivals for control of the agricultural lands that stood between them along the coastline. Recently, at Gambacorta's urging, the Knights of St. John had occupied the port of Talamone, Siena's only link to the sea. The Knights were in service to the pope, so the move had the effect of pressuring Siena at a time when it was leaning in favor of the Florentine alliance against the church. Gambacorta in Pisa was regarded as one of the pope's staunchest friends in the region. However, Gambacorta himself was under pressure. Pisa and its neighboring city of Lucca were also being courted by Florence to join its alliance. Publicly, at least, Gambacorta had not made a decision as to which side he would choose. The situation was very delicate.

Given the political climate, Catherine was surely conscious that a trip by her to Pisa, and discussions with its ruler, would disconcert leaders in Florence and Siena. She and Raymond were on the record as opposing the Florentine league, which Catherine believed was tantamount to rebellion against God's church. To her, those who plotted against the pope severed themselves from the source of divine grace. In different language she said as much in her letter to Gambacorta. The letter condemned those who "have lost self-mastery and let themselves be possessed by anger and other faults." She added, "Now what would it be, dearest father, if we were masters of the whole world but not of the vices and sins within us? These rob us of the light of reason so that we cannot see how lost we are, nor how secure is the soul bound to the gentle Jesus. We have forfeited the life of grace because we are cut off from true life, like a branch cut from the vine, dry and barren. Anyone cut from the true Vine is just that dry and rotting, deserving of eternal fire."

In order for them to visit Pisa without upsetting people back home, Catherine and Raymond needed another legitimate reason that would give them cover for the trip. And Gambacorta's invitation held out one—his daughter who wanted to join the Dominicans. But an even better possibility was emerging. In 1371, Pope Gregory XI had announced a crusade aimed at stopping Turkish advances in the Adriatic and perhaps even, if everything went well, going on to recover Christian shrines in the Holy Land. It was an old, old dream. Crusading was a balloon oft floated by pontiffs who wanted the European powers to focus on an external enemy instead of fighting among themselves. Actually arranging for a crusade, though, was an awkward business, and this crusade, while announced, was still waiting to be put in motion. Crusades needed an appropriate historical moment— a *tempus acceptabile*—when the enemy was vulnerable and friendly forces available. Such a moment seemed to be emerging early in 1375. The French and English were talking truce and actually agreed in March to a one-year respite in the Hundred Years War. Likewise, papal forces were negotiating with the Visconti of Milan for a truce in their long struggle for dominance in northern Italy. The Visconti accord would not become official until June 1375, but the pope was already casting around for persons who could preach the crusade and grant papal indulgences to those who enlisted. Three individuals were finally selected. One of them was Raymond of Capua.

While his appointment was not announced until July, Raymond, being well connected, surely knew which way the discussions were headed. Promoting the crusade would provide a perfect excuse for visiting Pisa during the crucial time when that city was teetering between Florence and Avignon. Thus late in March, after she had recovered her strength, Catherine set out for Pisa with a large party that included Raymond, the Augustinian Giovanni Tantucci, Dominicans Tommaso dalla Fonte and Bartolomeo Dominici, and at least three Mantellate—Alessa, Lisa, and Cecca—as well as Catherine's mother, Lapa. Like most travelers in the Middle Ages, they covered the distance on foot. Dominicans were actually forbidden to ride horses, which were associated in the public mind with knights and nobles.

Pisa in 1375 was a bustling city of 50,000, situated just a few miles from the sea on the Arno river and surrounded by malarial but fertile lowlands. It had much in common with Catherine's own city. One could find in it works by Giovanni Pisano, the great sculptor and architect who had designed the facade of the duomo in Siena. As she entered Pisa, Catherine may have stopped and stared at the Campo dei Miracoli, larger than Siena's Campo and covered with grass instead of stone. On the campo was the duomo with its famous bell tower, completed the century before and already leaning dramatically. By Catherine's day Pisa had passed its political apogee when it had vied with Genoa as a maritime power. Now the city survived on a reduced amount of sea trade, agriculture, and fishing. It had just founded a university that two centuries later would produce Galileo Galilei. In the fourteenth century Pisa was, like Siena, an old Ghibelline town that had learned to live in the shadow of Florence.

Inside the city the travelers established themselves in the home of Gherardo Buonconti, a wealthy young nobleman, next to the church of Santa Cristina. Catherine quickly became friendly with the whole family, including Gherardo's wife, Caterina, and his brothers Tommaso and Francesco. The Buonconti house was convenient because the church next door was the meeting place of the local Mantellate. The Pisan women greeted Catherine by crowding about excitedly, even kissing her hand. Raymond watched uneasily. He feared such fawning displays would scandalize her critics and give her an inflated sense of herself. When he told her so, she brushed it off, saying that she hardly noticed what people did, adding, "I wonder that a creature, knowing herself to be a creature, can have inflated self-regard."

It was clear to everyone in the city that Caterina di Giacomo was a person of consequence. A short time after they had arrived, Piero Gambacorta came calling. Catherine spoke to the ruler about his daughter and about the need to remain loyal to Gregory XI.

Catherine had come to Pisa fully cognizant of the political situation in Tuscany and determined to plead the pope's cause. That doesn't mean she took the matter of a crusade lightly. She was deeply and passionately committed to a crusade for reasons that were at once religious, political, and personal. In a letter to Gregory XI some months later she spoke of the undertaking as a "sweet holy crusade." She strongly supported the church's obligation to defend its heritage and holy places. She accepted the commonly held belief that becoming a crusader was a way of living out the Christian vocation. In fact she had a powerful yearning to be a crusader herself. To Catherine, who had grown up listening to stories of early Christian martyrs, giving one's life for Christ was a way of sharing in Christ's passion and death. She believed with most people of her era that martyrdom guaranteed instant access to heaven, but even more than that—since Catherine seldom reflected on "heaven" as a place—martyrdom was an act of generous love that engrafted her to Christ and mirrored his love for humankind.

As mentioned, while still in Siena Catherine had written to the pope imploring him to let her and some of her Mantellate sisters travel to Jerusalem with the crusading army, knowing they might very well lose their lives in the process. Her letter to the pope has been lost, but we know she wrote it because she described her request in a separate letter to Bartolomeo Dominici and Tommaso Caffarini: "I have written a letter to the holy father asking him for love of that most sweet blood, to give us permission to offer our bodies for every sort of torment. Beg supreme eternal Truth [God], if it is for the best, to grant this mercy to us and to you: for all of us as a splendid company, to give our lives for him." Her eagerness to travel to the Holy Land and face death was not uncommon in that age. Francis of Assisi a century and a half earlier went to Egypt during the siege of Damietta and preached to Sultan al-Kamil. The sultan listened to him courteously but would not be converted. Francis later visited the crusader city of Acre until illness forced him to return to Italy. Ignatius Loyola in the sixteenth century likewise planned to go to the Holy Land and convert the infidels, but again illness and other events got in the way.

Catherine seemed quite certain that taking part in a crusade would result in her death—indeed, it was an outcome most ardently desired. Writing to William Flete she exclaimed, "Oh how blessed will our souls be when we hear this sweet message that we are to leave our homeland, our poor wretched body!" There is no record of a papal reply, but it seems Gregory did not respond with a "sweet message" but instead threw cold water on Catherine's project. So did Flete. He and Catherine had much in common, but Flete did not share her wanderlust or her enthusiasm for engagement in the events of the day. The Augustinian hermit believed the best place for a contemplative was in the hermitage and the best form of engagement was prayer.

One can't help wondering whether Catherine checked with her Man-tellate companions before volunteering them for her proposed journey to the Holy Land. Her letter to the two Dominican friars seemed to assume, without asking, that, naturally, they would be part of her "splendid com-pany," "*la bella brigata*," whose members would give their lives for Christ. While we have no evidence, it seems more likely that she did confer with her close companions among the Mantellate—either before writing her let-ter in Siena to the pope, or soon afterward. On the long road to Pisa, as on other trips, the party made a practice of walking in pairs or larger groups, talking, praying together or singing songs. It is hard to believe they could spend so much time in close company without sharing their plans for the future, especially plans that involved possible martyrdom.

While her crusader balloon was still up in the air, Catherine tried to enlist as many followers as possible—priests, nuns, and laypeople—who could accompany the crusading knights to the Holy Land and there meet their fate. She extended an invitation to an entire convent of women in

Fiesole, near Florence, in a letter written probably in the summer of 1375. The letter is remarkable because it casts martyrdom in a larger spiritual context—viewing it not merely as participation in Christ's passion but as a way of joyously submitting oneself to God's judgment. Here is an excerpt, full of Catherine's vivid imagery: "There is no way we can have this driving force of great and boundless desire except through the most holy cross—I mean, through the driven and crucified love of God's Son. For he is a peaceful sea that provides drink for all who thirst, for all who hunger and long for God. He gives peace to all who have been at war, yet want to be reconciled with him. The sea pours out a fire that warms every cold heart, warms it so powerfully that all slavish fear is dispelled and only perfect charity remains, with a wholesome dread that keeps us from offending our Creator.

"Don't be afraid—I don't want you to be afraid—of the plots and attacks of the devils who might come to pillage and take over the city of your soul. No, don't be afraid, but be like knights drawn up on the battlefield, armed with the sword of divine charity. This sword is the whip that beats the devil. Understand that if we don't want to lose the weapon with which we have to defend ourselves, we must keep it hidden in the house of true knowledge of ourselves. For when we know what we are not, and that we are constantly producing nothingness, we at once become humble before God and before everyone else for God's sake. We recognize that every grace and favor comes from him. And we see so much of God's goodness flowing down on us that love makes us grow severely judgmental of ourselves—so much so that we would gladly take vengeance on ourselves but wish that everyone else would take vengeance on us as well. We judge everyone else to be better than ourselves. And a fragrant patience is born that sees no burden too heavy or too bitter to bear for love of that loving engrafted Word.

"Yet more, dearest daughters: let's run, all of us a splendid company, to engraft ourselves into this Word! I am inviting you to the wedding feast of this engrafting—I mean, I am inviting you to shed your blood for him as he shed his for you. Specifically I am inviting you to the Holy Sepulcher, there to give your lives for him. The holy father has sent a letter with his seal to our provincial superior and to the minister of the Friars Minor and to Frate Raimondo, saying they should enroll all those who desire and are willing to go to win back the Holy Sepulcher and die for the holy faith. He wants them to send him a written list of all these people. So I am inviting you to get ready."

We don't know how the women in Fiesole responded to this invitation or whether they began compiling lists of names of people willing to die for their faith. We do know that a great number of people were profoundly moved by Catherine's advocacy—which is why her letters were extensively copied and why so many of them were saved. There was usually more than one level of meaning in her exhortations. She was dealing with the crusade, yes, but she was also dealing more broadly with the spiritual life and the invitation to give oneself unreservedly to God. People in the fourteenth century lived more easily with symbol and metaphor than we do today. They saw in Catherine's passionate pleading a summons to engage in spiritual warfare against the dark forces that afflict the human spirit. By reading her letters on this level one finds a measure of protection against disappointments that inevitably follow from placing all one's hopes on political solutions. Later that year, after her dreams of joining the crusade had been squashed, and while the crusade itself was still not off the ground, Catherine could write to Cecca, who had gone back to Siena: "The business of a crusade is continually progressing from good to better, and God's honor is growing daily. You, too, ought to be continually growing in virtue, provisioning the ship of your souls, because our time is coming closer."

In fact plans for the crusade were not going well. Raymond preached and met with civic and church leaders. Catherine gave public talks, met with leaders, and wrote letters, yet enlistments were disappointingly few. Perhaps the crusading spirit that had gripped Europe since the late eleventh century was losing its hold on the public imagination. Churches still had collection boxes to gather money for crusading; special prayers during mass still raised a clamor for battle, but the ardor exhibited by the First Crusade three hundred years earlier had definitely cooled. When the idea of a crusade was first launched in 1095, Europe was going through a period of burgeoning growth. There had been overflowing harvests for several years in a row and a growing population that provided surplus manpower for armies. Now, in 1375, the situation had changed dramatically. Even without the plague European populations had been shrinking, and harvests had been poor for several years. Tuscany right then was going through another period of famine. Added to these natural conditions, the seemingly interminable war between England and France placed demands on the manpower of those kingdoms. The credit of Italian bankers was stretched to the limit. The only political power that stood to gain from a new crusade was the papacy, since crusades by their very nature were demonstrations of the moral leadership of the church. They allowed the pope to exercise his symbolic primacy among the rulers of Europe while simultaneously beating back Muslims in the East and flaunting muscle in the face of the Eastern Orthodox. All of these ends were eagerly desired in Avignon. Yet regardless of how much Gregory XI might wish for a crusade, in order to mount one he had to depend on the European powers for men and money, and for that there was no political will at all.

It is hard to plan an overseas adventure when local security is under threat. In the summer of 1375 the cities of Tuscany were facing grave danger. The temporary truce between the Visconti of Milan and the pope had left unemployed the fierce mercenaries who had been fighting on the papal side. They were free to terrorize and plunder the city-states of Italy. A large force under Sir John Hawkwood had already extracted a bribe of 130,000 gold florins from the Florentines to leave their city untouched and another 30,000 florins from Pisa. Now his men were threatening Siena. Hoping to ease the pressure on her own city and at the same time recruit soldiers for her crusade, Catherine prepared a letter to Hawkwood and had Raymond carry it into the mercenary camp in late June.

"Oh dearest gentlest brother in Christ Jesus," she wrote, "would it be such a great thing for you to withdraw a little into yourself and consider how much pain and anguish you have endured in the devil's service and pay? Now my soul wants you to change your course and enlist instead in the service and cross of Christ crucified, you and all your followers and companies. Then you would be one of Christ's companies, going to fight the unbelieving dogs who have possession of our holy place . . . You find so much satisfaction in fighting and waging war, so now I am begging you tenderly in Christ Jesus not to wage war any longer against Christians (for that offends God), but to go instead to fight the unbelievers, as God and our holy father have decreed." She continued, "I find it very strange that you should be wanting to make war here after pledging (as I've heard) your willingness to go and die for Christ in this holy crusade. This is hardly the holy preparation God is asking of you for going to so holy and venerable a place! It seems to me you should be readying yourself now by virtue until the time comes, for you and the rest who are so disposed, to give your lives for Christ."

There is no record of Hawkwood's reply. Certainly the invitation had its attractive side. The condottiere maintained control over his troops by providing them with a continuous flow of booty, surely obtainable in a march through the Balkans to the Holy Land. Yet even in June Hawkwood could have perceived an overland campaign to be unlikely. In the end he contented himself by taking yet more bribe money—35,000 florins from Siena.

While all this was going on Gregory XI took inventory of the prospects for a crusade and did not like what he saw. There were rumors that Milan would join forces with the Florentines, threatening a wider and more dangerous war against papal forces in Italy. In late July that alliance became a reality. By October Gregory was trying to dampen the crusading enthusiasm of Queen Giovanna of Naples, suggesting that a land attack on the Holy Land might prove too difficult. Instead he proposed a sea campaign against the Turks. "Opposing the said Turks can not only be considered a work of Faith," he wrote, "but it is a better contribution toward the defense of the said Principality [Achaea] and Kingdom [Naples]; it is easier and more important to help those in danger, lest they perish, than to attempt, at present, the recovery of the Holy Land, which has been occupied for so long."

It appears that Catherine and Raymond did not know a change of plans was being contemplated. In August Catherine, believing that the crusade was still directed against Jerusalem, wrote to Queen Giovanna in glowing terms, exclaiming, "Oh what a great joy will it be to see you giving blood for blood! May I see the fire of holy desire so growing in you at the remembrance of the blood of God's Son that you may be leader and patroness of this holy crusade just as you bear the title of queen of Jerusalem. Thus the holy place will no longer be held by these evil unbelievers but honorably possessed by Christians, and by you as something of your own."

She added that she would like to see Giovanna lead the campaign in person: "I would like to ask you to make this holy crusade—you in particular, and all the other Christians who might want to join you. For if you stand up and declare your willingness to do this, and if you put your holy resolution into action, you will find Christians very willing to follow you. I beg you for love of Christ crucified to be zealous about this."

Giovanna might seem an unlikely subject for Catherine's blandishments, since the queen of Naples was notorious for her serial marriages and many lovers. Catherine, though, always felt that she could appeal to the best in people, no matter who they were. Just as she addressed the unprincipled mercenary John Hawkwood as a "dearest gentlest brother in Christ Jesus," so she saluted Giovanna as "honorable and dearest mother." Yet Catherine was not blind to the human faults of her correspondents, whether they were commoners or queens. While she addressed Giovanna respectfully, she promptly added, "I long to see you a true daughter and spouse consecrated to our true God and come forth from him." She reminded Giovanna that even queens are made in the image of Christ who "washed away the filth of humankind, his spouse."

Earlier this same summer she had written a long letter to another notorious figure—Bernabò Visconti, the tyrant of Milan, who twice had been excommunicated for making war on the papal states but with whom the pope had now reached a truce and who, Catherine hoped, might join the great crusade. Again, she began her letter by expressing her longing to see Visconti "sharing in the blood of God's son . . . so that you may walk in love and in holy fear of God." She then proceeded to preach to him about lordship: "No lordship we possess in this world allows us to consider ourselves lords"; rather, the only lordship available on earth is "the most satisfying, most gratifying, most mighty lordship there is—lordship over the city of our own soul." The letter pleaded with the Milanese leader never again to "rebel against your head" (the pope) but to make "sweet and gracious amends" by waging war against unbelievers, "offering your possessions and your body to Christ crucified."

As is the case with most of Catherine's letters, we are not privy to the response, if any, from Visconti. Clearly he was not tempted to join the crusade. A few weeks after having agreed to a truce with the pope, the cynical Visconti threw in his lot with Florence and against Avignon.

The Visconti letter serves to highlight the twofold purpose of Catherine's trip to Pisa in 1375. Previous biographers have insisted the trip had the overriding purpose of promoting Gregory's crusade. Indeed, Catherine and Raymond were willing to let people believe that was the sole reason. But as a matter of practical politics the crusade was linked to a settlement of the dispute between the pope and the Italian city-states. There could be no crusade if the Italian states turned to war. Merely promoting the notion of a crusade served to strengthen the political hand of the pope at home. For the pope to exercise his symbolic primacy and command the crusade to go forward, his primacy had to be accepted by the Italian states presently threatening rebellion.

It must have been disheartening for Catherine to learn soon after writing Visconti that the Milanese ruler had allied himself with Florence. If so, she was not discouraged for long. Her youth and conviction, coupled with a naturally buoyant spirit, restored her determination. When one door was closed in her face, she would try to open another. In this case she attempted to exercise some influence over Bernabò Visconti by appealing to his wife, the "imperious, avaricious, ambitious" Beatrice Regina della Scala. It is not known exactly when the letter was written. It may have been around Christmas of 1375.

Calling her "dearest mother and sister in Christ," Catherine appealed to the tyrant's wife to detach herself from the world and live in the knowledge of her own value and worth. "For it would be very displeasing to God if you were to set your heart on something of less value than yourself. That would be nothing but a surrender of your own dignity. For people become like what they love."

It was a long letter, compassionate, earnest, pleading—a letter from one woman to another—willing to acknowledge the writer's own failings ("poor wretch that I am, full of sin and wickedness") and only at the end asking the lady of Milan to influence her spouse: "Challenge him, beg him with all of your might, to behave like a true servant and son of Christ crucified, to be obedient to the holy father, his representative, and to cease being rebellious."

Like so many of Catherine's letters, it dropped into the void of history. Did it reach its addressee? Did she read it? And if she read it did she ponder it or just smirk?

Catherine's letters during this period went out indiscriminately to women and men—to bishops, monks, youths, nuns, tradesmen, rulers, saints, and scoundrels. She spoke the same fearless way to everyone—and "spoke" is the correct phrase, because these letters were dictated to Cecca or one of her other regular scribes. It was expected in the fourteenth century that women would be deferential to men. Catherine was respectful—but she was never deferential. To Bartolomeo Smeducci, a young condottiere allied with the pope, she commanded: "Up, dearest father! No more carelessness! No more turning back to look at the world's wretchedness—for its pleasures pass like the wind." She spoke to women in the same straightforward manner. The remarkable thing is that she never missed an opportunity to appeal to women. A male correspondent in that age would have dealt primarily with other men, but Catherine understood that women in their culturally subordinate roles could still be influential.

One of her letters, probably in the fall of 1375, was sent to the mother of King Louis I (Louis the Great) of Hungary. Louis's kingdom included Croatia, so naturally he would want to stop the Turkish threat to the Balkans. To the queen mother Catherine pleaded, "Urgently ask your son to offer himself with love to serve holy Church. If our Christ on earth [the pope] should decide to impose this task on him and should ask him, urge him in fidelity to accept his petition . . . and to support him in his holy resolve to make this sweet holy crusade against the wicked unbelieving dogs who have possession of what is ours. And even more, for according to what I hear, they are continuing to advance as far as they can . . . The time has passed for just watching. No, like children hungry for God's honor, you should be rising up to take back what is yours, for the salvation of their souls and the exaltation of holy Church."

Not all of Catherine's time that year was spent working for the pope's causes. She returned briefly to Siena in June to minister to a condemned prisoner from Perugia (as described in the next chapter). During her stay in Pisa she visited many churches and shrines. Surely she would not have missed San Sepolcro, the octagonal church built for the Knights Templar in the twelfth century and intended to replicate Jerusalem's Holy Sepulcher. Where better to promote the idea of a crusade? Pisa had two other places that would have recalled the Holy Land for Catherine: The stunning white marble chapel of Santa Maria della Spina was constructed in high Gothic style to house a thorn, said to be from the crown of thorns worn by Jesus. It was just a short walk along the river from Santa Cristina Church, next to which she was staying. And then there was Camposanto, the great cemetery adjacent to the duomo, landscaped with soil taken from Calvary and carried back to Pisa in merchant ships. A number of hermitages were located near the Camposanto. It was told Catherine knew and visited at least two hermits there named Bartolomeo and Giacomo.

Sometimes she walked farther from town. On several occasions she visited the village of Calci several miles to the east, on the slopes of Monte Pisano where there was a Carthusian monastery. Most likely she met the prior, Giovanni Opezzinghi. Being a woman she could not enter the cloister or the huts of the monks, but the church would have been open to her.

On another day she and Raymond and a party of about twenty went by boat down the Arno river and out on the Ligurian Sea to the island of Gorgona to visit the monastery there. The monks who lived on Gorgona had been chased away by pirates but recently returned under the protection of Pope Gregory. Catherine and her Mantellate remained overnight in the women's guesthouse while the men slept in the cloister. The next day she addressed the assembled monks on the demands of religious life, until the entire party returned to the mainland in a boat supplied by the monks.

In this way the summer passed. Catherine and Raymond continued their work, although as time went on they focused less energy on the crusade and more on fomenting resistance to the Florentine alliance. Some of their original traveling companions went home to Siena. Her mother left. Cecca went back to be with her grown daughter who was preparing to enter the convent, and Tommaso dalla Fonte returned to his duties at San Domenico. However, Neri di Landoccio Pagliaresi and Tommaso Caffarini came over from Siena to join the Pisa contingent. Neri took over the duties of scribe. Apparently there was murmuring in Siena about Catherine's activities. She brushed off the news, writing in a letter to Tommaso, "To think the world is opposing us! I don't deserve such mercy from them . . . that they should give me the cloak our sweet eternal father wore. Anyway, this is a little thing, such a little thing that it's almost nothing." A short time later she wrote to Tommaso again, apologizing to the Sienese Mantellate who wanted her home: "Tell them I'm sorry, and bless them all and the others a million times in the name of Jesus Christ and for me and these others."

In early September 1375 Catherine and her party left Pisa for the walled city of Lucca a short distance to the northeast. There is no record of the day they left or arrived, but everyone agrees that—because she was promoting the crusade—Catherine would have been present for Lucca's celebration of the Exaltation of the Cross on September 14 that commemorated finding the "true cross" in Jerusalem. The famous *Volto Santo* of Lucca—a wooden cross with a robed corpus of Jesus—was carried through the streets in a candlelit procession. Catherine's presence in the city likewise stirred much curiosity among onlookers. Caffarini described how people craned their necks to see the Sienese *santa* pass by. She may have stayed at a house outside the walls. Certainly she worshipped at the church of San Romano, since that was the meeting place of the local penitential women.

Catherine arrived in Lucca to find its leaders and population jittery. A few months earlier the city had been threatened by the combined forces of the

Milanese and Sir John Hawkwood, who, after he had left papal employ, sold his services to the Visconti. Now it looked like war was brewing between the papal forces and Florence, with Hawkwood and the Visconti siding with the latter. Poor Lucca was afraid of being caught in the middle. Yet for it to take sides with one or the other would only lay the groundwork for more problems in the future. Catherine recognized the anxiety. In her discussions with leading citizens of Lucca she argued that the cure for anxiety was deciding for the church, since the church possessed the light of Christ. Florence and Milan could not make such a claim.

Lucca was the place where Catherine, according to legend, was able to discern the difference between consecrated and unconsecrated bread. The story is not told by Raymond but by Caffarini in his *Libellus*, written to support the cause for canonization after her death. According to Caffarini, Catherine was sick in bed one day when a priest came to give her communion, accompanied by lighted candles and incense. In order to test her the priest had substituted unconsecrated bread for the consecrated host. She smelled it out at once and scolded him, saying, "Aren't you ashamed, Father, to bring me ordinary bread as if it were the Blessed Sacrament and turn me into an idolater?" The story may be invented, since it parallels a similar legend told about Margaret of Cortona, a Tuscan saint of the previous century. The two stories serve to underline a fascination with the real presence of Christ in the eucharist that emerged in the late Middle Ages. Until about the tenth century, few believers questioned exactly "how" Christ's presence could subsist in the consecrated bread. By the twelfth century scientific curiosity was beginning to infiltrate society. People became fascinated about the way things worked. In regard to the eucharist, they asked, if the bread was the "real" presence of Christ, what did that "real" mean? By receiving the bread did a person touch Christ? Bite Christ? Layers of awe and even fear began to cloud eucharistic devotion. Popular piety subtly shifted from taking the eucharist as food to beholding it as a holy object. So, while the story of Catherine's encounter with the bogus eucharist was meant to showcase her spiritual discernment, it also signals the direction of eucharistic piety in her day.

After some weeks, since there was not much they could do in Lucca after making their case for the crusade and urging loyalty to the pope, Catherine and Raymond returned to Pisa, intending to continue on to Siena. Because the political situation still hung in the balance, however, they remained in

Pisa a while longer. She wrote to Tommaso dalla Fonte, "I want you to know that I'm afraid I have to put off doing as you told me [i.e., coming home], because the archbishop [of Pisa] has asked the master general [of the Dominicans] whether I might stay several more days, as a favor."

Florence had dispatched an envoy to the Tuscan cities in an effort to pressure them to join the Florentine side. Siena, for one, was preparing to announce it had joined the league; Pisa and Lucca were still noncommittal. Catherine was hopeful she could influence their decision, but events were working against her. In Perugia early that December the nephew of the papal legate in that region caused the death of the wife of a prominent citizen. In an effort to escape his amorous advances, she had tried to climb from an upstairs window to a neighboring house but instead fell to the street. Faced with angry protests from the woman's husband and other citizens, the legate responded airily, "What then! Did you suppose all Frenchmen were eunuchs?" The story of the outrage quickly spread from city to city.

Already smarting from mercenaries who had been loosed on them by Avignon, citizens in the Italian states had had enough. Their leaders could no longer shape events but had to submit to the public mood. A discouraged Catherine and Raymond returned to Siena for the Christmas holiday amid stories of revolts breaking out against papal governors in the towns of northern Italy.

Shortly after the first of the year they had an urgent request to make another flying trip to Lucca, on the brink of deciding its allegiance. There is no record of who went with them. They stayed at the home of a nobleman, Bartolomeo Barbani. While they didn't get a promise from the Luccan leaders to opt for the papal side, at least the city did not announce for the Florentines while they were there.

Back home again in Siena, Catherine dictated a long letter to Gregory XI with a report on their efforts. It was the first of her many letters to the pope for which we possess a text.

Forsaking her usual opening of "I Catherine," she began, "Your unworthy, poor and wretched daughter Caterina, servant and slave of the servants of Jesus Christ, is writing to you in his precious blood." Her letter to the pope opened with comments on the perils of self-love, "whether . . . [among] rulers or the ruled," adding that rulers fall into this vice when due to self-centeredness or fear they fail to correct wrongdoers. "Sometimes, it's just that they would like to keep the peace, and this, I tell you, is the worst cruelty one can inflict. If a sore is not cauterized or excised when necessary . . . not only will it not heal, but it will infect the whole [body], often fatally."

She continued, calling the pope "My dear *babbo*!" (daddy), yet warning against the danger of excessive softness, deploring those doctors and shepherds who use ointment when they should use the knife or fire. "A shepherd such as this is really a hireling! Not only does he fail to rescue his little sheep from the clutches of the wolf; he devours them himself! And all because he loves himself apart from God. He does not follow the gentle Jesus, the true shepherd who gave his life for his little sheep."

Catherine reminded Gregory of his famous predecessor, Gregory the Great, who had a reputation for a firm hand. Yet, she added, "The flesh he was made of was no different from yours, and God is the same now as then."

Catherine concluded her encouragement of Gregory by urging, "If till now you haven't been very firm in truth, I want you, I beg you, for the little time that is left to be so—courageously and like a brave man—following Christ, whose vicar you are. And don't be afraid, father, no matter what may happen, of those blustery winds that have descended upon you—I mean those rotten members who have rebelled against you. Don't be afraid for divine help is near. Just attend to spiritual affairs, to appointing good pastors and administrators in your cities, for you have experienced rebellion because of bad pastors and administrators. Do something about it! . . . Pursue and finish with true holy zeal what you have begun by holy intent— I mean your return [to Rome] and the sweet holy crusade."

After this long homily, Catherine got down to Pisa and Lucca and faulted Gregory for not being in touch with them. "Forgive me, father, for talking to you like this. Out of the fullness of the heart the mouth speaks, you know . . . I beg you to communicate with Lucca and Pisa as a father, as God will teach you. Help them in any way you can and urge them to keep holding their ground. I have been in Pisa and Lucca until just now, and have pleaded with them as strongly as I could not to join the league with the rotten members who are rebelling against you. But they are very anxious, since they aren't getting any encouragement from you and are being constantly goaded and threatened by the other side. Still, they haven't up to now entirely given in. I beg you to write Messer Piero [Gambacorta] an urgent letter about this; do it for sure and without delay."

It was too little, too late. In mid-January 1376 the elders of Lucca decided to join the antipapal league. Sadly, Catherine wrote to the governing magistrates of Lucca, "I had been happy, jubilant, about the courage you'd had, up to now, to be strong and steadfastly obedient to holy Church. But now, when I heard the opposite, I was really sorry . . . You should know that if you were to do it [join the league] to save yourselves and to have peace, you would fall into greater warfare and ruin than ever—physically as well as spiritually. Don't get involved in such stupidity."

On March 14, Lucca formally entered the league, and Pisa soon followed. The Sienese hadn't needed as much time. They had thrown in their lot with Florence four months earlier.

Despite her warnings, it appeared the states of Italy were opting for war.

8

"THE BED OF FIRE AND BLOOD"

In the same letter that scolded Gregory for failing to communicate with the leaders of Pisa and Lucca, Catherine had the temerity to give the pope advice on the selection of cardinals. Her presumption must have startled Gregory. Very few women in the 1300s other than Catherine or Birgitta of Sweden would have dared give the pope advice regarding appointments. The pope had just created nine new cardinals, three of whom were related to him in one way or another. In her letter Catherine didn't object to any of his appointments specifically, but she did warn that when he chose people "I believe it would be in God's honor and better for you to be careful always to choose virtuous men. Otherwise it will be a great insult to God and disastrous to holy Church." Without quite saying so, she implied he had elevated men of little virtue in the past. Almost in the same breath she mentioned a rumor in circulation that Élias of Toulouse, master of the Dominican order, was being considered for a higher position. In which case, Catherine already had a successor in mind to replace him. She stopped short of revealing his name to the pope, instead referring him to Nicola da Osimo, one of the papal secretaries, whom she had written regarding her preference.

It is easy to see Raymond's hand in this. He would have been more aware than she of a possible change in the Dominican leadership, and no doubt he was better informed about the qualifications of cardinals. In prompting Catherine to raise these matters with the pope, however, Raymond found a willing collaborator. Even before she met Raymond, Catherine had been passionately committed to church reform, converted to that cause by William Flete and Bartolomeo Dominici. In addition, she had inherited the predilection—common among Sienese—for tweaking the machinery of government. Yet Catherine was no mere dilettante when it came to church reform. In her eyes reform was an essential element in the church's self-proclamation. She, who was committed to the conversion of individual sinners, knew that institutional conversion must follow in step if her penitents were to find a safe haven for their new faith. The reform she had in mind was moral rather than systemic since, like most of her contemporaries, Catherine tended to look upon church structures as God-given. The human qualities of church leaders, however, and the holiness of their lives, cried out for improvement, especially in the papal court at Avignon, the city that Petrarch called "Babylon on the Rhône." It was not the popes who were personally corrupt—on the whole the Avignon popes were capable and decent men—as much as the retinue and bureaucracy that surrounded them. The callous selling of church offices and indulgences was widespread. The lifestyles of some cardinals and bishops were scandalous, and this behavior trickled down to the local clergy. Boccaccio poked fun at friars whose "predecessors desired the salvation of men, [while] the friars today desire riches and women." Discontent with Avignon was further exacerbated in Italy by the insensitive qualities of many French-born legates sent down to govern papal territories in the Italian peninsula.

Over the years reform in the church became one of the three pillars of Catherine's preaching and political agitating, taking a place alongside crusading and the return of the pope to Rome. She was still working for reform toward the end of her life when she wrote her *Dialogue*. There she complained bitterly about rampant bribery, nepotism, and disgraceful behavior of clerics high and low. "Who are those who are clothed and fattened on what belongs to the Church?" she asked. "You and the other devils with you, and your beasts, the great horses you keep not because you need them but for your perverse pleasure . . . Such pleasures are for worldly people. Your pleasure ought to be with the poor and visiting the sick, assisting them with their spiritual and material needs." She spoke to those proud hierarchs with the voice of God: "How true it is that [such bishops] have made a robber's den of my Church, which is a place of prayer. They sell and buy and have made the grace of the Holy Spirit a piece of merchandise. So you see, those who want the high offices and revenues of the Church buy them by bribing those in charge with money and provisions. And those wretches [who took bribes] are not concerned about whether [the candidates] are good or bad, but only about pleasing them for love of the gifts they have received. So they make every effort to set these putrid plants in the garden of Holy Church, and for this the wretches will give a good report of them to Christ on earth [i.e., the pope]." The pope, she added, bears the weight of the responsibility: "If my Son's vicar becomes aware of their sin he ought to punish them . . . If Christ on earth does this, he is doing his duty. If he does not, his sin will not go unpunished when it is his turn to give me an account of his little sheep."

The little sheep from Siena was reminding her shepherd of the gospel mandate that he lay down his life for the flock. She expected nothing less from him. And if martyrdom was on her mind when she wrote *The Dialogue*, it was more intense still in 1375 when she was proclaiming a glorious crusade to the people of Tuscany. Just as the popes had their own reasons for supporting a crusade, Catherine had hers—and her reasons were only distantly related to preventing war in Europe or even recovering the Holy Land from the infidels. She had no particular dislike for the Muslims. In one breath she could call them "wicked, unbelieving dogs," but then turn around and acknowledge, "they are our brothers and sisters, ransomed as we [all] are by Christ's blood." She eventually had a vision that brought her to the conviction that the Christian and Muslim people were equally welcomed by God.

The real passion that inflamed her desire for a crusade was, as we have seen, the wish to pour out her blood—hers and the blood of other Christians—to God as repayment for the blood of Jesus. She dearly wished to be a martyr herself, but if that proved impossible to arrange, then the death of others would suffice if offered generously and ardently. Blood was the coin of payment. In late medieval times people were just beginning to discover how the human body worked and had come to recognize blood as the juice of life, the essential liquid that vivified earthly bodies just as Christ's blood enlivened the mystical body of believers. Students of medicine at the University of Bologna and elsewhere were taught that blood was the "father of all humors." A major part of the physician's art in that day (and indeed right through the eighteenth century) was managing the volume of blood in the body through the use of prudent bloodletting and restorative liquids. "Sanguine" people were considered the healthiest.

The medieval fixation on blood, however, went far beyond science and medicine. Blood was a religious image that filled them with fear and awe. By the Late Middle Ages, certainly in the north of Europe but in Italy as well, there was a religious "frenzy" for blood. According to one historian, "devotional art and poetry seem[ed] awash in blood." The phenomenon manifested itself in several ways. The new interest in the physical qualities of the eucharist led people to imagine they saw bleeding hosts on the altar—that the consecrated bread produced real blood. This "blood" was sometimes collected, preserved, and venerated by the faithful as Christ's blood. Held in equal awe were the bloodstained garments, said to be the clothing of martyrs, or bloody wooden relics allegedly of the cross, brought back to Europe by crusaders. Communion practice reinforced that sense of awe. Since about the twelfth century lay Christians were increasingly denied access to the cup of consecrated wine. Because the doctrine of concomitance held that the whole Christ was present in every fragment of bread, every drop of wine, people grew morbidly anxious about crumbs being lost or wine spilled. In some places the laity had to be satisfied with a cup of ordinary wine with just one drop of consecrated wine added to it. Later that, too, was withdrawn. As always, the human response to deprivation is heightened desire.

Catherine was undoubtedly affected by this desire. Denied the cup, she drank from Christ's side. The blood of Christ was constantly in her thoughts and on her lips. Nearly all of her letters opened with some reference to the blood of Christ. As she wrote to Queen Giovanna of Naples in June 1375, "I Caterina, servant and slave of the servants of God, am writing to encourage you in the precious blood of God's Son." To Tommaso dalla Fonte a few months later she wrote, "I . . . long to see you drowned and transformed in his overflowing blood." Her use of the image, though, was not founded on misguided awe or bogus relics. Blood for Catherine was a dynamic and life-giving image. It had the power of blessing, in the same way that the eucharistic chalice is sometimes called the cup of blessing. She who yearned to be a martyr knew that according to church teaching believers who were martyred before they could be baptized received the so-called baptism of blood. For them their own blood was a baptismal font, as though their blood became Christ's. She relished the belief that this life-giving fluid watered and permeated human existence, and she called on her followers to immerse themselves in it. Her wholehearted desire to submerge herself in the river of grace flowing from the cross was idealized as a goal for them all. She expressed it to Raymond of Capua in a letter written some years later: "Give your life to Christ crucified, and immerse yourself in the blood of Christ crucified. Eat souls as your food on the cross with Christ crucified. Submerge and drown yourself in the blood of Christ crucified. Keep living in God's holy and tender love."

As one can sense from this exalted language, Catherine's conception of the undertaking was festive and celebratory. She compared it more than once to a bridal feast and invited people to enlist in the crusade, for instance, and possible death as though they were joining a wedding party. In her eyes it ought to be spontaneous and communal—a joyous parade to the altar of sacrifice. "I am inviting you to the wedding feast of everlasting life," she wrote from Pisa to her Florentine friend Niccolò Soderini. "Fire up your desire to pay blood for blood. And invite as many as you can to come too (no one wants to go to a wedding alone), and then you will not be able to turn back." Catherine willingly threw herself into this journey of self-sacrifice, and her friends trailed along behind her. It was already too late to turn back.

The time she spent in Pisa and Lucca in 1375 was eventful for Catherine in ways that went beyond her advocacy for the crusade. For the very first time she was representing powerful interests in a foreign city. No longer the obscure tertiary from Siena, she carried the stamp of approval from the master of the Dominican order and, behind him, the pope. She was escorted by a distinguished and politically connected friar and accompanied by a crowd of male and female disciples. She made her residence in houses of wealthy patrons. She was recognized in public and fawned over in private.

No wonder Raymond of Capua was concerned that all this adulation might go to her head and cautioned her in the famous episode involving hand-kissing. He needn't have worried. Catherine was disposed to attribute honors she received to God and claim nothing for herself. Yet she could not have avoided that sense of entitlement that comes from bearing powerful credentials—oracle of God, bride of Christ, emissary of the pope—and she could not have been too surprised when a further distinction fell on her, although in this case it was the mark of suffering.

Just a few short days after she had arrived in Pisa, Catherine was praying in Santa Cristina Church next door to her residence. She had just received communion at a mass celebrated by Raymond. It was the fourth Sunday of Lent, Laetare Sunday, which that year fell on April 1. As was her custom,

Catherine slipped into an ecstatic state after receiving the eucharist. She lay face down on the church floor with her arms spread wide. After a time, Raymond and the others noticed that she rose to her knees, still with her eyes closed and her arms spread. As he later described it, "her face grew radiant. For a long time she knelt like that, bolt upright, her eyes closed. Then, whilst we still looked on, of a sudden she pitched forward on the ground as if she had received a mortal wound." They rushed to pick her up. She returned to consciousness with Raymond hovering over her. She murmured, "Father, I must tell you that, by his mercy, I now bear the stigmata of the Lord Jesus on my body." Raymond confessed he suspected something like that had happened, although by looking down he could see her hands were unmarked by wounds.

Catherine told them that during her prayer, Jesus had come down from the crucifix and walked toward her. Rays of blood shone from the wounds on his hands and feet and from his right breast striking her hands and feet and her left side. In the seconds before she collapsed she begged God to keep her wounds invisible. While no one else could see them, she told Raymond the wounds were excruciatingly painful—so painful, indeed, that she did not know how she could bear them. Her companions helped her back to her room where she collapsed again and hovered at the edge of consciousness. Raymond and the others were so worried that they immediately began to pray for her survival. Only slowly, over a period of days, did she regain her strength.

As far as we know, Catherine never spoke again about this experience. There is no mention of it in her letters and only an oblique reference in *The Dialogue*. That didn't stop her disciples from spreading stories about it and making it part of her popular legend. Raymond, obviously, related the whole incident in his biography written after her death. It was rumored that the marks of the stigmata, hidden during Catherine's life, appeared on her body after death. Several posthumous paintings show the wounds of the nails on her hands, so clearly the belief that she received the stigmata was part of contemporaneous lore.

On one level Catherine's stigmata can be taken simply as a private prayer experience. It has little bearing on her larger mission of bringing peace to Tuscany or reforming the church. One could write it off as an example of overwrought medieval spirituality without diminishing her other accomplishments. Yet to the extent that the stigmata became a part of her legend, it contributed to her notoriety and immeasurably strengthened the way people came to see her as a person favored by God. In the words of a modern historian, it became part of her "self-authorization"—a claim made on public credibility whose basis rests solely on the person making the claim. During Catherine's lifetime, her legend, enhanced by the stigmata, was used by her and others to leverage political and social ends.

For us, looking back, Catherine's stigmata provides a window on the religious sentiments of the age. Stigmatists were unknown to Christianity until Francis of Assisi in the early thirteenth century was said to have received the miraculous marks of Christ's passion on his hands, feet, and side. In the centuries after Francis, reports of people receiving the stigmata multiplied many times over. Nearly all of those who received the sign were women, and almost without exception the episodes occurred while the subject was in a state of ecstatic prayer—periods of intense emotional excitement. It can hardly be doubted the manifestations of Christ's wounds on a human body had a strong psychological basis. The wounds of some stigmatists bled copiously while others bled little or not at all. Frequently the wounds would go away, then reappear. The periodic nature of the bleeding (sometimes only on Fridays or once a year on Good Friday) did not strike its subjects as odd. Women were thoroughly used to periodic blood flow. Catherine, who had no menses because of severe fasting, likewise had no bleeding from her "hidden" wounds.

It is not surprising that the first stigmatists appeared in the 1200s. People in much of the Middle Ages were fascinated by the suffering Christ. In earlier Christian centuries the crosses in most churches had been unadorned wood, without a human form attached to them. From Carolingian times onward the figure of Christ attached to the cross became a new focal point. Very often the corpus would be twisted in agony to dramatize the horrendous suffering of the God-man. Preachers in medieval and later times would declaim at length on the public torture of Jesus, sometimes whipping their own bodies while in the pulpit to demonstrate the brutality of the passion. The crusades had drawn people's attention back to the land and the places of Christ's suffering. Pilgrims to the Holy Land relished the experience of following the way of the cross and imagining the punishment Jesus accepted at the hands of unbelievers. Carved or painted Stations of the Cross—miniature versions of the Jerusalem experience—began to appear in European churches during Catherine's lifetime. Bloody passion plays were performed in city squares. The drama in all of these displays served to center public attention on the violent passion and death of Jesus, obscuring the older theology that looked upon the cross as an image of triumph. By the late Middle Ages Christians were inflamed with the desire to replicate in their own bodies the suffering of Christ—whether that meant joining a crusade and being martyred in the Holy Land, or beating their bodies until they bled, or, for a select few, to have the marks of the passion miraculously imprinted on their bodies.

Theirs was a bloody era. People in the late Middle Ages did not turn away from gruesome suffering. Executions of criminals were public events and often involved the public torture of the victim prior to the final blow—thereby affording maximum suffering for the victim and maximum fascination for the crowd. The connection between these public deaths and the execution of Jesus was not lost on the audience, since medieval passion plays were frequently staged at the same places that were used for public executions—sometimes utilizing the real instruments of torture as props in the play. Blood figured prominently in staged dramatizations; large quantities of animal blood were provided by butchers to ensure that a generous amount would be available to lubricate the staged death scenes.

The spilling of blood, of course, has an ancient—even archetypal—significance as a rite of purification. It had always been used for that end in ancient Mediterranean cultures. For pagans the sacrifice of animals appeased the gods. For the people of Israel blood of the slain lamb, smeared over the lintel, sheltered them from the avenging angel at Passover. For Christians the life-giving blood of Jesus flowed in a mystical way over the human race, cleansing it and freeing it from sin.

One event in particular heightened this symbolism for Catherine during the spring and summer of 1375 when she was pursuing her double objective of promoting the crusade and urging the city of Pisa to support the pope. It took place in Siena, where authorities were engaged in their usual intrigues. There was in Siena a senator named Pietro Marchese del Santa Maria, a strong supporter of the pope and an ally of Catherine. Pietro had in his employ a young man from Perugia named Niccolò di Toldo, the son of a noble family. Niccolò's situation in Siena was delicate because the Sienese regarded citizens of Perugia with distrust, Perugia being one of the papal states. Not only that, Perugia maintained friendly ties with the power-hungry Salimbeni family in Siena. So Riformatori leaders in Siena were doubly wary of young Niccolò. They regarded him at the very least as an unfriendly visitor and at worst as an enemy agent.

Whatever his real role, Niccolò should have been more careful, especially during this period leading up to war between the Florentine league and the pope. Just a few careless words could be interpreted as subversion, for which a person could lose his head. Whether out of youthful innocence or genuine malice, Niccolò was heard to utter "certain rash words . . . against the Sienese state" and was arrested and hauled before the podestà. He was quickly found guilty and condemned to death. When the papal legate and de facto ruler of Perugia, Gerard du Puy, heard of the conviction he wrote two letters to authorities in Siena, the first inquiring about the nature of the crime and the second pleading for mercy. It was no use.

How Catherine in Pisa heard about Niccolò is not clear. She may have been alerted by the Sienese senator, or she may have been tipped off by Neri di Landoccio Pagliaresi, member of her own familigia who was then in the senator's service. Whichever way she got the news, it is clear that Catherine and Raymond were already familiar with Niccolò because she wrote a letter to Raymond—careful not to mention Niccolò by name—concerning "the one you know" who was facing execution.

Catherine had to act fast. Executions in Siena were normally carried out soon after being pronounced. It was early June. She gathered a few things together and with a couple of companions—we don't know who—made a flying visit back to her native city. There she met Tommaso Caffarini, and together they went to visit Niccolò in his prison cell. It was the afternoon or evening before his scheduled execution. They found him full of rage and despair—in Caffarini's words, pacing his cell "like a ferocious and desperate lion." Catherine spoke with him. Their conversation is not recorded, but we can imagine it. It is also possible to guess the impression made on the handsome young Perugian by this passionate young woman as they spoke of life and death in the intimate confines of his cell. Men could not help being attracted to her. In appearance she was pale, thin, and virginal, yet she spoke quietly with such blazing words that both men and women were simply bowled over by the force of her personality. For Niccolò she reiterated the message he had learned in childhood—that faith in God offered a way out of his predicament. This God of hers (and of his) promised freedom that was greater and more enduring than earthly justice or political solutions. She, Catherine, guaranteed it. Niccolò listened and wept. His anger dissolved and fell from him, washed away by her tenderness and absolute conviction. He had not been especially faithful to his religion, but at her urging he confessed his sins to Caffarini who came out of the shadows for that purpose. Before Catherine left, Niccolò begged her to be with him the next day at the place of execution. He could bear anything, he said, with her at his side. She promised to come again in the morning and then wait for him at the block.

In her letter to Raymond that described these events, Catherine treated her conversation with Niccolò in three sparse sentences. It must have been far more wrenching in person than she made it out to be. It was enough to turn Niccolò's life around. She came away from their meeting marveling at the grace that allowed people in extremis to grasp the offered hand.

In her role as angel of mercy to a condemned man, Catherine was taking on a ministry that during the Middle Ages was handled primarily by lay Christians. Prisons in that era did not have the established chaplaincies we know today. Prisoners condemned to death were usually accompanied to the scaffold by laypersons known as comforters. Often the *conforteria* ministry in a given city became the responsibility of tertiaries trained in the work. Siena had such a group, although why those designated ministers were not caring for Niccolò di Toldo has not been explained; perhaps they offered their services, but he in his despair drove them away. It may have been unusual for a female comforter to care for a male prisoner, but in general her role as a layperson comforting another at the moment of death was understood perfectly by those involved in the execution.

The next morning, even before the curfew bell sounded from the Mangia tower, Catherine rose and went to Niccolò in his cell. It isn't mentioned who accompanied her. Probably Caffarini again. At this point in her narrative all other human beings, both individuals and crowds, utterly disappear. Her focus shrinks to the intimacy of a bridal chamber, with room only for Catherine, Niccolò, and God. "I went to him," she wrote, "and he was greatly consoled." Niccolò, whose last night on earth was spent in solitude, was enormously relieved to have her back. She took him from his cell to another room to attend mass with her. There he received communion that he had for so long neglected.

Back in his cell again they had time for a short talk. Niccolò confessed that his only fear was not being strong at the moment of execution. Once more she assured him that she would be there. "Stay with me," he pleaded.

"Don't leave me alone. That way I can't help but be all right, and I'll die happy." At this point she was holding him. "His head was resting on my breast," she wrote. "I sensed an intense joy, a fragrance of his blood—and it wasn't separate from the fragrance of my own, which I am waiting to shed for my gentle spouse Jesus."

The intense affection—even eroticism—of the moment must have been apparent to them both. She was both lover and mother nursing him, crooning into his ear, his head resting on her breast. Catherine knew their emotions were conflicted but did not pull away from them. It is a "trick" that God makes use of, she thought—using Niccolò's love for her to gain a soul for heaven. So was her love for Niccolò, although she failed to mention that.

Holding him, she whispered, "Courage, my dear brother, for soon we shall reach the wedding feast. You will go to it bathed in the sweet blood of God's son, with the sweet name of Jesus, which I don't want ever to leave your memory." Consummation was approaching. "I shall be waiting for you at the place of execution."

He pulled away from her, his face shining. "What is the source of such a grace for me, that my soul's sweetness will wait for me at the holy place of execution?"

Niccolò, Catherine reflected, had made such progress that he was able to see the place of execution as "holy."

"I shall go joyful and strong," Niccolò announced, "and when I think that you will be waiting for me there, it will seem like a thousand years until I get there!"

He followed this with "such tender words as to make one burst at God's goodness!" Catherine recalled.

And so the lovers parted—he to ride in a cart through the streets of the city to the place of execution, and she to walk there directly. It was a custom for the conforteria minister to ride in the cart with the prisoner, holding an icon before the prisoner's face so he could keep fresh in his mind the salvation awaiting him. Catherine did not ride with Niccolò; perhaps it was beyond the bounds of what a woman could do. During the ride the prisoner was usually tortured. Often his skin would be pinched and torn by red-hot instruments. This seems not to have happened in Niccolò's case. The appeals of the Perugian government on behalf of the nobleman Niccolò might have spared him from that indignity, since he was not in pain when he arrived at his destination.

Catherine reached the place of execution well before him. She mounted the platform with her spirit still swimming with feelings left from her meeting with Niccolò and the fate awaiting him. She had long dreamed of martyrdom for herself. Now Niccolò was going to achieve it, or something like it. In a sense, death by martyrdom was like mysticism. Both aspired to union with God. But where a mystic, in ecstatic prayer, could come close to union, the martyr, it was believed, entered the court of heaven directly and beheld God face to face. No wonder Catherine was envious, gazing at the block where Niccolò would soon place his neck.

She walked over to it, oblivious to the crowd that was pushing into the area in front of the scaffold. Delicately she knelt and placed her own neck on the block. As she described the experience: "I knelt down and stretched my neck out on the block, but I did not succeed in getting what I longed for up there." Centuries later we try to picture the scene: we see the avid faces of the crowd, the platform with the executioner and witnesses already in place, the young woman in a Dominican habit kneeling and putting her neck on the block. The crowd, watching, suddenly falls silent, their eyes on her alone. There is a moment of utter stillness. Then she rises and moves aside.

She prayed. "I waited there in continual prayer and in the presence of Mary [the mother of Jesus] and Catherine, virgin and martyr . . . I prayed and pleaded with Mary that I wanted this grace, that at his last moment she would give him light and peace of heart and afterwards see him return to his destination. Because of the sweet promise made to me, my soul was so filled that although a great crowd of people was there I wouldn't see a single person."

The reference to "Catherine, virgin and martyr" was an allusion to Catherine of Alexandria, the legendary early Christian martyr and patroness of the medieval Dominicans. Like her Sienese namesake, the first Catherine was married mystically to Christ. By mentioning her name at this moment Catherine was once more introducing a marriage motif into Niccolò's execution.

At last the cart bearing Niccolò arrived. He dismounted "like a meek lamb" and, seeing Catherine waiting for him, laughed. Whether it was joy or nervousness we don't know, but he seemed genuinely reassured by her presence, asking her to make the sign of the cross over him.

They had eyes only for each other. She led him to the block, saying, "Down for the wedding, my dear brother, for soon you will be in everlasting life!" Again he complied "very meekly." She described the events that followed: "I placed his neck [on the block] and bent down and reminded him of the blood of the Lamb. His mouth said nothing but 'Gesù!' and 'Caterina!' and as he said this, I received his head into my hands, saying 'I will' with my eyes fixed on divine Goodness."

With a thump of the axe Niccolò's head was severed from his body and fell into her hands. Kneeling next to him, her hands and habit were splattered with his blood. The words "I will" were spoken almost as a bridal vow.

It was an extraordinary moment. The complex feelings of the principals were mirrored by the complex symbolism in Catherine's description of it, as parsed by one scholar. Catherine "stands in for Christ" as Niccolò's spouse, yet "scripts herself" as Catherine of Alexandria who was both a martyr and a bride of Christ. Lastly, she imitates the Virgin Mary by "standing over" Niccolò, whose mystical marriage has been "consummated in his execution."

Catherine had worried almost to the end that Niccolò would not bear up under the pressure. According to the accepted theological view of that time the state of a soul at the moment of death is crucially important; a denial of God in the last second of life could doom one to eternal punishment. Niccolò was safe now, she believed. Gazing with her inner eye upon Christ, the "divine Goodness," Catherine saw Niccolò, "bathed in [his] own blood," enter the side of Christ. Just before he disappeared "he made a gesture sweet enough to charm a thousands hearts . . . He turned as does a bride when, having reached her husband's threshold, she turns her head and looks back, nods to those who have attended to her, and so expresses her thanks."

Her work was done. She felt utterly fulfilled and at the same time strangely alone. As she wrote, "Now that he was hidden away where he belonged, my soul rested in peace and quiet in such a fragrance of blood that I couldn't bear to wash away his blood that had splashed on me . . . Poor wretch that I am, I don't want to say any more! With the greatest envy I remained on earth!"

The entire episode involving Niccolò di Toldo was related in a single letter written by Catherine while she was still in Siena to Raymond of Capua back in Pisa. We can only guess what ran through Raymond's mind when he read it, so filled was the letter with deep human feeling and complex symbolism. We will never know for sure because Raymond, when he came to write her biography years later, never once mentioned the letter or

Niccolò's execution. Indeed the absence of the execution in Raymond's *Life* has led some scholars to doubt it really happened or to claim that the whole story was a concoction of Tommaso Caffarini. Today, despite some ongoing problems with the letter (especially the fact that Catherine never once mentions Niccolò's name in it), the event itself and Catherine's participation in it are generally accepted as historical.

As evidence of its authenticity, the letter is so brimming with Catherine's spirit and style that it is difficult to consider it a forgery. In addition, her reputation as a truth-teller is so secure that one can't fathom her trying to pass off a private vision as a historical event involving real people. Records from the city of Siena confirm that a political criminal named Niccolò di Toldo was executed around the time of Catherine's narrative.

There may be good reasons why Raymond chose to make no mention of the Niccolò incident in his *Life*. His biography of Catherine was written with the aim of advancing her cause for canonization. He may have felt that a letter so marked by conflicted emotional feelings could only muddy the process for sainthood. Even more likely, Raymond may have avoided the incident deliberately because the account of Niccolò's life and death would have raised anew the matter of Avignon's intelligence operations against Siena and Florence, since most likely Niccolò *was* a spy for the papal court working to subvert the commune of Siena. Raymond, who spent a lifetime serving the popes, may have preferred to keep the whole matter under wraps.

And there may be still another reason. Catherine's account of the Niccolò episode was likely the first letter she ever wrote to Raymond. Certainly it is the first that has come down to us. Her relationship with her mentor was barely a year old at the time, and Raymond, the esteemed son of Neopolitan nobility, may have been unsettled, even shocked, by the tone of it—by its ravishing language and bold claim of self-authorization. Like most of her letters this one was written not merely to inform him of what happened but to challenge him personally. In this case Catherine wanted Raymond to free himself from gentlemanly constraints and become more charismatic, throwing himself into events of daily life as she did. She spoke to him as though he was the disciple and she the teacher.

In the opening of the letter, she went after him in her typical way: "I long to see you engulfed and drowned in the sweet blood of God's Son, which is permeated with the fire of his blazing charity . . . I am saying that unless you are drowned in the blood you will not attain the little virtue of true humility, which is born from hatred as hatred is from love, and so come forth in the most perfect purity as iron comes out purified from the furnace."

Fresh from her experience with Niccolò, Catherine was demanding from Raymond nothing less than passion—a passion for life and a passion for God. She wanted him to do as she did and hurl himself onto the bridal bed where sin is burned away and truth made clear.

Or, as she wrote, "I want you to shut yourself up in the open side of God's Son, that open storeroom so full of fragrance that sin itself is made fragrant. There the dear bride rests in the bed of fire and blood. There she sees revealed the secret of the heart of God's Son."

The good, discreet friar may have read it with a sinking heart. Who was this woman he had been put in charge of?

9

ENCOUNTER IN AVIGNON

"You know that a member cut off from its head cannot live, for it is not joined with the source of its life. It is the same, I tell you, with people cut off from God's love and charity." This was Catherine writing to Niccolò Soderini, the wealthy Florentine merchant. She was in her sermon mode but imparting more than just religious wisdom. Catherine used metaphors to assert several things at once, and in this case she was warning Soderini that Florence risked very much by cutting itself off from the pope. For a brief period in 1376 Soderini was a member of Florence's Signoria, or executive council, and Catherine wanted him to use his influence to prevent a final break. "You know what I'm talking about," she said to him. "Now who are we—poor, miserable, proud, and wicked as we are— that we should act against our head. Oimé! Oimé! [Woe! Woe!] The blind sight of our pride and arrogance shows us the flower of prestige and power, but we don't see the worm that has gotten under the flowering plant and is gnawing away at it. And it will soon die if it doesn't set itself right."

Soderini was aware of the worm as clearly as she, but there was little he could do about it. Florence was preparing for war. In a sense, armed conflict had already begun. In November of the previous year, while Catherine was still visiting Pisa and Lucca, citizens in Città di Castello, a town near Perugia, had heeded Florence's cry for liberty and overthrown their papal governor. Perugia itself soon did the same, followed by Viterbo. In March 1376, Bologna—the northern anchor of the papal states—likewise rebelled. If this wasn't war, it was the nearest thing to it. Agents of Florence were busy trying to convince the people of Rome not to accept the pope should he ever attempt to return there.

There were many who, like Catherine and Soderini, equated the rebellion against the church as an attack on divinely instituted power. Theirs was a medieval understanding of society in which human relationships mirrored the divine order and where the church had a central and sacred place. Medieval society was organized on a hierarchical and largely rural, feudal pattern. The later Middle Ages, however, especially in Italy, experienced the growth of cities where people came together in more egalitarian ways. In Florence, as in Siena, political leadership had passed into the hands of the lower guilds that were less respectful of the prerogatives of wealth, family, and church. The guildsmen, in turn, were being pressured from below by poor laborers who wanted citizenship and a measure of power. So for the people of Florence the demand for liberty was not just a political slogan but reflected the aspirations of people who suddenly felt unbound from old restraints.

Predictably, because he, too, was a medieval man, Pope Gregory's response to these aspirations was clumsy and insensitive. He offered written assurances that the consolidation of the papal domain in Italy was no threat to Tuscany. But actions spoke louder than words. When Florence experienced a crop shortage back in 1374, its leaders attempted to purchase grain from lands controlled by the papal legate but were turned down. Despite the threat of famine, Florence would get no grain from the pope. Citizens of Florence were outraged. The grain fiasco convinced many moderates that the pope was working against their best interests.

For Catherine the church was more than a mere social entity. The church was a divine institution, so a break with the church severed persons and groups from life-giving grace. As she explained it to Soderini, "If you should say to me, 'I'm not scorning [Christ's] blood!' I say that is not so . . . How can you tell me that you can attack a body without attacking the blood within the body?" She closed her letter to him with a plea: "I beg you, Niccolò, by the ineffable love with which God created you and so kindly redeemed you, to try as hard as you can . . . to bring about peace and unity between yourselves and holy Church, so that you and all of Tuscany may not be endangered. It doesn't seem to me that war is so lovely a thing that we should go running after it when we can prevent it."

Surely war was an unlovely thing. Yet in making that charge Catherine was possibly forgetting her recent advocacy of a bloody crusade. The disconnect between deploring war in Italy and desiring war in the Holy Land had not yet come home to her, although it soon would.

Around the same time that she was urging the Florentines to make peace, Catherine was imploring Pope Gregory to refrain from armed retaliation against them. She laid it out for him as if it were a children's story. "I long to see you a good shepherd, my dear *babbo*, for I see the infernal wolf carrying off your little sheep . . . Then along comes God's infinite goodness and sees the sheep's sorry state. He knows he cannot use wrath or war to entice [the wolf] away from them. Supreme eternal wisdom doesn't want it that way, even though the sheep had wronged him." Then she got personal. She begged the pope—as a favor to *her*—to treat the people of Florence with kindness. "Oh my dear most holy *babbo*! I see no other way, no other help for getting back your little sheep who have left the fold of holy Church, as rebels disobedient and unsubmissive to you their father. So I am begging you in the name of Christ crucified, and I want you to do me this favor, use your kindness to conquer their malice. We are yours, father, and I am certain that all of them realize they have done wrong."

Of course the leaders of Florence realized no such thing. If anything, their opposition to the pope was hardening. As mentioned, after Gregory XI had made a truce with Bernabò Visconti of Milan in June 1375, the pope's former mercenaries under John Hawkwood began to prey on the cities of Tuscany. Florence had to pay Hawkwood a huge sum to escape his predations.

The city fathers of Florence were determined to recoup from the church the money they had paid Hawkwood, and so they created an eight-man board called *Otto dei preti*, popularly known as the Eight Saints, to levy a forced loan on the clergy of the Florence diocese. It was a fateful step. Historically the church had claimed immunity from state levies on the grounds that church property was not subject to secular power. King Philip the Fair at the turn of the century had attempted to tax church property in France, and now Florence was goading the pope with the same weapon.

Florentine leaders knew this was bound to escalate the conflict. One month after creating the first eight-man board, they created a second to oversee further operations. This one was called *Otto di balìa* but on the street was dubbed *Otto della Guerra*—the Eight of War.

All this was taking place while Catherine and Raymond of Capua were touring Pisa and Lucca, preaching the crusade while working behind the scenes to keep those two cities from joining the Florentine alliance against the pope. Their efforts were in vain. The actual war began slowly as city after city overthrew its papal governor in the name of *libertas*. It took Gregory XI several months to respond. As pope, he had several advantages on his side. While he had no standing army to speak of, he had the wealth to hire mercenary forces. In addition, his papal office gave him moral leverage that could be exploited by a cadre of clergy scattered throughout the rebelling states, reinforced by a devout laity. Lastly, the pope possessed a still more powerful weapon: he could place groups or even whole cities under interdict, closing churches and stopping the administration of the sacraments. This was no slap on the wrist in a society where the church provided the only hope of salvation, the only sure guarantor of happiness in the afterlife. Persons under interdict could not receive communion, confess their sins, or have a church funeral.

On February 11, 1376, Gregory issued an ultimatum to the leaders of Florence ordering them to appear before him in Avignon by the end of March or suffer the consequences. The threat of interdict was in the air. Florence was not surprised by the summons or inclined to submit meekly, but leading citizens thought it wise to go through the motions of conciliation so it could not be said later that they had been intransigent. They searched their minds for a person or persons in good standing with the pope who could serve as an intermediary. The name they came up with was Catherine of Siena. She had the advantage of being nearby, was undoubtedly a holy woman esteemed by the pope, and on good terms with influential men in Florence. Last not least, she was an advocate of peace. The Florentines weighed the propriety of being represented in Avignon by a woman, especially by a young woman (Catherine was then twenty-eight). In the end they settled on Raymond of Capua to go "in Catherine's name." The invitation was duly forwarded.

There are no letters or testimony to indicate how this news was received in Siena, but there is reason to believe it was eagerly welcomed. Raymond set off almost at once, accompanied by someone named Papo, going first to Florence and then to Pisa. In Pisa he was joined by the Augustinian Giovanni Tantucci and a Dominican, Felice da Massa. Catherine had thought that he might need a secretary or messenger during the trip, so she sent Neri di Landoccio Pagliaresi bearing a letter with greetings for Raymond and other friends in Pisa.

The season of Lent was just beginning. It would have been her first Lent with Raymond, and now Catherine had to go through it without him. Echoing the words of Jesus to his disciples, she wrote Raymond, "With tremendous blazing desire I have longed to celebrate this Pasch with you"— but it was not to be. To take her mind off the worsening political situation, she dictated a series of letters to female disciples in Lucca exhorting them to greater faithfulness to God and the practice of voluntary poverty. Other letters went out to Bartolomeo Dominici, who was preaching a Lenten mission in Asciano.

Lent began as a time of spiritual favors. In her letter to Raymond, Catherine announced that "the day after I was separated from you gentle First Truth, my eternal Spouse, decided to treat me as a father does his daughter, or a bridegroom his bride, not being able to bear her grieving at all but finding new ways to give her joy. Imagine . . . ! The supreme eternal Word and exalted Godhead gave me such joy that even the parts of my body felt as if they were melting, disintegrating like wax in the fire." She said it was an experience of simultaneously loving God and loving herself, the way one might look into a fountain and see water but also see the self reflected there. Mixing her metaphors, she added that the Word of God becomes "engrafted into our humanity," so that one can't tell where the human ends and the divine begins. It is heaven on earth, or heaven *and* earth. "In no other way could we ever experience him in everlasting life or see him face to face, except by first experiencing him in this life through affection and love and desire in the way I've described."

Then just before Holy Week she had another revelation. She specified that it happened "on the night of April first," so it must have been a dream or maybe a shadow vision that played out on the walls of her room as Catherine lay on her pallet. Describing it in another letter to Raymond, she said God "showed his marvels in such a way that my soul seemed to be outside my body and was so overwhelmed that I can't really describe it in words." It was a vision about love. Her heart was so full that she demanded Raymond and all who read the letter should "Love, love, love one another! Be glad, be jubilant! Summertime is coming!"

Catherine had been worrying about the church, trying to make sense of the Florentine rebellion. She had wondered why God allowed it to happen—why sin in any shape or form happened. It was the problem of evil that believers in every age have wrestled with.

The answer, she said, was love. God *allowed* evil to happen. He *needed* evil so that love could restore the church to its original purity. When put through the furnace of charity, sin would be melted down and transformed into love.

She described her nighttime vision in more detail. "The fire of holy desire was growing within me as I gazed. And I saw the people, Christians and unbelievers, entering the side of Christ crucified. In desire and impelled by love I walked through their midst and entered with them into Christ gentle Jesus. And with me were my father Saint Dominic, the beloved John [the Evangelist], and all my children. Then he placed a cross on my shoulder and put the olive branch in my hand, as if he wanted me (and so he told me) to carry it to the Christians and unbelievers alike. And he said to me: 'Tell them, "I am bringing you news of great joy!"'"

"Then," Catherine continued, "my soul was fuller than ever. It was immersed in the divine Being, along with the truly joyful, in union with love's affection. So great was my soul's delight that I was no longer conscious of the pain I had felt at seeing God offended [i.e., by the rebellion]. In fact I said, 'Is sin blessed now?'" In her vision Jesus responded that sin is indeed blessed and transformed, quoting Gregory the Great, a famous pope of the early church, who called sin a "blessed fault."

It was a vision worthy of the book of Revelation or Dante's *Paradiso*, in which all people, believers and infidels, are swept up and gathered in the shelter of God's reconciling love. Like most of Catherine's visions, it also involved a commission. She believed herself sent into the world bearing the cross of love's suffering on one shoulder and the branch of peace on the other. It gave her a feeling for the role she could play in the crisis that was developing.

That was April 1. The news hadn't reached her yet that on the previous day in Avignon, Gregory XI had pronounced sentence on Florence. He had considered the arguments put forward by Florence and rejected them outright. The punishment was harsher than expected. Florence and its allied cities would be placed under interdict; churches would be closed, priests forbidden to say mass or hear confessions. And there was more: all debts and loans owed to Florence by outsiders were cancelled; an embargo was placed on Florentine goods; citizens of Florence who traveled outside their state could be captured, imprisoned, or even enslaved. For a mercantile city like Florence it was the equivalent of a death sentence.

Once the news reached her, that's the way Catherine saw it too. Writing to the "Lords of Florence" a week or so later, she compared their city to a gangrenous limb on the body of the church. "It is clear that by your disobedience and persecution (believe me, my brothers, I am saying this with heartfelt sorrow and tears), you have fallen into death and into hatred and contempt for God. Nothing worse could happen to you than to be deprived of his grace." She urged them to "Get up and run to your father's arms!"

Florence was not ready to run into the pope's arms. It was still winning the war on the ground. Yet some cooler heads among the citizenry were beginning to question the long-term benefits of the struggle. Reports had reached them that Avignon was assembling a force of Bretons, the fiercest and most brutal of all the mercenary bands, to send down against them. And who could tell what toll the economic sanctions might take if the war stretched into months or years? Now that Florence had made its point, some of its citizens wondered if this might not be a good time to sue for peace. They began to discuss names for a possible delegation.

At this juncture Catherine came back into the picture. There is some question about how she got involved. Previous accounts of her life have maintained that Catherine offered her services to Florence, but the letter cited as evidence—the one addressed to the Lords of Florence—is ambiguous. It concludes with the routine offer of services "if I can be of any use." Raymond of Capua guessed that the initiative came from Florence, saying that the same people who commissioned his trip to Avignon "brought" Catherine to Florence. Most likely these were private citizens rather than the Signoria or the Eight of War.

In any case, the invitation she received mentioned only a trip to Florence, not Avignon. Yet Catherine was already weighing the longer trip. There was a list of matters she wanted to discuss with the pope, and the Florentine business provided an opportunity to do it. There was still the crusade, for instance; Gregory had announced it but had not put it in motion. There was the whole matter of church reform that distressed her terribly. In mid-April she had written to Cardinal Giacomo Orsini, Siena's official "protector" stationed in Avignon, begging him to "do what you can about seeing to the appointment of good pastors and administrators . . . Don't make us and God's other servants keep dying of heartbreak!" Last but surely not least was the issue of the pope's return to Rome. Having the pope in Rome was connected to reform, since he could not know what was going on in Italy from faraway Avignon. In the same letter to Gregory that had advocated kindness for Florence, Catherine had added an urgent plea: "Come, come," she wrote, "don't resist any longer the will of God who is calling you! The starving little sheep are waiting for you to come and take possession of the place of your predecessor and model, the apostle Peter. Come! Come! Come! Don't put it off any longer! Take heart and don't be afraid of anything that might happen, for God will be with you."

Catherine was not the only one imploring the pope to return. Most Italians wanted the pope to come back and restore Rome to its old glory. Almost from the beginning of his term in office, Gregory XI had expressed the intention of going back someday. He had told Edward III of England that returning was his "dearest wish." In February 1374 he had informed a consistory of cardinals of his plans to go. What restrained him was his cautious nature. He was an honest but conventional man who fretted over difficult decisions. The cardinals and members of his court had grown used to the easy life in Provence and opposed the idea of returning to Rome. He, like them, feared the volatile Roman mob and how it might react to a French pope and his Frenchified curia. As a result, he equivocated. Catherine had expressed "joy upon joy" in January 1376 when the archbishop of Otranto, then in Avignon, had told her the pope was going to move soon. When in late March there was no sign of movement she wrote Gregory again, even more firmly, telling him to be a man: "My dear father! I am begging you, I am *telling* you: come! . . . In the name of Christ crucified I am telling you! Don't choose to listen to the devil's advisors. They would like to block your holy and good resolution. Be a courageous man for me, not a coward. Respond to God, who is calling you to come and take possession of the place of the glorious shepherd, Saint Peter, whose vicar you are."

One wonders what Gregory thought of Catherine's demands. Whatever his feelings about that particular letter, on April 18 he responded to promptings from many quarters and arranged for Venetian galleys to wait for him at Marseille on September 1 and take him to Rome. It is doubtful Catherine knew those plans were in the works when she set out for Florence in the first days of May.

She was accompanied by Stefano Maconi, who was acting as her secretary, Bartolomeo Dominici, who had returned from his preaching mission in Asciano, and three Mantellate companions, her sister-in-law Lisa, Alessa Saracini, and Cecca Gori. In his account of her life Raymond declared that

Catherine was brought to the "neighborhood of Florence" (another translation says the "outskirts" of Florence) and met there by "the Priors of the city" who begged her "in a most pressing way" to go to Avignon and negotiate peace between the city and the pope. This is questionable in several respects. First of all, we know Catherine and her party remained in Florence for about a month, so she likely stayed in the center of the city, probably at the home of Niccolò Soderini. Second, it is still unclear who invited Catherine to Florence. By naming "the Priors," Raymond suggests they were members of the Signoria, but there's no mention of such a meeting in city records, and anyway the Eight of War, rather than the Signoria, were really running things then. Lastly, while her friends in Florence may have urged her on to Avignon, it would not have required a great deal of pressure since Catherine was planning to go anyway.

She spent her time in Florence meeting people in an effort to learn what sort of peace terms the commune would accept. It was hard to get a clear picture because she did not have access to those who were making policy. The chancellor of Florence at that time was the eminent humanist Coluccio Salutati, whose letters and proclamations had laid out the city's case against Avignon. He was inaccessible to Catherine, as were members of the Eight. Her briefings came primarily from elite members of the old Parte Guelfa—men like Soderini, Carlo Strozzi, Piero Canigiani, and Lapo di Castiglionchio, who were more disposed in the pope's favor and therefore inexpert barometers of Florence's mood.

During the weeks she spent in Florence the papal interdict formally went into effect. Churches were locked and the city hunkered down to see if it could ride out the economic sanctions. Catherine was saddened to see it happening. While the Florentines were outwardly defiant, the interdict at least nudged them to test the waters of peace. An official delegation was being readied to go to Avignon and see what terms might be forthcoming. Catherine hurried her own preparations, intending to get there first. She left Florence the last week of May, accompanied by Stefano Maconi, Bartolomeo Dominici, the three Mantellate women, and the three Buonconti brothers, Gherardo, Tommaso, and Francesco, in whose family house Catherine had lodged during her stay in Pisa.

The trip, mostly on foot, took three weeks. Catherine rarely described details of her travels and left no record of that journey. Speculation has routed them north to Bologna, where the party would certainly have visited the tomb of Saint Dominic in the Bolognese church of San Domenico. The road led next to the Ligurian coast, past Genoa, and into Provence along the Côte d'Azur. In June the weather would have been warm, the sky brilliant. Upon reaching the mouth of the Rhône, they likely took a boat up through the Camargue and past Arles to the city of the popes.

Arriving in Avignon in 1376 by boat would have been a memorable experience. Moving against the stream, powered by the last breaths of the mistral, the travelers would see flowers and fruit trees in abundance along the riverbanks, while farther off vineyards marched in neat rows up the hillsides of Provence. After rounding the last bend in the river, they would behold the walls of the city, and behind these the massive facade of the Palace of the Popes and the cathedral, outlined against an intensely blue sky. Everything here on the east bank of the Rhône—the papal buildings and the city itself—belonged to the Holy See, purchased from Queen Giovanna of Naples in 1348, while on the west bank the town of Villeneuve-lès-Avignon was French territory. Crowning the highest point of the French town was the massive fortification with towers built by Philip the Fair in the late thirteenth century. There were farms and arbors on both sides of the river and a scattering of estates and manors half hidden under the trees— signs of the wealth that had come to Avignon in the seventy years since the popes first made their residence here. Cardinals, nobles, and diplomats lived a languid existence in the verdant, rather sleepy capital. Many of the prelates had become immensely rich. According to one report the typical estate housed a score of servants as well as "troupes of buffoons to make the owners laugh, singers, male and female, musicians to play concerts . . . such attendants as officers of the hunt and falconry, captive monkeys and even lions," not to mention mistresses and other companions. It is little wonder the cardinals resisted every attempt by the pope to move back to Rome.

As the boat moved farther upriver, visitors would finally come in sight of the twenty-two stone arches of the bridge of St.-Bénézet —the famous *pont d'Avignon*—angling across the Rhône to connect the two riverbanks and two states. Built in the twelfth century, the bridge was one of only two places between Lyon and the sea where one could cross the Rhône dry-shod. It had the effect of making Avignon an important trading center, the river itself being the north-south axis for transporting goods while the bridge and its road formed the east-west axis. It gave Avignon an edge over its neighbors. Arles to the south was larger than Avignon and served as the archbishop's see, but Avignon controlled the crossroads. The town was also blessed to have a pope in residence to provide an ongoing spectacle for its citizens and visitors alike. A historian has left us a picture of a pope setting off from his palace on a cavalcade to a neighboring estate: "[There were] the pope's white palfreys, led by a groom, equerries carrying the *pallium*, or white wool band worn by the Pontiff as a symbol of might—and three red hats set on poles. Then would come two papal barbers, each holding a red case, one containing the pope's garments, the other his tiara in its box. After a subdeacon holding up the cross, followed by a horse or mule bearing the Corpus Christi . . . then came the pope himself on a white horse, half a dozen nobles around him holding a canopy over his head, behind him an equerry carrying a *montatorium* to help him mount or dismount. A great crowd of courtiers, prelates and members of the pope's household were next, the most useful being, perhaps, the pope's almsgiver whose function was to break up traffic jams by scattering little coins."

It is unlikely Catherine would have enjoyed that spectacle or that she was thrilled to behold the city and its palaces. She looked forward to meeting the pope, the man she called Christ on Earth, but the place itself held no allure for her. For Catherine, Avignon symbolized the dissipation and corruption that was eroding the soul of the church. It stood for everything that she was struggling against. She would have agreed with Petrarch:

> From the impious Babylon, from which
> all shame has fled, all good is banished,
> the house of grief, the mother of error,
> I've also fled, to prolong my life.

It was said she had a preternatural ability to *smell* sin. She always knew when one of her male followers had surrendered to carnal desires—one sniff and she would send him off to confession. Now, as she stepped off the boat at the landing place near the east end of the bridge, one can imagine her sampling the air and frowning. She did not want to spend any more time in Avignon than was absolutely necessary.

The attitude of Avignon toward its famous visitor was something else again. Avignon was both suspicious and fascinated by her. Gossip about Catherine was already circulating on the streets and in palace corridors. Quite possibly a copy of the *Miracoli* had made its way to Avignon to be passed around and read avidly. Prelates warned each other to guard against the dangerous young woman and her trances. Yet many others were captivated by her story and eagerly looked forward to meeting the maiden of Siena, or at least catching sight of her. One of those who quickly attached herself to Catherine was the countess of Valentois, the pope's sister. Another was Siena-born Francisco di Bartolomeo Casini, the papal physician. The pope himself had arranged for Catherine and her party to be lodged in an elegant mansion that once belonged to a cardinal—"a fine house with a beautifully decorated chapel," according to Stefano Maconi. Finding their way around town was made easier by the presence of Raymond, Neri, and Giovanni Tantucci who had been in Avignon for some weeks as an advance party.

Two days after she arrived, Catherine had her first audience with Gregory XI. She and Raymond made their way to the massive Palais des Papes—more fortress than palace, in fact, with walls fifteen feet thick—and were ushered into a private meeting room. When Gregory appeared, he proved to be a man "short of stature, pale, with grave gestures and sorrowful eyes." Initially he was reserved. Apparently he had been unsettled by the boldness and familiarity of her letters. But as they spoke longer his prejudice evaporated. Like many men he found her charming—vivacious, enthusiastic, yet respectful. With Raymond translating (she did not speak Latin or French, and Gregory did not speak Italian), they reviewed the terms of possible peace between Avignon and Florence and found themselves much in agreement. She thought the terms he outlined would be acceptable to her contacts in Florence. On that high note they adjourned, promising to meet again.

She was pleased to have reached the pope before the official delegation from Florence. She looked forward to informing them that she and the pope had outlined a framework for peace. Gregory, who referred to the Florentines as "those merchants," was not so optimistic. During their meeting he predicted the delegation would never appear or, if they did, would agree to nothing. He cautioned her that the Florentines "have deceived you, as before now they deceived me."

When after some time the ambassadors still had not arrived, Catherine grew worried. Late in June she dictated a letter to the Eight of War, first chiding them for the tax they had levied on the clergy ("when the holy father finds out about it he will be even more angry"), then revealed that she had spoken with the pope who showed an "enthusiastic love for peace" and was ready to be merciful. She promised to explain it all to the Florentine ambassadors, adding, "I am surprised they still haven't come."

At last the three-man delegation arrived in Avignon. They had delayed leaving Florence until after a scheduled election. Catherine immediately invited them to visit her so she could outline the terms she and Gregory had discussed. They declined the invitation, declaring that she had not been empowered to negotiate on their behalf.

The next few weeks proved Gregory right. The peace terms he offered Florence were completely unacceptable to the ambassadors, just as their terms were to him. The papal side demanded that Florence pay an indemnity of three million florins. When he heard about the amount, Chancellor Salutati complained to King Louis of Hungary, "He [the pope] doesn't want to make peace, he wants to sell it!" By early September the talks reached a complete deadlock and the ambassadors departed.

Catherine directed an angry letter to Buonaccorso di Lapo, a member of the Signoria and at that time Florence's ambassador to Siena. She felt the Florentines had misrepresented themselves to her. "When your ambassadors came here they did not act as they should have ... I was never able to confer with them, in spite of what you told me when I asked for a letter of credentials. You said that you would tell them that we would confer together about everything ... Just the opposite has been done." She pleaded with the Florentines to change their ways: "I beg you, for the love of Christ crucified, to accept the treasure of the blood given you by Christ's bride [i.e., the church]. Be reconciled, be reconciled with her by that blood! Recognize your sins and offenses against her, for those who recognize their guilt, and prove by their actions that they recognize it and are humbled, always receive mercy." But the opportunity for reconciliation had passed them by.

Although locked out of the peace negotiations, Catherine still had a list of things to discuss with the pope. It is not known precisely how many times they met, but they certainly had several meetings during the three months she spent in Avignon. High on her list of issues was the pope's return to Rome. When he sought her advice about it at one of their early discussions, she reportedly answered, "It is not meet that a wretched little woman should give advice to a Sovereign Pontiff"—overlooking the fact that she had not hesitated to offer him advice prior to this.

Gregory tried to make it easier for her. "I will not ask you for advice," he said, "but tell me the will of God on this matter."

Catherine answered, "Who knows the will of God better than your Holiness who vowed to God that he would do this thing."

Her reply startled the pope. True, he had made a vow when he was elected pope to bring the papacy back to Rome. But it was a private vow, revealed to no one.

Later on Gregory told her that he had received a warning that he would be poisoned if he went back to Rome. He showed her the anonymous letter. Catherine told him the letter was the work of a devil—a devil nearby in Avignon, not in Rome. Anyway, she said, isn't it proper that a shepherd should lay down his life for his sheep?

They talked and talked. Gregory, whose natural tendency was vacillation, was emboldened by her confidence that his return to Rome was God's will. The more they talked, the more he believed it. But after she left his presence other courtiers would get his ear to suggest the move was unwise, or untimely, or dangerous, and Gregory became anxious again. There were times when she felt his advisors were keeping her from him. In an effort to open a private line of communication, Catherine had one letter carried to the pope by Neri di Landoccio Pagliaresi, with the suggestion that he use Neri to deliver a message back to her.

Whether carried by Neri or Raymond, she wrote him letters from her mansion a few blocks away reminding him that he was pope and could do what he wanted. "Don't make light of the works of the Holy Spirit that are being asked of you," she wrote. "You can do them if you *want* to. You *can* see that justice is done. You *can* have peace, if you will put aside the world's perverse pretensions and pleasures and keep only God's honor and what is really due holy Church." She closed with a semiserious threat: "Don't make it necessary for me to complain about you to Christ crucified. (There is no one else I *can* complain to, since there is no one greater [than you] on earth.)"

It may not have been a complaint, but she certainly did pray for Gregory during the weeks in Avignon. One of her prayers was taken down by a scribe. It reads, in part:

> Punish my sins, my Lord
> and do not look at my wretched deeds.
> I have one body,
> and to you I offer and return it.
> Here is my flesh;
> here is my blood;
> let me be slain, reduced to nothing;

let my bones be split apart
for those for whom I am praying,
if such is your will.
Let my bones and marrow be ground up
for your vicar on earth [the pope], your bride's only spouse.
For him I beg you to deign to listen to me.
Let this vicar of yours be attentive to your will,
let him love it and do it
so that we may not be lost.

One of those who tried to counter Catherine's influence was Louis, duke of Anjou and brother of the French king. France desperately wanted the pope to stay where he was, in French-dominated territory. For one thing, it gave France a moral edge over its enemy, England. Hoping to sway her, Louis of Anjou invited Catherine across the river to his castle for a few days on the pretext of comforting his ailing wife. But rather than changing her mind, Louis found himself entranced by her ideas for a crusade. He was on fire to commit himself to the holy cause. But after Catherine returned to Avignon he was injured in a fall from his horse and his ardor cooled.

During her whole time in Avignon, Catherine was under scrutiny of various kinds. There was still deep suspicion of her among prelates at the papal palace who feared that she had an undue influence on the pope. With Gregory's permission, they arranged an interview to test her orthodoxy. Three cardinals came to her residence. Catherine was ready for them and asked Giovanni Tantucci to sit in as a witness. She did not need his help. After questioning her on points of theology for a couple of hours the prelates pronounced themselves completely satisfied and left with smiles all around.

On another occasion the wife of the pope's nephew devised a test of her own. Admitted to the chapel where Catherine was lying on the floor praying, the woman bent as though to kiss her heel when she suddenly jabbed it several times with a needle. Catherine did not flinch, but when she came out of her ecstatic state later she complained of a sharp pain in her foot.

All the pain and stress seemed worth it in September of that year when Gregory announced he would at last leave Avignon for Rome. The ships waiting in Marseille had become public knowledge. Aides were dispatched to Italy to let the Romans know he was coming. On September 13 he left his papal palace for the last time, stepping over the prostrate form of his father who had thrown himself on the ground in protest. A few cardinals opted to stay behind, but most joined the papal entourage despite their misgivings about the dangers awaiting them in Rome. The papal cavalcade made its way overland to Marseille, and on October 2 it set sail for Italy.

The day after Gregory had left Avignon, Catherine and her retinue likewise departed. The pope had given them one hundred florins to cover the expenses of their return trip. The first leg of the journey took them overland south and then east to the city of Toulon where the bishop came out to meet Catherine and escort her to a residence. The crowd following along demanded that she say a few words in the town square, which she did, with Raymond translating. She was becoming a skilled street preacher. That her preaching ministry should blossom just at this time says a great deal about her developing vocation. The south of France had been the scene of Dominic Guzmán's ministry the previous century, so the sermon in Toulon placed Catherine squarely in the Dominican preaching tradition. Even more, Catherine's preaching linked her to Mary Magdalen who, according to local legend, had lived her final years in Provence. Her supposed tomb was in Toulon itself. Christian tradition considered Magdalen to be the first witness to the resurrection, the archetypal female preacher, and "apostle to the apostles." So the flowering of Catherine's preaching mission at this time and place seemed to mark her as a new Magdalen whose knowledge of the risen Christ came not from others' testimony but from firsthand experience.

After a short layover in Toulon, Catherine's party took a boat along the Riviera coast eastward. It was a season of storms and erratic winds. Raymond of Capua recounted one episode when the wind died during the middle of night and the captain feared their boat would be pushed onto the rocky shore. Raymond—never known for his physical courage—begged Catherine to do something. Like Jesus on the Sea of Galilee, she commanded the captain to turn his wheel in a certain direction while she prayed. Sure enough, a wind sprang up that carried them to safety. At dawn, reported Raymond, "we came into port in a happy mood, raising the echoes with the joyful strains of *Te Deum laudamus*."

It may have been that incident, or another one, that soon led them to abandon sea travel in favor of walking. Coming ashore near Saint-Tropez, they followed the coast road past Cannes (possibly visiting the famous monastery on the isle of Lérins), then to Antibes and Nice, and finally entered Italian territory at Ventimiglia. On October 3 they reached the town of

Varazze, birthplace of the Dominican Jacopo da Varazze, author of the *Golden Legend*. Catherine had been looking forward to it, recalling the book Tommaso dalla Fonte would read to her as a girl in her parents' kitchen. However they found the town contaminated by plague, so rather than staying they pushed on to Genoa, reaching it the next day.

In Genoa Catherine and her party were invited to stay at the palazzo of a noblewoman, Orietta Scotti, on the Via Canneto near the harbor. It was a welcome respite from all their walking. Shortly after their arrival, Neri became ill with abdominal cramps that caused him so much pain everyone in the house was upset, particularly since they had just gone through a plague-infested area. Two doctors called to the scene by Raymond were not able to help. At this point Stefano Maconi, who was especially close to Neri, appealed to Catherine to do something. She promised to pray for him. After mass the next morning, she told Stefano, "You have your wish."

"Will Neri be cured, mamma?" Stefano asked.

"He will for certain, for our Lord has given him back to us," Catherine said.

Stefano ran off to tell Neri of the news, and Neri—according to Raymond—began to improve from that moment.

Unfortunately, just as Neri began to get well, Stefano got sick. Stefano was a young man with a sunny disposition and a favorite of everyone in the famiglia. Catherine hurried to his bedside and told him, "I command you, in virtue of holy obedience to suffer this fever no longer!" The way Raymond describes it, the fever left him before she left the room.

Their time in Genoa lasted one week, then two, which was not because of sickness or the need to rest from their travels. Catherine was most likely waiting for the papal galleys that were scheduled to stop in Genoa on their way to Rome. The storm-battered ships finally pulled into port on October 18, having taken two weeks to come from Marseille. Much of that time was spent sitting in coastal towns while the Mediterranean tossed and bellowed. The cardinals were uniformly unhappy, telling Gregory this was God's way of counseling them to go back to Avignon. The pope was as sick of the cardinals as he was of the sea. Learning that Catherine, too, was close by in Genoa, Gregory one evening put on a hooded robe and crept out of his quarters, heading across town to where Catherine lived. It was dark when he knocked on her door. She rushed to meet him, kneeling in the doorway and calling him *il doce Cristo in terra* (sweet Christ on earth). The two of them went into a room together with only Raymond to translate, shutting the door behind them.

Raymond's discretion in this instance was absolute. No word of their discussion—which went on for hours—ever escaped him. The nighttime encounter does not appear in his account of Catherine's life, yet it was witnessed by too many persons to be kept entirely secret. The sovereign pontiff had put on a disguise and gone out alone to seek the guidance of an unschooled female. His reasons are not hard to imagine. There had been rumors of riots in Rome as well as armed battles in the war with Florence. One unconfirmed report (which turned out to be true) claimed that the Florentines had met and defeated a force sent by the pope's ally, Queen Giovanna of Naples. Gregory—exhausted by the trip and harassed by his advisors—needed to feast once more on Catherine's certainty, on her absolute conviction that he had made the right decision and that going to Rome was God's plan for him. He needed assurance that everything would turn out all right. She told him in as many ways as she knew how. She encouraged him, exhorted him, most likely prayed with him, until together they rested once more on a narrow ledge of resolve. So comforted, he put on his hooded mantle, said goodbye at the door, and disappeared into the night. They never saw each other again.

The boats carrying the papal party left again on October 28, heading south for Corneto, near Rome. Catherine delayed still another week. Before she left she addressed a letter to Lapa back in Siena. A letter had reached them saying that Lapa was "going to pieces" with worry over her daughter's safety. In response, Catherine sought to console her. She also demanded that Lapa show fortitude, advising her to imitate Mary who first let go of her Son and then the disciples.

"Your poor unworthy daughter Caterina wants to comfort you in the precious blood of God's Son," she wrote. "How I have longed to see you truly the mother of my soul as well as of my body! For I know that if you love my soul more than you love my body, any excessive attachment you may have will die, and my physical absence won't be so wearing on you. No, it will even bring you consolation, and you will be ready to bear any burden for God's honor, knowing that I am being used for that same honor . . .

"I want you to learn from that sweet mother Mary, who for God's honor and our salvation gave us her Son, dead on the wood of the most holy cross. When Mary was left alone after Christ had ascended into heaven, she stayed with the holy disciples. And then she willingly agreed to their leaving . . . even though it was wrenching, since they had been a great consolation to each other. She chose the pain of their departure over the consolation of their staying . . . Now it is from her I want you to learn, dearest mother."

She added, "You know that I must follow God's will, and I know that you want me to follow it. It was God's will that I go away—and my going was not without mystery, nor without worthwhile results. It was also God's will that I remain away; it was no mere human decision, and whoever says anything else is lying. And so I must go in the future, following in his footsteps however and wherever it shall please his boundless goodness."

As a letter it was loving but uncompromising. It shows Catherine claiming a place for herself that few medieval women up to then had claimed. She would be no passive devotee. In her eyes Mary was a fitting model for her mother, but Catherine identified herself with the male disciples who had been entrusted with the risky business of preaching the word to an unbelieving, sometimes hostile, world. She had just returned from the seat of power. She had met princes of the church on their own ground and held the hand of an anxious pope, and she had come to see herself in a new light. She would not be fitted into institutional slots or submit docilely to family expectations. She was an apostle, and she answered to God alone.

In November 1376, Catherine and her band of followers, not unlike the Apostle Paul, continued their mission journey by ship, sailing from Genoa to Livorno, then proceeded on foot to Pisa. Stefano Maconi went on ahead to Siena carrying messages from Catherine to various people, while in the opposite direction Lapa hurried to be reunited with her daughter. Their large party settled into the hospital next to the Dominican church in Pisa. A few days later Catherine preached to a crowd that gathered in the square that fronted the church. Just before Christmas, Catherine and her famiglia returned to Siena.

PART THREE

WOMAN OF THE WORLD

10

NEW FOUNDATIONS

Just as Catherine came home to Siena, so Gregory XI returned the papacy to Rome. His ships reached Corneto, just north of Rome, in mid-November. After two months of delicate negotiations, the citizens of Rome agreed to accept him back. He was paraded into the city with singing and dancing and was taken, smiling but uneasy, to his residence beside old St. Peter's Basilica on January 17, 1377.

Catherine's reentry was less festive but also much less anxious. Her return was made easier by several privileges she had secured in Avignon. First, she had received the right to have three confessors in her entourage. Several priests were often required to hear confessions of the many people who felt called to conversion when Catherine preached. The usual three in her party were Raymond of Capua, Bartolomeo Dominici, and Giovanni Tantucci, whom Catherine referred to as *il maestro* (the master) in deference to his academic credentials. She had also secured for her chaplains the right to celebrate "private" masses—i.e., masses outside a church or chapel. These were necessary because of the amount of time she was spending on the road with no house of worship nearby, and with the churches in her own city—as an ally of Florence—under interdict; but also because her public masses were becoming spectacles with people clamoring to witness her religious raptures. The papal permission guaranteed that she would have privacy when she prayed. William Flete provided her with an altar stone that had an embedded relic of a saint—a necessity for celebrating masses outside of a church.

There was another concession from Avignon that brought Catherine particular satisfaction. She had long desired to found a women's monastery—not because she wanted to live there herself (she could never abide being confined in one place for a long time), but as a place of domicile and prayer for female followers. In recent years she had been guiding many noblewomen in their spiritual lives. Yet once they were brought to a more ardent faith, women of her day had fewer options than men did. They could become tertiaries like the Mantellate, but serving the poor and infirm was not for everyone. On the other hand, if they joined one of the established monasteries they would be subject to the rule of the place and could no longer be guided by Catherine. The idea was to have a convent that was not closed to her, where she could visit and serve as an anchoring presence.

Almost a year earlier she had written to Giovanni di Gano da Orvieto, an abbot she knew in the Orcia Valley, to ask his help in locating "a suitable place for establishing a really good monastery." Shortly after that she was approached by Nanni di Ser Vanni, the man she had freed from the compulsion of incessant feuding. Luxuriating in his newfound docility, Nanni wanted to repay Catherine for her kindness. He had recently purchased a small, fortified estate named Belcaro about three miles southwest of Siena. The place was partly a ruin, having been devastated during Guelph–Ghibelline conflicts in the thirteenth century and once again more recently. It needed a wall of enclosure before it could serve as a monastery. Hearing that Catherine had expressed a desire to found a house for women, Nanni was willing to give her Belcaro free of charge if she wanted it. Catherine was delighted. On inspection, the place looked ideal to her.

To found a monastery, one needed the consent of civil and ecclesial authorities. The latter permission had been granted by Pope Gregory XI during one of their meetings in Avignon. An additional clearance had to be secured from the commune of Siena, predictably nervous about a privately owned fortress so close to the city walls. Catherine and Nanni assured the Defenders of the Commune that the site would not be used for military purposes. On January 25, 1377, a vote by the city fathers cleared the way for turning Belcaro into a monastery.

The date and vote tally are matters of record, but nearly everything else about Belcaro, rechristened the monastery of Santa Maria degli Angeli (Saint Mary of the Angels), is conjecture. What sort of monastery was it? What rule did it follow? Raymond tells us it was founded for "ladies of the upper classes," but how many and who were they? One biographer asserts that Belcaro was a Dominican convent. That is unlikely, since it was not formally blessed by a Dominican friar. Instead, the blessing and opening ceremonies were conducted by Catherine's abbot friend Giovanni di Gano, a member of the Williamite order. William Flete was persuaded to leave his hermitage at Lecceto to celebrate and preach at the first mass in April. Catherine herself remained at the monastery until later that month, helping to get it organized, relaxing into its silence, and no doubt counseling its new members.

Part of her commitment to the new house, as she saw it, was recruiting. One person she hoped to attract was Benedetta Salimbeni, the daughter of the noble clan that had been exiled to its country estates. The unfortunate woman's husband had died, followed by the death of her fiancé in a proposed second marriage. Catherine, who was acquainted with the young woman and her mother, wrote to Benedetta, urging her to find solace in the "gracious and glorious bridegroom who had given you life and who will never die." Earthly husbands, she said, "pass away like the wind" and are often the cause of spiritual death for their wives. "You have experienced how constant they are, for in a short time the world has kicked you twice, and divine Goodness permitted this to make you run from the world." She begged the countess Benedetta to flee "the world's poison," no matter how handsomely packaged. She ended the letter by reporting that work on her new monastery was moving ahead swiftly, adding, "If you come, you'll be coming to a land of promise!"

However promising Belcaro seemed to Catherine, recruitment was not easy. Benedetta's brother Agnolino opposed her entry into a monastery. Being the head of the family, he controlled his sister's destiny. Catherine had to plead with him in another letter to let his sister go. Benedetta's sister Isa was similarly interested in religious life—not at Belcaro but as a Franciscan —so Catherine wrote a third letter to encourage Isa's vocation. In the end neither sister entered the convent, although in time Isa did become a Dominican Mantellata.

During the short time Catherine spent at Belcaro the nasty little blaze between Florence and the pope, known in history as the War of the Eight Saints, flamed up into an inferno. The town of Ascoli, close to the Adriatic coast, had fallen to Florentine forces in December 1376. Viterbo, north of Rome, was taken in January. During the latter battle, the brother of Raymond of Capua was captured by the Florentines and held for ransom. Catherine pulled what strings she had in an effort to get him freed, apparently without success. The reality of war and the loss of life were distressing to her. Also in January she wrote to Gregory XI, then still in Corneto, imploring him to use kindness rather than the sword to overcome his enemies. She pleaded, "Peace! Peace, most holy father! May it please your holiness to receive your children who have offended you, their father. It will be no shame on you to bend down to placate your naughty child. Rather it will be the greatest of honors, and very advantageous to you before God and the people of the world. Oimé! No more war, my *babbo*!" If he wanted to fight someone, she added, there were always the infidels.

Gregory, however, was determined to punish Florence by force of arms. He had placed the papal forces in the hands of his cardinal-legate, Robert of Geneva, a cousin of King Charles V of France. After failing to retake Bologna, the legate and his Breton mercenaries turned their attention to the town of Cesena, south of Ravenna. By first promising clemency, Cardinal Robert persuaded Cesena's defenders to lay down their arms and open the gates. As soon as they were helpless, he loosed his mercenaries on the town, ordering the Bretons to "exercise justice" on its citizens. For three days in the first week of February they raped and looted, destroying what they could not carry away, and slaughtering Cesena's people, including women and children. The dead numbered between 2,500 and 5,000, while another 8,000 fled to neighboring towns. Cardinal Robert became known as the "Butcher of Cesena."

Catherine, at Belcaro, was horrified by the reports that reached her. She couldn't believe Gregory condoned the atrocities, but she had to acknowledge them as fruits of policies he put in place. Writing to the pope in Rome a few days later, she deplored "the great slaughter of souls and dishonor to God that comes from war!" and she questioned the mind-set that placed the conquest of cities above the welfare of people. To the pope she said, "even though you have the responsibility to conquer and protect and rule over the treasure of the cities the Church has lost, you are much more obligated to regain all these little sheep, who are a treasure within the Church."

"Forgive me!" she continued. "I am not saying this to lecture you. I am compelled by gentle First Truth and by my desire, my dear *babbo*, to see you at peace, at rest, body and soul. For I don't see how, with these disastrous wars, you can have a single hour of good. What belongs to the poor is being eaten up to pay soldiers, who in turn devour people as if they were meat!"

It was clear to her that the war was devouring people and treasure. And if this was true for the war against Florence, it must be true—Catherine was beginning to see—for all wars, even the crusades. She made her letter to Gregory a discourse on recovering lost treasures. She tried to lay it out for him in measured terms: "[T]here are two things that have made and are still making the Church lose temporal goods: war and dearth of virtue. For where there is no virtue there is always war against our Creator. War, therefore, is the cause of all this. Now I am telling you that if you want to regain what is lost there is no other remedy except to use the opposite of what has caused the loss. I mean using peace and virtue to regain it . . . In this way, too, you will realize your other holy desire and the desire of the servants of God and of poor wretched me, that is, to win back the souls of the unbelievers who are not sharing in the blood of the slain, consumed Lamb."

The "other holy desire" she spoke of was an allusion to the crusades. It was dawning on her that a bloody crusade could never achieve success if its object was limited to the liberation of Jerusalem and the holy places. The true object of a crusade must be the "winning back" of people, reclaiming their souls and their loyalty, which could be achieved only through acts of charity. Catherine held this conviction deeply, yet imperfectly. In the future she would continue to agitate for an armed crusade. The notion of a "just war" as outlined by Thomas Aquinas a century earlier had not been fully absorbed, with the result that Catherine and most people of her time lacked perspective for weighing a state's motivations for waging war. Civil and ecclesiastical authorities, she believed, had the right and duty to use arms. Pacifism, to the extent that it existed at all in her day, was founded on the biblical mandate of love, augmented by natural human compassion. It applied to persons rather than states. Still, the full horrors of war revealed in the massacre at Cesena had brought Catherine to a new understanding. She never went back to the unthinking, jingoistic Christianity of her earlier years. For her, infidels were now souls to be "eaten"—taken in, absorbed into the social body—instead of fodder for armies.

Her own city of Siena was suffering the effects of war. Suspicion was everywhere. Strangers were scrutinized and even citizens were watched. As in the case of Niccolò di Toldo two years earlier, an imprudent word spoken in public could get one thrown into prison, perhaps executed. The state of affairs troubled Catherine extremely, not least because some of the suspicion seemed directed toward her. She urged the Riformatori government to be more tolerant and refrain from "tearing [God's servants] apart with rumors and unwarranted suspicions." In addition to political prisoners arrested on the thinnest of pretexts, Siena's jails held prisoners of war taken in battles against papal forces. One of these was a nameless Knight Hospitaler whose plight especially touched Catherine, perhaps because the knights were associated in her mind with crusading. In March 1377 she addressed a letter to the "prisoners of Siena" appealing to them to accept their suffering as Christ accepted his. In a remarkable image, she described Christ as a wet nurse who consumed bitter medicine in order to pass it through his body and heal the babe who nursed at his breast. It was another instance of her envisioning Christ as a mother figure, and it calls to mind instances when she herself claimed to have "nursed" at Christ's wounded side.

Here again, though, Catherine's letter to the prisoners contained no criticism of authorities who jailed and sometimes executed people for scant reason. To be sure, she understood that injustice caused suffering, yet suffering in itself was not an evil. Indeed, suffering endured in love was redemptive. So she encouraged the prisoners to accept their fate in the knowledge that they would find justice in the afterlife. "Keep living in God's holy and tender love," she wrote. "And remember that you will surely die, and you don't know when. Those who can, see that you get ready for confession and holy communion, so that you may be resurrected in grace with Jesus Christ."

This letter, like the one in January to Gregory, was probably written from Belcaro. She remained at the monastery until late in April when she returned to the city, some say to minister to prisoners. There are anecdotal reports (but no documented evidence) of her interacting with prisoners beyond the case of Niccolò di Toldo. It certainly would be in keeping with her character for Catherine to get involved with the jailed much as she had done with the hospitalized. We know the Knight Hospitaler was released from prison the same month she came back to the city, but we don't know why. Perhaps he was ransomed, or perhaps Catherine successfully intervened on his behalf.

The fate of prisoners, the war, the treatment of infidels—all of these burning issues say something about the way Catherine was living out her mission to the world in these months. She had a deeply felt desire to serve as a reconciler. She felt it was her particular calling to heal old wounds and bring people together. This desire, so clear in the spring and summer of

1377, brought her into an especially bitter division between two cousins of the Salimbeni family residing in their respective castles about thirty miles to the south of Siena. While the roots of the disagreement between the cousins were petty, their feud threatened the peace of the surrounding country-side. The Salimbeni in their various branches, like many noble and wealthy families of their day, maintained private armies. The tinder of their disagreement was ready to burst into an armed struggle that would bring suffering to residents of the Sienese contado. On one side of the feud was Cione di Sandro Salimbeni, a perennial hothead in his fortress at Castiglioncello di Trinoro. Cione had been one of those who tried to overthrow the Sienese government six years previously when Catherine saved her brothers from the mob. On the other side was Agnolino di Giovanni Salimbeni—the same man with whom Catherine had pleaded to allow one of his sisters to enter Belcaro. Agnolino made his home at the Rocca d'Orcia, a dramatic pillar of rock that rose from the floor of the Val d'Orcia, or Orcia Valley, southeast of Siena. The cause of the dispute between these two was yet a third castle that Agnolino had inherited from his father but which Cione believed had been promised to him.

At some point in this family squabble the Salimbeni women got involved by recruiting Catherine to enter as peacemaker. Most sources believe she was invited to mediate by Biancina di Giovanni, Agnolino's mother, although Monna Stricca, Cione's wife, may have had a hand in it as well. The invitation struck a responsive chord in Catherine. Clearly, bringing peace between the cousins was women's work that suited her sense of vocation. In a small way the restoration of peace to the countryside mirrored what she hoped to accomplish in the church and among the city-states of Italy. Restless as usual, she may also have been drawn by the opportunity of getting out of the city and into the country during the summer months. She discussed it with Raymond and members of her famiglia, and soon a sizeable number of people had signed on for a trip to the south. In addition to Catherine and Raymond the party included Lapa, Tommaso dalla Fonte, Neri di Landoccio Pagliaresi, Francesco Malavolti, Bartolomeo Dominici, Giovanni Tantucci, Matteo Tolomei, the hermit Fra Santi, several Mantellate—including Alessa Saracini, Lisa Colombini, and Cecca Gori—and a few others.

It was sometime in early July when they left. We see them on the road—a large band of people plodding along in twos and threes under the Tuscan sky, chatting, sometimes singing together, and other times silent or in prayer, passing other travelers in both directions—farmers with oxcarts laden with produce, tradesmen with donkey-drawn wagons stirring up dust, mendicant friars sweaty under their robes, and (because this was the Via Francigena, the great pilgrim road) scores of pilgrims from northern Italy and all corners of Europe on their way to Rome, once more the center of Christendom. At wells and resting places along the way the various travelers would share food they carried, trade stories, and exchange news. The road was a living organism that stirred them together, changed identities, and dropped them off in new places. In Catherine's case, the stop at Montepulciano wasn't entirely new. She had been there before, most recently with Raymond after the plague summer in Siena three years previously. Once more the party made its way to the Monastery of Sant'Agnesa, the resting place of Blessed Agnes, where Cecca was reunited with her daughter Giustina, a novice in the community.

Apparently the Salimbeni did not require immediate attention, since Catherine and her party seem to have remained in Montepulciano for some time. Raymond had many friends there. Catherine probably preached to the nuns in the convent—who included her niece Eugenia, Lisa's daughter —and to crowds in the square. This entire trip to the Sienese countryside has been described as a "preaching mission" for her. In addition, while in Montepulciano she took the opportunity to begin mending fences in the family of Spinello Tolomei, a distinguished citizen of the town. Spinello's nephews had become embroiled with the sons of a certain Lorenzo, apparently related to the Salimbeni family. Somehow she was able to sort it all out. Her skill as a mediator was welcomed by the city fathers of Siena who in a letter she received around this time expressed their earnest hope she could pacify the Salimbeni. She assured them the work of reconciliation had already begun.

Eventually Catherine and a small group of followers made their way further south to Castiglioncello di Trinoro, the home of Cione Salimbeni. Cecca remained behind in Montepulciano to spend more time with her daughter, and Lapa stayed with her. There was some coming-and-going among famiglia members throughout the summer. At some point Alessa Saracini took a side trip to Montegiovi, while Tommaso Caffarini came down from Siena to join the party.

Catherine may have been worried about confronting the volatile Cione on his own preserve, but the Salimbeni elder proved to be remarkably docile.

We don't know the details of their negotiations, yet it seems Cione's differences with his cousin quickly evaporated under the spell of Catherine's earnest charm. Like many semifeudal lords, he was generous when approached in the spirit of deference, which Catherine could produce when she really had to. With that difficult part out of the way, she spent the week at Cione's estate under the care of his wife, Monna Stricca, and most likely preaching in the town.

From there the mission band turned north and then west to the valley of the Orcia river, passing through the town of Vignoni where as a girl Catherine had burned herself in the hot spring, to the towering hill Rocca d'Orcia, with Agnolino Salimbeni's fortress perched on its top. Once more Catherine presented herself to the lord of the keep and outlined the general terms of Cione's concession. These were entirely suitable to the younger cousin, and so very easily the dispute that threatened the peace of the countryside and worried even the city fathers was settled to everyone's satisfaction.

With the major goal of her mission already accomplished, Catherine moved into the Salimbeni fortress as a guest of Agnolino and Monna Biancina, his mother. It was a strange, austere place, set high above the valley floor with a view for miles. The dwelling was buffeted by a constant wind that funneled up the valley and whistled around its ramparts. One could lie awake at night and watch as it billowed the curtains or listen as it nibbled at the very stones of the walls. She found the place entirely suitable. During the day crowds came, attracted by her presence. Then she would go down to the lower town and the church of San Simeone and preach to them, and afterward the priests would hear confessions of those who felt called to conversion. It was here, too, that, according to Raymond, she found herself in combat with an evil spirit that had inflicted a local woman so dreadfully that "the news spread throughout the neighborhood." Catherine tried to avoid the troubled woman. She knew what it was like to wrestle with her own dark spirits and wanted no part of it. Unfortunately, there was no place to hide in the Salimbeni castle. Monna Biancina arranged an "accidental" meeting between the two women. When Catherine drew close, said Raymond, the spirit began to howl until Catherine demanded that it leave the poor woman alone. He said the spirit fled, leaving its victim sane but bone weary and with no memory of her distress.

It was not the first time Catherine had vanquished an evil spirit. Raymond tells about a time in Siena years earlier when she healed an eight-year-old girl. On that occasion, too, Catherine had tried not to get involved. She complained that she was tormented enough by demons, and asked, "How can you think I need other people's evil spirits as well?" In that instance it was Tommaso dalla Fonte who planted the troubled girl in Catherine's room, making a confrontation unavoidable. According to Raymond, Catherine prayed with the girl all night and in the morning the evil spirit was gone. Whether these were cases of demonic possession or hysteria or some other emotional disturbance, we have no way of knowing. What seems clear from both stories is that Catherine's reassuring and calming presence brought peace to the sufferers.

There was something about her time spent at Rocca d'Orcia that Catherine found especially nourishing. Between episodes of preaching and letter writing, there was still ample time for prayer and personal reflection. She settled into her aerie and let Monna Biancina care for her needs. Members of her famiglia would drift away and then come back. These were the hot days of August, and most of her party adjusted to the languid schedule of the countryside. Not all persons were happy with this quiet existence, however. In Siena and Rome there was still a war to be fought, and officials in those cities were beginning to wonder what Catherine was doing with her time in the Orcia Valley. The rulers of Siena were always wary of plots being hatched against the state and were suspicious of her attentions to those inveterate plotters, the Salimbeni. They first mentioned these worries when she was still in Montepulciano. At that time she replied sharply, "How can you tolerate fearing and passing judgment on those who are ready to die for your welfare and for your republic's preservation and growth in peace and prosperity? . . . [T]ruly, dearest brothers, this is the perverse fear, the perverted love, that killed Christ. For Pilate, out of fear of losing his authority, was blinded and failed to recognize the truth." She warned the council members about listening to those who are "worrying and wagging their tongues over me. It seems that they have nothing better to do but speak ill of me and the company that is with me."

Her protestations didn't make the rumors about her go away. From Rocca d'Orcia she wrote to the wool worker Sano di Maco, a disciple who held a high place in the Riformatori government, about the "opinionated presumption" rife on the streets of Siena. She complained it was the work of the devil "sitting on people's tongues," and she directed Sano to read her letter "to all my children" in order to calm the storm of gossip back home.

Still later she contacted the Sienese goldsmith Salvi di Messer Pietro, who had warned her of rumors flying about town. She replied, "All the rumors and suspicions heaped on both me and my father Frate Raimundo had made me fear I was offending God by staying." But she said when she had asked God directly, God told her, "'Continue to eat at the table where I have put you. I have put you at the table of the cross to eat—in your pain, with all these grumblings—to seek and savor my honor and the salvation of souls.'"

As her time away from the city stretched on and on, friends as well as critics began to voice complaints. Sano di Maco reported the sisters at Belcaro were unhappy with her long absence; they had expected Catherine to spend more time with them. She responded airily that her trip was good for the sisters, since "good children do more when their mother is away than when she is there, because they want to show their love for her and get more into her good graces." Likewise, when some of the Sienese Mantellate expressed their longing for her, she told them they were being selfish. "I know my presence is a great comfort to you," she wrote. "Still, you as obedient women should for God's honor and the salvation of souls give up the pursuit of your own selfish comfort. Don't yield to the devil who makes it seem you have been deprived of my loving affection for you." The loving mamma suggested it was time for them to grow up and fend for themselves: "Don't be satisfied to keep living on milk forever; we have to get the teeth of our desire ready to chew on bread that is hard and moldy, if necessary."

Last of all there was Lapa, still in Montepulciano and impatient to see her daughter again. Catherine wrote Lapa at least two short notes during the summer begging her to be patient. "If you think I am staying here [at Rocca d'Orcia] longer than you would like," she wrote, "I beg you to be content, because I cannot do otherwise. I believe that if you knew the circumstances you yourself would be sending me here."

Not all of her time in the valley was spent at the Salimbeni fortress. She had promised her good friend Abbot Giovanni di Gano da Orvieto, who had presided at the blessing of Belcaro, to visit his abbey of Sant'Antimo. So late in August she and Raymond, along with Francisco Malavolti and Bartolomeo Dominici, traipsed to the abbey located a few miles west of Rocca d'Orcia. They spent some weeks there visiting and trying to settle a dispute between the abbot and the archpriest of nearby Montalcino. Catherine wrote the city fathers in Siena to warn them of the archpriest's "evil deeds." The priest had spread rumors about the abbot and once even attacked him with a knife. In Siena they seemed to believe the rumors. It was the same old story. Catherine guessed that by siding with the abbot she would become the target of still more gossip. To the rulers of the city she wrote, "As for my coming here with my family, I am told that people are suspicious and are grumbling about it. I do not know, however, whether this is true. But if you valued yourselves as much as they and I value you, you and all the other citizens would not to lightly harbor such thoughts and feelings. You would stop your ears so as not to hear."

Almost everyone, it seemed, found some reason to resent the time Catherine was spending in the Val d'Orcia. She, on the other hand, was finding the experience enormously fruitful. Large crowds were turning out to hear her preach wherever she went. She exulted that "so many demons are being eaten up that Frate Tommaso [dalla Fonte] says he has a stomach ache!" She added, "You can imagine how sweet it is to see God being honored and souls being saved!"

Nevertheless, when she, Raymond, and the others got back to Rocca d'Orcia, they found a letter sent by Gregory XI begging them to come to Rome. The pope was ailing and insecure in his Roman palace, harassed by townsmen he didn't know and by courtiers who pouted because Rome wasn't Avignon. He longed for people he could rely on. There is some mystery surrounding this invitation. Later Raymond would claim it was Catherine who sent him to see the pope regarding "certain church affairs." He may indeed have carried a message from her to the pope, but there is ample reason to believe the invitation originated with Gregory and was extended to them both. Catherine adamantly refused to go. There was more work to be done in the valley. Here crowds were flocking to hear her speak, whereas in Rome, she knew, her voice would be muted in the patriarchal surroundings of the papal court. She might have a few private meetings with the pope but her public preaching would necessarily come to an end. So around the middle of September Raymond went by himself to Siena and then Rome while Catherine continued her mission to the countryside. They both believed it would be a temporary separation. Once apart, however, they were swept up by events that made the break a lasting one: after arriving in Rome Raymond was elected prior of the Dominican church of Santa Maria sopra Minerva, and was not able to return to Siena or the Orcia Valley. His mentoring relationship with Catherine had lasted a little more than three years.

Catherine was glad that she had stayed. In late September her hostess, Monna Biancina, learned that her bother, Trincio, the lord of Foligno in the territory of Perugia, had been assassinated. Only the week before Catherine had written him at Biancina's request in an effort to get him to change his lascivious and despotic behavior. Alas, there had been no time for him to mend his ways. An irate crowd of citizens stabbed him and threw his body from a balcony. Biancina grieved. Catherine tried to comfort her while reflecting herself on the persistence of evil.

Evil was stalking the streets of Rome as well as Foligno. In September or early October Raymond reported by letter that, contrary to their expectations, the papal resettlement to Rome had not been accompanied by significant reforms in church management. The nepotism, rampant simony, and loose living of the papal court were as bad in Rome as they had been in Avignon. He also informed her the pope was annoyed that she had stayed behind in Val d'Orcia.

On the big issue—church reform and the continuing bloody war—Catherine was blunt. She gave Raymond a message to pass on to Pope Gregory: "Oimé, Oimé, Oimé, most holy father! Had you only . . . [begun church reforms] the very day you got back where you belong! I trust in God's goodness and in your holiness that you will do what had not yet been done . . . You know (for you were told) that is what you were asked to do: to see to the reform of holy Church; to attend to the punishment of sins and the planting of virtuous pastors; and to grasp the opportunity for holy peace with your wicked children in the best way possible and the manner most pleasing to God." She went on to say that his failure to make peace was a direct cause for so much "devastation and harm and disrespect [that] have befallen holy Church and her ministers."

As for the pope's annoyance, Catherine told Raymond she regretted that he had to bear the brunt of the "displeasure or indignation from Christ's vicar" on her account. She acknowledged she had disobeyed God by not staying near the pope "with my presence and my words." But having said that she still didn't offer to go to Rome.

She wouldn't go to Rome because a new idea was stirring in her. In one sense it was the culmination of ideas. From the very beginning of her public life she had longed to communicate the wisdom that grew in her cell of self-knowledge—that flowered from years of living in solitude and through experiences of intense prayer, a wisdom that was nourished by fasting and service to others. It seemed to her that people hungered for this wisdom. As evidence she had only to consider the multitudes that turned out to hear her preach. Even Pope Gregory in his incapacity to do what seemed manifestly obvious sought her counsel. The world, it must have seemed to her, lay under a cloud of darkness and discouragement. Certainly Raymond was discouraged; he had written her in October, on the feast of Francis of Assisi, grieving over the state of the church. The antidote for grief, she knew from long experience, was found in "a water peaceful, clear and unpolluted" that flowed from the rock of faith. In earlier years the desire to share that blessing had overflowed in the formation of her famiglia where she acted as mamma and guide. It spilled out in letters to disciples and others given to her care. It overflowed into preaching—at first conferences to nuns and monks and then, after Avignon, preaching to large crowds who were moved to tears and conversion by her words. Now the waters were tipping again. In her mind she imagined a flood that would sweep well beyond the Orcia and even the Tiber.

She would write a book. She knew in general what she wanted to say, yet the shape of it was still unclear to her. She prayed over it in her tower room at Rocca d'Orcia, listening to the wind moaning outside. The message began to come together one night and morning in October. After praying through the dark hours she went down to morning mass. It was Saturday—Mary's Day—she told Raymond. She took her place by the altar "with true knowledge of herself, ashamed of her imperfections in God's presence," and "rising above herself with restless desire and gazing with her mind's eye on eternal Truth" she made four petitions to God. These petitions and the responses she heard—seemingly from beyond—coalesced into a framework for her book. Reading her long letter to Raymond that described the process, one can sense her descending to a place deeper than ego where truth and compassion lay together. People of her day would call it a state of ecstasy; indeed much of the book she subsequently produced was dictated in this state. Today this state might be called accessing the unconscious, or simply "bliss" (if it means being in touch with the deepest reality). Through long practice Catherine could enter this state easily; and she could maintain it in the presence of others by her posture and by guarding her eyes. Tommaso Caffarini later described the way it happened:

"I have very often seen the virgin in Siena, especially after her return from Avignon, rapt beyond her senses, except for speech, by which she dictated to various writers in succession sometimes letters and sometimes the book, in different times and different places, as circumstances allowed. Sometimes she did this with her hands crossed on her breast as she walked about the room; sometimes she was on her knees or in other postures; but always her face was lifted toward heaven . . . When emergencies would cause several days to pass in which she was kept from pursuing her dictation, as soon as she could take it up again she would begin at the point where she left off as if there had been no interruption or space of time."

Her book, Catherine decided, would come out of this interior place where she was most sure of herself. It would be like the voice of God echoing in her soul. The decision to make God the central narrator was an acknowledgment of the way the words rose up inside her as well as an act of deliberation on her part. After all, would readers accept the message if they believed it came from a common woman? No, they would not. But if God spoke to them—if she could channel God's intentions to them—then the message might be heard.

With mounting excitement she outlined it in the long letter to Raymond written soon after the idea had taken shape. She described her four petitions and the way "divine Goodness" heard and responded to them. She wrote the letter in part to comfort Raymond in Rome in his discouragement, but her own enthusiasm kept getting in the way: "Oh dearest and sweetest father," she wrote, "when I saw and heard so much . . . from gentle First Truth, my heart felt that it would break in two! I am dying and cannot die! Have compassion on your poor daughter, who is living in such torment because God is so offended, and who has no one to whom she can unburden herself—except that the Holy Spirit has provided for me interiorly by his mercy, and outwardly has provided me a diversion in writing.

"Let's all take heart in Christ gentle Jesus, and let suffering be our refreshment. And let's eagerly and without hesitation accept the sweet invitation, dear father. Rejoice, because you have been called so sweetly. Suffer with great joy and patience, without being crippled by pain, if you want to be a spouse of Truth and comforter of my soul. In no other way could you have grace, and that would deeply sadden me. That is why I said I long to see you a follower and lover of truth."

This is the letter that Catherine was supposed to have produced without the help of a scribe—the result of a spontaneous and presumably miraculously acquired ability to write. In the quoted passage she describes the act of writing as a "diversion," but not until her final paragraph does she state plainly that the letter was "written with my own hand on the Isola della Rocca with so many sighs and tears that I couldn't see even when I was seeing." She goes on to explain that God, assisted by John the Evangelist and Thomas Aquinas, "provided for my refreshment by giving me the ability to write—a consolation I've never known because of my ignorance—so that when I come down from the heights I might have a little something to vent my heart, lest it burst . . . [H]e fixed it in my mind in a marvelous manner, the way a teacher does when he gives his pupil a model. Shortly after you [Raymond] left me, I began to learn in my sleep."

Scholars are divided about Catherine's supposed ability to write. Some who remain skeptical maintain the final paragraph (or even the whole letter) is a forgery generated by a later editor. The letter itself is very long; the printed translation covers ten pages. It is difficult to imagine Catherine laboriously bent over the writing desk for all that time given her state of excitement. And if she could write, it is fair to ask why she went back to dictation for her other letters as well as the book that was germinating in her. Last of all, when he came to write his *Life of Catherine of Siena*, Raymond never acknowledged receiving this letter and was silent about her sudden acquisition of writing skills, even though the *Life* recalled other "miraculous" events such as healings and her ability to read—which likewise occurred spontaneously.

Recent speculation has suggested that Catherine's announcement of her ability to write may have been a kind of wordplay rooted in a desire to be present to those distressed by her absence. By joining heart to hand (*mano*) she could be "manifest" to the pontiff and the famiglia who yearned for her physical closeness. According to this explanation, she imagined there were no intermediary scribes. The letter was an expressed dream that bridged the solitude of her stay in the valley. "[T]he dream of writing may well have granted her the possibility or illusion of control, of being in charge of her life when the Rocca is being assailed by *venti*, winds, and she by the demands of a pope, of a confessor [Raymond], of the crowds who supposedly sought her out."

The explanation is provocative and far more detailed than outlined here, yet not conclusive. There are other scholars who, regardless of the problems involved, maintain that Catherine *did* learn to write at this time, "at least in an elementary way."

Catherine's supposed ability to write was surfacing at a moment when a great many issues were emerging in her life. Chief among them was her book—*il libro*—that was taking shape in her consciousness and bursting to get out. It would be a book of direction, of consolation, and of challenge. It would serve as a manual for her disciples who looked to her for guidance, as consolation to Raymond and for people like him who were weighted down by the pain of war, discouragement, and spiritual exhaustion. Finally, it would be a challenge to God's church that purported to be his body on earth but in reality was crippled and defaced by human weakness.

First the framework came to her, then the voice, and last of all the words. She begged one of her scribes to take them down, probably either Bartolomeo Dominici or Lisa Colombini, both of whom were with her on the Rocca (later joined by Neri di Landoccio Pagliarisi and other disciples). We don't know which section of the book was spoken first. It may have been the prologue—in which case she began the book with herself, described in the third person:

"A soul rises up, restless with tremendous desire for God's honor and the salvation of souls. She has for some time exercised herself in virtue and has become accustomed to dwelling in the cell of self-knowledge in order to know better God's goodness toward her, since upon knowledge follows love. And loving, she seeks to pursue truth and clothe herself in it."

She continued, describing the four petitions to God: "Now this soul's will was to follow truth more courageously. So she [the soul] addressed four petitions to the most high and eternal Father, holding up her desire for herself first of all—for she knew she could be of no service to her neighbors in teaching or example or prayer without first doing herself the service of attaining and possessing virtue.

"Her first petition, therefore, was for herself. The second was for the reform of the holy Church. The third was for the whole world in general, and in particular for the peace of Christians who are rebelling against holy Church with great disrespect and persecution. In her fourth petition she asked divine providence to supply in general and in particular for a certain [unspoken] case which had arisen."

And so the book that became known as *The Dialogue—Il Dialogo—* began to take shape. Raymond of Capua would later describe the creative process as rapid and intuitive. Catherine, he said, begged her secretaries "to be alert and take down whatever they should hear her say. It was this way that, in a brief space of time, a certain *Book* was compiled, containing a *Dialogue* between a Soul and the Lord." Pious legend claims the whole thing was finished in five days. Most scholars believe the composition took closer to a year. Although the book came out of a deep place in the psyche where Catherine encountered her God, the finished work also shows signs of careful editing and revision. It was at once spontaneous and calculated—a completely synthetic creation.

Catherine's *libro* was the end result of her preaching mission to the Sienese countryside. Its message was nourished by days and nights spent in her room in the Salimbeni fortress, which provided a safe distance from the politics of the day. She had to fend off the muttering of enemies, the demands of friends, and even an invitation from the pope, in order to get the book well started. There were days when she was too ill to work, "suffering the weakness I usually do in this sort of [summer] weather." She was sometimes lonely and sad without Raymond, who was similarly discouraged in Rome. She wrote to him with a heartbreaking mix of desolation and hope, "As for me, if it be [God's] will, let him take from me this dark life, for life is burdensome to me, and I long for death. Take heart, and let's be glad and joyful, because our happiness will be complete in heaven."

Yet still the dictation went on as *The Dialogue* progressed. Catherine sought strength and inner light from the Holy Spirit in a prayer that, again, she is supposed to have written with her own hand:

> O Holy Spirit, come into my heart;
> by your power draw it to yourself, God,
> and give me charity with fear.
> Guard me, Christ, from every evil thought,
> and so warm and enflame me again
> with your most gentle love
> that every suffering may seem light to me.
> My holy Father and my gentle Lord,
> Help me in every need.
> Christ love! Christ love!

The days of 1377 ticked away. October flowed into November and then December. Catherine labored on her book, making no move to return to Siena. But soon events snatched at her again, and when they did she could no longer avoid moving on.

II

ᔕᕐᕐᔑ

FULFILLMENT AND DISINTEGRATION

During the months that Catherine spent in the Orcia Valley, Florence and Rome continued to circle around each other, paying lip service to peace while practicing war. Late in the summer of 1377 delegations from both sides met at the papal residence in Anagni to discuss terms of peace. The result was not encouraging. Sensing that the struggle was turning in its favor, the papal side demanded that in exchange for lifting the canonical interdict, Florence must return confiscated church property, renounce its allies in the antipapal league, and pay a fine of one million florins. Florentine delegates agreed to carry the terms back home but predicted they would not be accepted. Nor were they. When the magistrates of Florence learned of the outcome they took steps to increase political pressure on Rome. In October they announced they would no longer obey the interdict the pope had levied on their city. By government decree churches were reopened, priests compelled to preside over services, and bishops ordered back to their sees. The papal side raised the ante once more by proclaiming the Florentine Eight of War heretics who no longer had to be obeyed. Catherine and her allies were scandalized by these developments. In their eyes waging political war against the papal states was one thing, but flouting the interdict was an assault on the church's spiritual authority. Florence's bishop, Angelo Ricasoli, refused to obey the government order, fleeing instead to Siena. Catherine knew Ricasoli from her first visit to Florence in 1374. She hadn't thought much of him then, but now she applauded his action. She wrote him a letter, urging him to be steadfast even if it meant losing his life. "Since you are a courageous man, you will do this, and will persevere in what you have begun." Again she said, "I long to see you a courageous and fearless man so that you might be better able to fulfill God's will and my desire for your salvation." Her admonition "to be a man" echoed words she had directed to Gregory XI months previously. For Catherine "being a man" was the ultimate test of a faithful apostle. Unspoken in the exhortation was the plea to "be a man—*like me.*"

The failure of the Anagni talks had the short-term effect of hardening positions in Rome and Florence, but eventually a long-term solution had to be found. Both sides were weary of war and had little to gain from its continuance. Gregory XI began casting about for another avenue to settlement. Just at this moment he received a letter—perhaps from Niccolò Soderini— suggesting that Catherine be sent to Florence as a mediator. Gregory leaped at the idea. What happened next is told by Raymond of Capua: "A messenger came to me from the pope one Sunday morning, commanding my company at dinner with His Holiness. I obeyed the command and when dinner was over the pope summoned me to his side and said, 'They have written to me to say that if Catherine of Siena will go to Florence, I will have peace.'"

Raymond answered that many persons besides Catherine were willing to do the pope's bidding, even if it led to their martyrdom.

"I do not want you to go yourself," said Gregory. "They would lay hands on you. But if she went, I believe they would not molest her; she is a woman, and besides they hold her personally in high esteem." The pope asked Raymond to prepare the necessary letters and return with them the next morning, which was done. Raymond closed his account by noting that he dispatched the letters to Catherine, who "undertook the journey without delay."

Well, perhaps there was a short delay. It took time to arrange things at Rocca d'Orcia, to notify her disciples of the change in plans, to contact her mother at Montepulciano, and to get everyone back to Siena. Once back home, there were obligatory visits to her Mantellate sisters, and probably to Belcaro, and, of course, the celebration of Christmas (if, in fact, she arrived in time for the holiday). It wasn't until early in 1378—probably in mid-January—that she set off for Florence with a party that included Stefano Maconi, Neri di Landoccio Pagliaresi, Fra Santi, Lisa Colombini, Cecca Gori, and Giovanna di Capo. Her unfinished manuscript had been left at the Rocca, since it didn't seem likely she would have an opportunity to work on it during her mission.

In Florence she found lodging once more in the home of Soderini on the south bank of the Arno, near the Ponte alla Carraia. It sufficed for Catherine's needs but was inadequate for those companions who could not find shelter in convents or monasteries. Soderini also had property near the Porta San Giorgio where he was planning to build a house, or perhaps already had one under construction. With financial help from his wealthy friends, Soderini soon completed the building with a walled garden where Catherine could stay with her famiglia. They moved in sometime during the spring.

Catherine had last visited Florence two years earlier on her way to Avignon. Now as then, her position in the city was ambiguous. On one hand, because she was not an official emissary from the pope she lacked the credentials needed to secure an audience with Florentine leaders or mediate in a formal way. On the other hand everyone in the city knew the Virgin of Siena was there at the pope's request. Her views reflected Gregory's; her very presence in their midst served to underscore his papal authority. In her first weeks she flaunted it freely. She made pronouncements on local politics in ways that may have been imprudent, considering that she was an outsider. As a consequence she was ignored by those in power and generally scorned by the more radical elements. Her warmest welcome came from extreme members of the Parte Guelfa who, while outwardly supporting the church, were waging their own factional war against the Florentine leadership and saw an opportunity to use her for their own ends. Catherine, especially at first, did not fully grasp the mixed motives of her associates. She tended to assume that allies who shared the same convictions must have the same goals. As time went on, however, she seemed to become more cautious. She may have been tipped off by Soderini who was not numbered among the radicals. In any event, after attending a few meetings of the Guelph leadership, she kept a low profile in Florence. As far as we know she addressed no appeals to the Signoria and did not preach in public. The letters she wrote to friends elsewhere hardly mentioned her activities in the city. Even the house Soderini provided for her, at the foot of San Giorgio hill, seemed ideal for keeping out of sight.

As she watched the political struggle between Florence and the pope play out from a distance, Catherine's mood fluctuated between discouragement and hope. To Nigi di Doccio Arzocchi, one of her disciples in Siena, she wrote, "it is time to weep and sigh and pray for Christ's dear bride [the church] and for the whole Christian people, so afflicted because of our sins." She was more upbeat in a note to Alessa Saracini when she expressed the hope that "[God's] providence will not fail. And it seems to me his providence is already beginning to appear." Indeed, the two sides agreed on a truce as they returned to the negotiating table early in 1378. Talks arranged by Bernabò Visconti were opened in Sarzana, on the border of Tuscany and Liguria. Catherine waited for some word of progress.

Raymond of Capua, likewise, waited anxiously in Rome. From Florence Catherine tried to boost his spirits, urging him to find "rest and pleasure" in the cross of Christ. Perhaps remembering their sea voyage home from Avignon on the storm-tossed Mediterranean, she reflected on the church as an ark. "Those who live in selfish love do not administer justice but are guilty of injustice," she wrote. "That is why we must strip ourselves of ourselves and clothe ourselves in Christ crucified. We must board the little ship of the most holy cross and fearlessly navigate this stormy sea. Those of us who are aboard this little ship have no reason for slavish fear, because the ship is provisioned with every food the soul can imagine. And if head winds blow that would beat against us and delay us so that we cannot fulfill our desires, we are not concerned. We stay there in living faith, because we have plenty to eat and the little ship is so strong that no wind, no matter how terrible, can dash it against the rocks and wreck it. True, [God] may often allow the little ship to be swamped by the sea's waves. But he does this not to drown us, but to make us better and more perfectly able to discern peaceful weather from stormy, so that we will not be over-confident in peaceful weather but will turn in holy fear, with continual humble prayer, and with holy and burning desire to seek the honor and salvation of souls aboard this little ship, the cross. This is why he permits the devil, the flesh, and the world, with all their harassment, to swamp us with their stormy waves. But those on board shouldn't simply stand at the edge but should leap into the hold at the heart of the ship, into the abyss of the blazing and anguished love of Christ crucified, and the waves won't hurt them at all. In fact, once they have experienced and tasted divine providence in the waves, they will emerge more strengthened and courageous, willing to endure pain and weariness and reproach in the world without sinning.

"So I beg you and I want you to board this little ship of the most holy cross, stripped of selfish love and clothed in the teaching of Christ crucified.

Use it to navigate the stormy sea with the light of living faith and the pearl of true holy justice toward both yourself and those in your charge."

News so eagerly awaited concerning the fate of the little ship arrived late in March. It did not come from Sarzana but from Rome, and it shocked them all. Gregory XI was dead.

Apparently the pope had been more ill than anyone realized, and more discouraged. A mere fourteen months after parading triumphantly into the city, he had died on March 27. If the suddenness of his passing was upsetting, the greater anxiety had to do with selecting a successor. Would a new pope return the papacy to Avignon? Many feared so, since French cardinals made up the majority of electors. The citizens of Rome were publicly demanding the election of an Italian—preferably a Roman—to the See of Peter. The cardinals were alarmed by threats of bodily harm. One of them, Jean de Cros, was told to elect an Italian "or all the cardinals from beyond the Alps will be knifed." The possibility that a Roman mob might dictate the selection of a new pope was a scenario the cardinals, when they were back in Avignon, had dreaded. Now they had to face it.

Sixteen cardinals sequestered themselves for the conclave on April 7. Of those, eleven were French. The French, though, were divided into two factions and couldn't agree on a candidate. The stalemate, in addition to the demands of the Roman crowd, convinced the electors that selecting an Italian was the most prudent option. They passed over Cardinal Giacomo Orsini, the Roman favorite, instead settling on a prelate who was not a cardinal and thus could not vote. Bartolomeo Prignano was archbishop of Bari in the territory of Naples. He was an experienced and respected church bureaucrat, having served Gregory as vice chancellor both in Avignon and Rome. He was not associated with any political faction, got along well with both the Italians and the French, and was considered able and honest. Prignano's election took place the following day, April 8. He took the name Urban VI.

Alerted by rumors of an election, an unruly crowd broke into the conclave and demanded to see the new pope. The cardinals were momentarily unnerved for having selected a Neapolitan pope instead of a Roman. They attempted to pacify the crowd by vesting the aged Roman Cardinal Francesco Tebaldeschi in papal attire and placing him on the throne. After the crowd dispersed, Prignano's election was formally announced without further interference. He was crowned in Rome on Easter Sunday, April 18.

Catherine's immediate reaction to Urban's accession is not recorded, although she doubtless knew what was going on. Raymond of Capua was serving as an aide to Cardinal Pedro de Luna during the conclave. De Luna, a moderate, was the only Spaniard there. Both Raymond and Catherine were acquainted with Prignano from their time in Avignon. They were most likely pleased with his selection since the Neapolitan was known to be a champion of church reform. He was on the record as a vigorous opponent of simony, the practice of selling church offices.

The election of a new pontiff immediately changed the political reckoning between the church and Florence. As a gesture of goodwill, the city fathers on May 1 announced they would henceforth obey the papal interdict, ordering the churches closed once more. Responding in kind, Urban renewed the truce that Gregory had originally mandated while peace talks were in progress. While these gestures were being exchanged, the citizens of Florence elected a new Signoria, ousted one of the Eight of War, and brought in Salvestro de Medici as *Gonfaloniere della Giustizia*, or dominant member of the Signoria—one of the first members of that illustrious family to hold high office in Florence.

All of these events, but especially the observance of the interdict, lifted Catherine's spirits. "It seems to me the dawn is beginning to break just a little bit," she wrote to William Flete. "I mean our Savior has enlightened this people to let them be roused from the perverse blindness in which they have sinned by using force to have [the liturgy] celebrated. Now, by divine grace, they are observing the interdict and beginning to turn toward obedience to their father. So I am begging you for love of Christ crucified . . . to pray especially, urging divine Goodness for love of the blood to send the sun of his mercy so that peace may be achieved soon—for that would truly be a sweet and lovely sun."

A short time later, though, she began to fear it was a false dawn. Urban VI was not proving himself the savior he first seemed to be. He did not lack commitment to church reform, but he pursued it in such an abusive and irascible manner that many of his cardinals were soon alienated. The day after his coronation he harangued his cardinals as "perjurers" for abandoning their dioceses and camping permanently in Rome. Two weeks later he denounced the same group as simoniacs who lived in ill-gained luxury. There was ample truth in both charges. Some cardinals had as many as ten or twelve dioceses or abbeys in their charge, each of them producing income but none ever visited. Still, the pope's offensive and even violent manner soon drove a wedge between him and his curia. He referred to Cardinal Orsini, from a distinguished Roman family, as a "blockhead," and he had to be restrained from physically assaulting the cardinal of Limoges. Speaking to the French cardinals, Urban vowed to nullify their influence by packing the Sacred College with Italians. The threat alarmed King Charles V of France. The new pope also managed to antagonize Queen Giovanna and the duke of Fondi from his native Naples. He seemed incapable of holding his tongue or his temper. Soon Urban VI stood almost alone in his righteous fury.

Raymond of Capua kept Catherine discreetly informed of these developments. His first reports were positive. Catherine wrote to Alessa Saracini that Urban "is beginning courageously" and "seems willing to give his attention to winning souls." Eventually, though, the darker aspects of the pope's character became known to her. The prior of the monastery on Gorgona, the island she had visited during her first stay in Pisa, complained to Catherine late in April that "this holy father of ours is a monster and is frightening people terribly with his words and actions." We do not have her reply. However we do have a letter she wrote (probably at Raymond's urging) to Cardinal de Luna whose loyalty to Urban was showing signs of erosion. In an effort to keep him on the pope's side she acknowledged hearing that "discord is arising [in Rome] between Christ on earth [the pope] and his disciples. This causes me unbearable sorrow, simply because of my fear of the heresy I am almost certain will come because of my sins . . . For it would be extremely hard to be fighting outside and internally at the same time. Tell [the pope] to provide himself with good pillars, now that he is about to appoint some cardinals. Let them be courageous men who are not afraid of death but who are prepared by virtue to suffer even to the point of death for love of truth and for the reform of the holy Church, ready to give their life if necessary for God's honor. Oimé! Oimé! Stop wasting time! Don't wait so long to do what is needed, or the stones will be falling on our heads!"

She wondered if she was overstepping propriety by raising this matter with the Spanish cardinal, yet concern for the church made her plunge ahead. "I think, dearest father, that it might be better for me to be silent than to speak about this matter. Still, I'm begging you, as much as I know how and can, to ask Christ on earth and the others to make this peace quickly, to do whatever is necessary for God's honor and the reform of the holy Church, and to eliminate this scandal."

The scandal she alluded to was schism, now openly being discussed among the disaffected cardinals. Some of them were claiming Urban's election was illegal on the grounds that it had been forced on them by the Roman mob. One by one they used the excuse of hot weather in Rome to drift away to the hill town of Anagni, about forty miles to the south, where they continued plotting. Even Cardinal de Luna went down to Anagni—not to plot, he assured Raymond, but just to listen. That de Luna should want to listen underscored the seriousness of the situation. It was not just the French prelates who were deeply disturbed by Urban's behavior.

The whole matter was distressing in the extreme to Catherine, especially since there was nothing she could do about it. She was trapped in Florence, unable to either advance the peace talks in Sarzana or stifle the plots in Rome. Her principal scribe, Stefano Maconi, had returned to Siena and was replaced by Barduccio di Piero Canigiani, the youngest son of her Florentine benefactor, and Cristofano di Gano Guidini. Now she wrote to Stefano and asked him to secure her manuscript left behind at Rocca d'Orcia. Working on the book would at least give her something to do.

Inactivity gnawed at her. So urgent was her desire to spend herself that she tended to see delays and setbacks as signs that she personally was unworthy or at least unready for God's kingdom. Thus she could tell de Luna that "my sins" bore the blame for the incipient schism. It was at once a formalistic expression of humility and a real feeling of guilt. For Catherine these "sins" did not so much jeopardize her personal salvation as contribute to the world's burden of evil and thereby inhibit progress. God, she believed, would not flood the world with goodness until humanity, which included her (maybe especially her), opened wide to grace. She said as much to Giovanni Tantucci in a letter written around this time. "This blood and fire, our redemption, are given to everyone. Nevertheless, not everyone shares in them—not because anything is lacking in the blood or the fire or in the gentle First Truth who had given them to us, but because of what is lacking in those who do not empty their vessel in order to fill it with this blood. The vessel of the heart, as long as it is filled with selfish love . . . cannot be filled with divine love or share in the power of the blood." Believing this, she had concluded that success or failure in the world depended to some measure on personal worthiness. Her whole life, she sometimes thought, was a chronicle of falling short. She had longed to become a martyr in a crusade, but that desire was not realized. She had yearned to purify the church but succeeded only with her famiglia, and perhaps not even then. She wished to be an instrument of peace but sat unemployed and marginalized in Florence. She still hoped that her book might advance the store of grace in a small way. Yet what she most desired was to place her body and her whole self on the altar of sacrifice. That greater gift, so earnestly offered, seemed to be ignored by God, and that, she concluded, had to be caused by some imperfection in herself.

Eventually the unfinished manuscript arrived in Florence and Catherine went back to dictating. Yet hardly had she begun when disturbances in the city interfered with its progress. Florence was entering a new period of political instability. The ongoing war and the interdict—especially the embargo on Florentine goods—had stirred old fault lines between social groups and set them grinding against each other. Salvestro de Medici used the discontent of the lower classes who had suffered most from the embargo to buttress his position against the conservative oligarchs. On June 18 he proposed penalties of banishment against some of the magnates. When the Signoria rejected his proposal, Salvestro dramatically announced his resignation and appealed to the people for support. The next day, June 22, riots erupted in the city. Guildsmen, led by the furriers, poured out of their halls to chase down and attack barons of wealth. Buildings were burned, shops looted, and an unknown number of people were killed outright. Niccolò Soderini's home was plundered; fortunately he was not home and so escaped death. Armed mobs poured across the Ponte Vecchio to the south bank of the Arno. Once on that side they remembered Catherine, the "witch" who lived near the foot of San Giorgio hill. They set off to find her.

Catherine heard them coming. Her disciples had been aware of the growing unrest for several days and urged her to flee, but she would not. Now she and her friends assembled in her garden and listened as the cries of the mob grew louder. In addition to her Mantellate companions, her group included Neri, Cristofano di Gano, and Barduccio Canigiani. Raymond of Capua (who was not present) relates what happened next: "[W]hile she was . . . praying in the garden, united to Christ, the rioters, satellites of Satan, came on the scene with swords and clubs, shouting 'Where is that wicked woman? Where is she?' When she heard them she, like one invited to a festive banquet, got ready for the martyrdom that she had so long desired. Stepping forward to one of them who, naked sword in hand, was shouting louder than the rest: 'Where is Catherine?' she knelt before him, her face radiant with joy, and said: 'I am Catherine. Do with me whatever our Lord may permit, but in the name of the Almighty I command you to harm none of my companions.' At her words the ruffian was so disconcerted and became so paralysed that he could not strike a blow at her, nor even to remain face to face with her."

In Raymond's account the two exchanged still more words, some of them, probably, of Raymond's invention. Yet the basic scene is perfectly clear. The mob leader threatened Catherine with a sword (a different translator calls it a "dagger"). She stood (in some accounts knelt) before him calmly, ready to take the blow, asking only that he spare her family. Confused, the ringleader and his companions shrank back, then crept away. Raymond's story concludes with her companions gathering around Catherine, congratulating her on her escape. She, however, wept bitterly, saying, "Oh! what a disappointment . . . I thought that he who in his mercy granted me the white rose of virginity would grant me also the red rose of martyrdom. But alas, no! . . . This is the result of my innumerable sins."

In this case Catherine's mea culpa may have been overstated by Raymond because two weeks later she wrote him a letter describing the event and expressing satisfaction with its outcome. In fact she felt as if "my eternal bridegroom played a great joke on me." True, she had missed martyrdom (yet again!) but God had tied the hands of the one who wanted to hurt her, which was a great miracle. Instead of his blade piercing her heart, her words had pierced his. "Oh my *babbo*!" she wrote, "Feel within yourself a wonderful joy, for I have never before experienced such joyful mysteries within me! There was a sweetness and truth in it, the happiness of a sincere and pure conscience." Nevertheless, delight was tempered by the knowledge of her imperfections "because such a great good [martyrdom] was prevented by my sins."

Although she escaped injury, Catherine realized that Florence in its present mood was not a safe place. Indeed, the city would experience riots throughout the summer of 1378. So she and her disciples found shelter for a short time in nearby Vallombrosa where there was a Benedictine abbey and hermitages. When they returned to Florence they did not go to the house on San Giorgio hill, since Soderini needed it for himself, now that his own house had been destroyed by the mob. Instead Catherine moved into the home of the tailor Francesco di Pipino and his wife Monna Agnesa, staying there secretly in case angry crowds should find her again.

At Vallombrosa and now at Francesco's she was making progress with her book manuscript. The early sections were most likely completed in the Orcia Valley. But no one is sure how exactly the book was put together—whether she dictated the various passages in the order we find them today, or whether she dictated passages randomly and organized them later. Here is a summary of the first two sections. After the prologue, God speaks:

Suffering by itself does not atone for sin, God says, but only suffering borne out of love. By themselves pain and suffering have no value. Heartfelt contrition, though, does have value, and the very desire for God is the way to God. The loving soul discovers within itself the breath of God's goodness that flowers into knowledge of the self and of God. It prompts the soul to serve God, and, when God cannot be seen, to serve the neighbor who can be seen. In this way virtues are born and grow in the one who is offering service—virtues of humility, justice, and courage that far surpass rote penances, which are but means rather than ends in themselves. Love is ordered by the power of discernment that finds the best way to serve others and guards the soul against sin, for even the noblest service is valueless if sin is involved. So service with love—suffering with charity—are always joined. Offering one without the other is like trying to offer water without a vessel to hold it. Service is the water, love the vessel.

But here the soul, moved by such kindness on the part of God, weeps for the fact that humans have produced such a polluted church, such a ruined world, both of them stained by sin and unworthy to be God's dwelling. To be sure, answers God, the house of the church is impure and its ministers, many of them, squalid and soiled. Still, divine mercy is not negated. Atonement has been paid in full by God's gift in Jesus and is available to all who would take it. Although the path to God on this earth is broken and in poor repair, it will still suffice with God's help. Across the waters of sin God has cast an arch by which souls can escape death. Bearing their burden of love and tears, these travelers derive power from their connection with the source of life, bringing God's mercy and their own acts of charity to places along the way.

Now Catherine has reached her great theme—for the arch over the flood is Christ himself, the bridge that joins flesh and spirit, earth and heaven. In the water below one encounters sin and destruction, but, God declares, "my chosen children keep to the higher way, the bridge. They follow closely the way of truth, and this truth is their gateway." The image is a powerful one for Catherine. The hilltop city of Siena did not have bridges, but here in Florence bridges were vital connections. The Ponte Vecchio, with its many shops, reminded her of the church that brings people to the other shore and succors them along the way, since "the bridge has walls and a roof of mercy. And the hostelry of holy Church is there to serve the bread of life and the blood, lest the journeying pilgrims, my creatures, grow weary and faint on the way." Perhaps, too, she remembered the bridge of St.-Bénézet over the Rhône at Avignon, with a chapel built into one of the piers near the eastern bank. "If [the soul] perseveres to the end she will come to the house of self-knowledge, where she shuts herself in watching and continuous prayer, completely cut off from worldly company."

Warming to this allegory, *The Dialogue* is not content to picture the bridge as a span between two banks. If the bridge is truly Christ's body then the soul must enter into it, learn from it, and grow in holiness. Catherine returns to an image she had used previously. One can enter into Christ's body through the wounds in his feet and climb up within, moving from space to space as one advances in the spiritual life (much as Teresa of Avila exactly two centuries later would imagine her *Interior Castle*). Catherine describes three major steps for the soul. At the level of the feet one deals with human affections. Just as the feet can lift from the earth, the soul severs itself from earthly things, frees itself from sin, and relishes the consolation of God. However, such warm feelings don't last. The soul next advances to the heart where it realizes how deeply it is loved by God and learns to love in return. Love prompts the third step, to the mouth, which is the realm of truth. Here different souls may respond in different ways "according to their hunger and their will." They may experience profound prayer, or learn true wisdom for the guidance of other souls, or pour themselves out in service to suffering humanity.

The bridge, then, is more than a route to a distant shore. It is a process, a path that one walks. For those who wish to make progress toward God, it is a map and school of perfection. The way is not always easy. Sometimes God seems to withdraw and abandon the traveler. Yet even in darkness the bridge carries one forward. To those who persevere God becomes "their bed and table," providing rest and food.

Catherine labored over her book through June and into July, interrupting the work only long enough to dictate letters to followers. She also dispatched her first letter to Urban VI, urging him to appoint cardinals "who will really be pillars of support for you . . . who will help you bear the burden of your responsibilities." She made no mention of Urban's behavior beyond asking him to act with kindness "and with only as much of the staff of justice as [people] can bear, no more." Other than that, she voiced her full support for the pope's campaign against simony. "Oh wretched me," she exclaimed, "I say it sorrowfully! Your sons are feeding on what they receive through their ministry of the blood of Christ, and they aren't ashamed to act like gamblers, playing their games with those holy hands anointed by you, Christ's vicar! And that's saying nothing of all the other wretched things they are doing! . . . Oimé! My dear *babbo*! Bring us a remedy!"

Considering the reception his pontificate was getting in Rome, Urban must have welcomed these positive words from Florence. Frankly, Catherine wished she could dictate her letters from somewhere—anywhere—else. She had gone to Florence as an act of obedience to Gregory XI but now found herself trapped there. Her wishes erupted only once in the letter to Urban when she cried, "Oimé! My *babbo*! I don't want to stay here any longer! Do with me later whatever you want."

But still she stayed. Things were getting dicey again in Florence as civic agitation escalated. From mid-July to the end of August there was constant turmoil, making it almost impossible for Catherine to concentrate on the book. On July 18 word reached the city that peace terms had been agreed to in the talks that had been moved from Sarzana to Tivoli, near Rome. Joy abounded in Florence, partly because Urban, in order to get a settlement, had agreed to reduce the city's fine from one million florins to 250,000 florins—and then consented to installment payments.

Two days later disenfranchised cloth workers, the *ciompi*, in Florence rose up in rebellion. They had taken part in the riots of June 22 and discovered their power in the process. Now they demanded their own guild and representation in the Signoria. Then, on July 22, the lower classes forcibly took over the government and named a wool carder, Michele di Lando, as Gonfaloniere della Giustizia.

The ciompi rebellion was a telling moment in European political history, since it was the first time the poorest classes were involved in the governance of a state. Unfortunately for their cause, the ciompi proved to be inept rulers and were overthrown in turn on August 31 by the major guilds and moneyed classes led by Salvestro de Medici. Catherine, who was left untouched during the entire affair, must have watched it with wonderment and not a little dismay. Both she and her Parte Guelfa friends were being pushed toward the margins, distrusted both by the ciompi and the forces around Salvestro.

While the rebels were still in power, other important events were occurring further south. On July 28 the peace treaty between Florence and the papal states was formally signed in Tivoli. Urban VI was eager to close the book on the Florentine war because another kind of rebellion, and perhaps war, was confronting him—the dissident cardinals who continued to weigh their situation in Anagni. The cabal of prelates had discreetly contacted European rulers to see which ones would support them in the event of a showdown with Urban. France's Charles V responded with a cautious affirmative.

News of the actual peace signing reached Florence on August 1. It set off another day of rejoicing. Catherine exultantly sent off a letter to Sano di Maco and other disciples in Siena. "Oh dearest children," she wrote, "the lame are walking, the deaf hear, the eyes of the blind see, and the mute speak, shouting with a loud voice: 'Peace! Peace! Peace!' They cry out with great joy at the sight of these children returning to obedience and their father's favor, their spirits reconciled. Like people who are already beginning to see they say, 'Thank you, Lord, who have reconciled us with our holy father.' Now Christ on earth, the gentle lamb, is called 'holy' where before he was called 'heretic' and 'Paterine.' Now they accept him as father, whereas before they rejected him. I am not surprised, because the cloud has fallen away and left the weather fair."

Happily, with the peace concluded, Catherine was no longer obliged to stay in Florence. She wanted to celebrate a little longer, but the hostility directed against her in some quarters propelled her to leave sooner rather than later. She quickly made plans—so hurriedly in fact that she left her manuscript and many personal papers with Francesco the tailor. On the day after the peace was formally announced, she and her party departed for Siena.

She was relieved and happy to come home but felt bad about her hasty departure. She wished she had brought the papal document giving her permission to celebrate private masses, because in Siena the churches still had not reopened. (As mentioned, Siena had also been under the interdict.) She wrote a quick note to Francesco asking for her papers and her manuscript. The same courier who bore the letter to Francesco also carried a letter to government leaders in Florence, still under ciompi rule, in which Catherine explained her reasons for running off so quickly. "I had wanted to leave and go back to Siena [only] after having celebrated and thanked divine Goodness and you," she said; "but now it seems the devil has so unjustly sown hostility toward me in [people's] hearts that I didn't want wrong to be piled on wrong, for the more of this thing there is, the greater will be the damage . . . But I go sad and dejected, leaving the city in so much bitterness."

The letter gave her an opportunity to weigh in on ciompi desires for social reform. Pulling no punches, she told the leadership that true reform would depend on their ability to put aside class hatreds. "You want to reform your city, but I'm telling you this desire will never be realized unless you do your best to demolish the hatred and rancor in your hearts and your self-centeredness. In other words, don't be concerned just for yourselves but for the general good of the whole city. So I'm begging you for the love of Christ crucified, for your own good, not to play favorites in choosing officials for your city but to choose virtuous men, wise and discerning, who with the light of reason will establish the order the city needs."

Home again in Siena, Catherine put aside politics to concentrate on her book and her famiglia. During the rest of August—while more storm clouds were growing over the papacy—she gave her attention to friends and acquaintances, writing letters of spiritual advice, with scarcely a word about church politics. She was silent in the days after August 9, when thirteen cardinals meeting in Anagni had declared the election of Urban VI to be invalid—or rather the election of Archbishop Prignano, since the Anagni group refused to recognize that a pope named Urban VI existed. In a followup document they called him an "Anti-Christ, devil, apostate, tyrant, deceiver, elected-by-force."

Not a word about this from Catherine. She had gone back to dictating her book. She had been searching for a quiet place to work and finally found it in the hermitage of her friend Fra Santi, probably the same hermitage where back in 1374 she had "miraculously" cured him from the plague. There she settled down with her scribes to complete her great work.

The long section in *The Dialogue* about the bridge is followed by shorter sections on tears and on truth. Catherine describes tears as the outpouring of compassion from the "fountain of the heart." Different kinds of tears are related to the stages in the spiritual life as she expresses it in the bridge section.

Catherine's treatment of truth considers the kinds of knowledge that are available to the soul. In its earliest stage, she writes, the soul makes progress by the light of reason, then it moves to the light of faith. As it comes closer to divine truth, it experiences a third way of knowing, when understanding pours into the soul in the form of fire. This section concludes with a discourse on discernment—the ability to tell when understanding comes from God and when it does not.

The next section, on the church, is a catalogue of the sins of the medieval church. Laypeople are faulted for disrespecting the clergy, especially the pope, who guards the storehouse of grace. Clergy are faulted at much greater length for licentious living and for violating each of the seven deadly sins. The poor quality of most of the clergy is mercilessly characterized: "My ministers should be standing at the table of the cross in holy desire ... But instead these have made the taverns their table, and there in public they swear and perjure themselves in sin upon miserable sin, as if they were blind and bereft of reason. They have become beasts in their sinning, lustful in word and deed."

After these bleak descriptions of the church, the section on providence is all sunshine and light as God describes how he will care for the soul "to make her grow in the light of faith, to make her trust in me and give up trusting in herself, and to make her see and know that I am who I am and that I can assist her in her need and save her." The virtue of obedience is treated in a section of its own, described variously as a key that unlocks heaven and as a ship that is sailed according to rules. Obedience is a particular concern for monks, friars, and nuns, so *The Dialogue* lays special weight on the religious rules of St. Benedict, St. Francis, and St. Dominic.

A brief conclusion follows. At the end the soul gives thanks to God for answering her prayers, saying, "You responded, Lord; you yourself have given and you yourself answered and satisfied me by flooding me with a gracious light, so that with the light I may return thanks to you. Clothe, clothe me with yourself, eternal Truth, so that I may run the course of this mortal life in true obedience and in the light of most holy faith. With that light I sense my soul once again becoming drunk! Thanks be to God! Amen."

Catherine finished dictating *The Dialogue* sometime in mid-October 1378, by which time the turmoil in Rome had clearly pushed its way into her consciousness. On September 20 the dissident cardinals had met in

Fondi, in the kingdom of Naples, and elected Cardinal Robert of Geneva as a counterpope, proclaiming him the legitimate successor to Gregory XI. It was an appalling choice. No one could have been more offensive to the Italians than the "Butcher of Cesena." He took the name Clement VII.

Now the great division of the church, the schism, was becoming a reality. Even before news of the election had reached Siena, Catherine wrote a letter of encouragement to Urban VI, telling him that if he clothed himself in charity "the bitterness in which you find yourself, most holy father, will be transformed for you into the most exquisite sweetness . . . By innocently suffering the blows of these wicked people who want to beat your holiness with the club of heresy, you will receive light."

Her message was not as sweet and naive as it may initially sound. She made it clear that along with "light" the pope received a knife for cutting out sin and vice—not merely in the enemy's heart but also in his own. "Now is the time to unsheathe this knife," she wrote, "the time to hate vice in yourself and in those in your charge and in the ministers of holy Church. In yourself I say because in this life no one is without sin, and the work of charity must begin with oneself, using it first on oneself for the love of virtue, and [then] on one's neighbors."

Urban was not about to use the knife on himself. Yet he did admire the Virgin of Siena, especially her wish, expressed at the end of the letter, to finish talking and go out on the battlefield to die for his cause. He wanted more people like that around him! A short time later he expressed his feelings to Raymond of Capua and suggested Raymond invite her to Rome. Raymond quickly passed along the papal invitation to Catherine in Siena. She, however, demurred. For one thing she was still putting the finishing touches on *The Dialogue*. But even more than that, she realized that people in Siena, including many Dominicans, would criticize her if she set off on yet another trip. If Urban really wanted her, she told Raymond, he should send her an order so that "if any are scandalized, they can be plainly shown that it is not by my own will I make this journey."

Raymond explained the matter to Urban, who told him to change the papal invitation to a papal command.

Catherine's life was evolving one last time. As September slipped into October she began to make plans for a trip to Rome. It was necessary to decide on her traveling companions, a place to stay in Rome, and the route they would take.

She wrote Urban again early in October, warning him to beware of assassination attempts and calling him "the cellarer who holds the keys of the wine cellar of holy Church in which is the blood of the humble spotless Lamb." She added that she would not be at peace "until I speak with your holiness in person."

It took some time to plan the journey. She wrote to Francesco di Pipino, the Florentine tailor, in late October to say the route was still uncertain, while welcoming a friend of Francesco's who wanted to join the party. On November 4 she wrote Francesco again to let him know "I'll be going to Rome from here about the middle of this month, more or less, as God pleases."

In the end almost forty people enlisted for the journey. Among them were Barduccio Canigiani from Florence (who was becoming her favorite scribe), Neri di Landoccio Pagliaresi, Bartolomeo Dominici, Giovanni Tantucci, Fra Santi, and a number of Mantellate, including Alessa Saracini, Cecca Gori, Lisa Colombini, and Giovanna di Capo. More friends would have come if Catherine hadn't forbidden it.

The middle of November came, then went. It was a few days later when Catherine and her followers passed through the Porta Romana of Siena and set their faces for Rome.

12

CATHERINE IN ROME

Rome in 1378 had long passed its grandeur as the city of the caesars and was only slowly becoming the Rome we know today. The medieval city had many ancient buildings, of course, such as the Pantheon, Hadrian's Tomb, and the remnants of the Colosseum, as well as many centuries-old churches and the Piazza Navona. But one would search in vain for the immense St. Peter's we know, with its familiar dome; that church wouldn't begin to be built for more than a century. The St. Peter's that Catherine and Urban VI knew was the old Constantinian basilica built in the fourth century on the same site. The street that took pilgrims from the Tiber to the basilica was known as the Portica or Via Sacra, lined on both sides by buildings. Yet just one block to the north were open fields where cattle grazed and crops were harvested. Rural sights intruded everywhere into the city. A grazing area near the ruins of the Forum was called Campo Vaccino (Cow's Field). It eventually became a swamp.

Seen from a distance, the city of Rome was remarkable for its multitude of towers—some of them fortifications but most of them churches. A twelfth-century visitor called Rome a "cornfield of towers." It had 400 churches for a population estimated at 20,000, and many of those churches flaunted campaniles. On major feast days the noise could be deafening. Rome was in fact larger than its official population, because it was the prized destination of pilgrims from France, Germany, Scandinavia, the British Isles, and every other corner of Christian Europe. The fourteenth century still belonged to the great age of pilgrimage. Across Europe on dusty roads pilgrims were trekking to Canterbury in England, or Santiago de Compostela in Spain, or Rome. In 1350, only two years after the catastrophe of the Black Death, Pope Clement VI had proclaimed a Holy Year and granted special indulgences for those who visited the Eternal City. The numbers that turned out were astonishing. Roads leading south were filled with pilgrims. It made no difference that Clement was in Avignon; the tombs of the apostles were in Rome. To serve the flocks of pilgrims, the city offered an array of national churches—St. Biagio in Mercatello for Castilians and Aragonese, St. Nicolò for Catalans, and churches for French, Danes, Germans, Scots, and others. In addition to churches for the travelers, Rome built hospitals, which were really hostels more than medical institutions.

It has been alleged that Rome fell into decrepitude during the years the popes were in Avignon. Birgitta of Sweden called it a city "deserted and without greatness," and Petrarch, who had a nostalgic attachment to classical Rome, exaggerated its disrepair as a way of pressuring the popes to return. The allegations were vastly overblown. When Urban V did come back between 1367 and 1370, he found St. John Lateran without part of its roof and St. Peter's with three bells missing, both of which he corrected. Pilgrims continued to pour into the city while the popes were away. New hospitals were built to care for them, and some major capital improvements were made. For instance, the Aracoeli Stairs on the Capitoline Hill were constructed in 1348 by the people of Rome as a thanksgiving for having survived the plague. One had to look closely to see the true vitality of the neighborhoods. Birgitta, the noblewoman who tossed alms to the poor as she strode past, did not look closely. Catherine, the dyer's daughter from Siena, lived more simply and settled in with the citizenry. As it turned out, Catherine loved Rome.

Catherine and her party arrived in Rome on November 28, 1378, the first Sunday in Advent. They found a place to live on Via del Corso, across the street from the church of Santa Maria in Via Lata. Whether the entire party of forty was housed there, or just Catherine and a few others, is uncertain. They had already agreed that while on the road and in Rome they would be like pilgrims, sharing household duties and begging for food. It was to be a grand adventure, and in that spirit they settled into their residence with contentment. Catherine was pleased with the location in the heart of Rome for two reasons. First, the church across the street was built on a site where, according to legend, the Apostle Paul was imprisoned while awaiting trial in Rome. Catherine had great devotion to Paul, whom she liked to call the "glorious apostle." She frequently quoted from the Pauline epistles. Just a few days after her arrival she wrote to a Carthusian monk, encouraging him to bear pain and difficulties with patience so that with "dear Paul we will glory in trials. We will want to be conformed with the pain and disgrace of Christ crucified." Catherine was also pleased because the residence was just a short walk from Santa Maria sopra Minerva, the Dominican church under the care of Raymond of Capua. One can imagine the joyous reunion between the Mantellata and her friend and confessor. It was more than a year since they had seen each other. She was eager to renew their bond.

Rome at this time was being roiled by fighting inside the city walls and in the countryside. Breton mercenaries loyal to Robert of Geneva—the counterpope Clement VII—had seized Castel Sant'Angelo that guarded the main entrance to St. Peter's, thereby preventing Urban VI from using his basilica. The Clementines also assembled a force of Bretons and Gascons in the nearby Alban Hills, threatening Rome from the south. Their ships patrolled the mouth of the Tiber to stop reinforcements from coming upriver to Urban's aid. Francesco di Vico from Viterbo, another Clement loyalist, was raiding papal states to the north. All of these threats— including the defection of most of his cardinals to Clement—put Urban in a very tight spot. He was forced to seek shelter at Santa Maria in Trastevere, one of Rome's oldest churches, about a mile from the Vatican.

However Urban was not without resources. His principal assets were the people of Rome who were solidly behind their Italian pope. The Romans could provide more than just moral support. They had mounted an army, which at the moment was surrounding Castel Sant'Angelo to prevent the Bretons from escaping. Urban was also completing arrangements to hire his own mercenary force, the Company of St. George under Alberico da Barbiano, made up entirely of Italians. Alberico had been trained in warfare by Sir John Hawkwood. He had served under Hawkwood and Robert of Geneva at Cesena, but—or so he claimed—the slaughter in that city had so disturbed him that he decided to go into the condottieri business for himself. He would prove to be an effective general in the papal cause. Urban's final advantage was the ending of the War of the Eight Saints. He momentarily enjoyed the backing of all the northern city-states, including Florence, Siena, and Milan.

Freshly arrived in Rome, Catherine was eager to help the pope any way she could. With Raymond at her side she crossed the Tiber to the Trastevere district on her second day in town and was heartily welcomed by the pope. The conversation that followed took place behind closed doors, but Catherine's presence in the city did not go unnoticed. Siena's ambassador to the Holy See, Lando di Francesco Ungaro, wrote to his government, "Catherine of Monna Lapa has come here and our Lord the Pope has listened to her. What he asked her is not known, but it is apparent he is happy to have her here."

What the pope asked her is not too difficult to guess. Catherine was to use her influence to bring recalcitrant leaders around to his side. Already the rulers of Europe were lining up behind one or the other of the papal claimants. Charles V of France was, of course, leaning toward Clement VII, and because the French king was supporting Clement, Richard II of England threw his support to Urban—and because England supported Urban, Robert II of Scotland sided with Clement. Most of the Germans, and all of Scandinavia, backed Urban. The Spanish appeared uncertain. (They would eventually take the Clementine side.) The Italians—at least all the states north of Rome—were solidly for Urban. That left Queen Giovanna of Naples, whose territory embraced much of the south. Giovanna and Urban had an intense disliking for each other. The queen felt slighted when Urban, at a papal banquet, seated her ambassador at the far end of the table. There were other considerations as well. Giovanna, as a member of the House of Anjou, had blood ties to the French king. On the other hand the people of Naples strongly preferred Urban (who was, after all, a Neapolitan), so Giovanna had to be careful about public expressions of favoritism.

Like Pope Gregory before him, Urban overestimated Catherine's actual political influence. Gregory had blithely sent her off to Florence believing the Florentines loved her and would listen to her. Some of them did, but many did not, and Catherine nearly paid with her life for Gregory's miscalculation. Urban now seemed confident that her gift for language coupled with her powerful faith would rally influential people to support his claim to the papacy. Catherine, who did not always appreciate political realities or the forces behind them, was more than willing to try.

While they were still considering her larger role, Urban begged Catherine to do him an immediate favor. In September he had created twenty-four new cardinals, nearly all of them Italians. Most of the honorees were still in

Rome, serving in his curia. The new cardinals shared Urban's sense of being surrounded by enemies, with foes both inside the city and out, and with many of the great European powers working to overthrow them. They could use words of encouragement—words that Catherine was endowed with and always ready to use. Two months earlier, while still in Siena, she had written a letter to the three Italian cardinals left over from Gregory's reign, imploring them not to support Clement. She had pleaded, "I long to see you come out of that great darkness and blindness into which you have fallen and return to true and most perfect light. Then you will be fathers to me, but not otherwise." The letter recalled the way the three had publicly acknowledged Urban at the time of his election, only to endorse Clement later. She maintained they were either living a lie then or were living a lie now; either way, they were living a lie. "No more of this, for love of God! Escape by humbling yourselves under the mighty hand of God and submitting obediently to his vicar while you still have time; for once time has passed, there is no way out."

Unfortunately her words did not sway the three who became permanent Clementines. Now, however, Urban wanted her to use the same eloquence on the prelates who remained loyal to him. She agreed to do it.

So on that same November day, the pope summoned his cardinals in the church of Santa Maria in Trastevere to listen to Catherine's discourse. It was an extraordinary moment—the illiterate daughter of a tradesman addressing the pope and his court in solemn assembly. An eighteenth-century rendering shows her in a pulpit preaching to the dignitaries, but such a setting is highly unlikely. Protocol would have arranged the cardinals on a platform flanking the enthroned pope while Catherine spoke from the floor below. There is no record of her words. Raymond reports she presented her case "with an easy flow of language." Most likely, as with her letter to the three cardinals, she reviewed the legalities of the two elections, assured the cardinals of God's blessing on their faithful support of Urban, and promised the eternal destruction of the Clementine cause in God's own time. Afterward the pope declared, "This weak woman puts us all to shame. I call her a weak woman, not to make little of her; but I want to emphasize that she *is* a woman and belongs to what is by nature the weaker sex . . . By nature, it is she who should show fear, even in situations where we would feel no danger. But on the contrary it is we who play the coward, while she stands undaunted, and by her rousing words imparts to us her own courageous spirit. Surely we should feel ashamed of ourselves."

A few days later, Urban came up with another idea. He proposed that Catherine travel to Naples to visit Queen Giovanna personally. Raymond apparently had reservations about the plan, but the pope and Catherine were swept along by its possibilities. As they considered it longer, Urban suggested adding another woman to the mission—Karin, the daughter of Birgitta of Sweden, who was presently in Rome and already acquainted with Giovanna. A final decision was postponed while the pope proposed the mission to Karin.

Catherine was enthusiastic about the Naples trip. A few days later, however, it all fell apart when Birgitta's daughter utterly rejected the idea. Karin detested Giovanna because the queen had once used her charms on Karin's brother Karl. Her opposition gave Raymond an opportunity to voice his own objections more forcibly, arguing that Catherine would not be safe in Naples. Raymond knew of Catherine's near assassination in Florence. What is more, he was familiar with Giovanna's court where discreet stranglings were known to happen. He had grown up only twenty-five miles north of Naples and had a brother in the queen's service.

Urban listened to Raymond's arguments and finally agreed with him. The mission to Naples was cancelled. Catherine was upset. She was annoyed with the pope, but even more annoyed with Raymond. She couldn't believe that her personal safety was the issue that finally scuttled the project. In her view, apostles were expected to risk their personal safety; it was a mark of their apostolic vocation. And if the risk eventually brought them to martyrdom— so what? Martyrdom was the laurel of victory! "If Saint Agnes and Saint Margaret [two early Christian martyrs] had reasoned as you do, they would never have won the martyr's crown," she told Raymond. "Your reasonings are worthless; they come from your lack of faith and not from the genuine virtue of prudence." Nevertheless, Raymond's arguments prevailed.

Still grumpy, she chose instead to dictate a letter to Queen Giovanna. "Dearest mother in Christ gentle Jesus," she began. "I Caterina, servant and slave of the servants of Jesus Christ, am writing to you in his precious blood. I long to see you grounded in truth, the truth we need to know and love in order to be saved." From this opening she moved into a lengthy treatment of truth as it subsists in God and humans. Then she got down to cases: "Oh dearest mother! I call you mother only to the extent that you are a lover of truth and obedient to holy Church, but in no other way. Nor do I address you with any respect, because I see the great change in your person. You who were a lady have become a servant and slave of that which has no being . . . You who were a trueborn daughter tenderly loved by your father, the vicar of Christ on earth, Pope Urban VI, who is truly pope and supreme pontiff, have pulled away from the breast of your mother, holy Church, where you have been nurtured for so long . . . Oimé! Oimé! Unless you abandon such a great error, we can mourn you as dead, cut off from the life of grace, dead in soul and dead in body!"

Having thus measured her own neck for a ligature should she ever appear in Naples, Catherine proceeded to lay out her case for Urban's legitimacy. At the end of it, she relented. She recognized that Giovanna had allowed some expressions of support for Urban among her people, which suggested that the queen may yet possess a measure of truth—"not a courageous and manly heart but effeminate weakness with no firmness or stability." She offered the queen a chance to amend her ways. "Return to the obedience of holy Church. Acknowledge the evil you have done. Humble yourself under the mighty hand of God, and God, who considers his servant's humility, will be merciful to us . . .

"I long for your salvation, and . . . I long to see you grounded in truth, because it is the truth that sets us free . . . I would much rather tell you the truth in person than in writing, for your own good and most of all for God's honor . . . I'll say no more. Keep living in God's holy and tender love."

As with most of her letters to government dignitaries, Catherine's long letter to Giovanna was not couched in diplomatic language. The weapon she employed was fear—the fear of being on the losing side and the fear of God. It was a religious argument. She sometimes called this approach "holy fear"—holy in the sense that it was grounded in compassion for the victim more than the dread of punishment. She used the same approach in a letter to an unidentified woman in Giovanna's court, pleading with her to help the queen see the light. Whether these letters were effective is another question. Undoubtedly Giovanna was attentive, but in the end she stayed in the Clementine camp.

During the last month of 1378 another blow fell on Catherine. Without forewarning to her, Urban VI appointed Raymond papal legate to the French sovereign and directed him north to call on Charles V. Raymond broke the news to her to see how she would take it. Saddened, Catherine nevertheless urged Raymond to go, which comforted him. A few days before he was scheduled to leave they met for a few hours to reflect on their interlocked lives and the many divine favors she had received while under his care. As Raymond remembered, "all other persons except the two of us were excluded—not that others were not present, but that they were not included in the conversation." When they were quite finished she said, "Go now with God, for I feel that never again in this life will we have a long talk together like this."

He sailed in December from the old Roman port of Ostia, some twenty miles away. She insisted on going there with him. Raymond recalled that when his ship pulled away she knelt on the shore "and then she made the sign of the cross with her hand, weeping as she did so." They must have known, both of them, that they would never see each other again.

She went back to Rome a much lonelier woman. From her residence she wrote a letter intended to catch Raymond during a stopover in Pisa, once more urging him to be faithful to his mission. It must have been tedious work for the ship toiling north in the winter sea, beating into the wind the whole way, but, as Catherine noted, Raymond had the truth to guide him. "[W]e have seen in the light that our gentle God finds pleasure in few words and many deeds. Without the light we wouldn't have known this and therefore would have done just the opposite, speaking much and doing little. Our heart would be sailing on the wind, for in happy times we would be frivolous and unduly self-confident, and in time of sorrow inordinately sad."

She was trying hard not to be sad. She didn't always succeed. She closed by saying, "And now, my soul, be silent and speak no more! I don't want to begin, dearest father, to say what I could neither write with pen nor speak in words. Let my silence tell you what I want to say. I'll say no more about this."

Even with her famiglia around her, preparing meals and sharing food, Catherine was lonely. Sometimes she had blamed Raymond for being too cautious, but she always knew that his concern was meant lovingly. The emptiness she felt after his departure may have provided the impetus for her idea to gather a council of holy men in Rome to advise the pope—and also, one suspects, to comfort herself. She wrote to people she knew, begging them to come to Rome. Among the invitees were Giovanni dalle Celle at Vallombrosa, with whom she had stayed when the mobs forced her out of Florence; Bartolomeo Serafini, prior of the monastery on the isle of Gorgona, near Pisa; three hermits from Spoleto; and William Flete and his secretary, Brother Antonio da Nizza, both hermits at Lecceto. To each of them she made the same argument: come, the pope needs you—Rome is the place where you can best serve the church. Knowing how much Flete relished the solitude of his hermitage, Catherine was especially direct. "You will come out of your woods and come here to the field of battle. If you don't, you will be out of tune with God's will. So I'm begging you, for love of Christ crucified, come soon, without delay, in response to the request the holy father is making of you. And don't worry about not having any woods, because there are woods and forests here!"

It is safe to assume that the council was Catherine's idea. The plan had her fingerprints all over it; the persons invited were *her* friends. Besides, she had long worried about the advice Urban was getting from his curia. She did not trust the self-interested advice of cardinals in the papal court. She must have discussed the idea for the council in general terms with the pope because he added his formal invitation to Catherine's. The invitees were summoned to gather in Rome on the Feast of the Epiphany: January 6, 1379.

To her great disappointment the council of sages never became a reality. Two or three of those invited may have come, but others never responded to the invitation. Still others, including Flete, flat out declined to attend. Catherine learned of Flete's decision early in January when a messenger arrived at her house with his letter. She dictated a snippy letter in reply and sent it back with the same messenger. Responding to Flete's argument that he could commune with God only at Lecceto, she said that true servants of God never presume that God is found only in one place. "It's my experience that for God's true servants every place is their place and every time is their time. When it's time to abandon their own consolation and embrace difficulties for God's honor, they do it. And when it's time to leave the woods and go to public places because God's honor demands it, they go."

Because she couldn't bring herself to answer her old mentor directly, Catherine addressed the letter to Brother Antonio, Flete's secretary. At the end she said, "As far as your and Frate William's coming or staying here, let God's will be done. I really didn't expect him to come, but I surely didn't expect him to respond with such disrespect for holy obedience or with such simple-mindedness. Give him and all the others my regards."

And so Catherine settled down for a long, quiet, and probably frustrating winter. Except for one letter to the rulers of Florence who were being courted by Clement, there is no evidence that she reached out to other rulers or influential persons during this period. Perhaps the siege conditions prevailing then in Rome made it a bad time to enlist support elsewhere. Urban had to prove, first of all, that he could command his own city. At Christmas Catherine sent him a gift of five bitter oranges gilded with honey in the Roman manner, along with a letter that played with the notion of the tree of life (the cross) that gives such "sweet bitterness." She wrote, "It seems, most holy father, that this eternal Truth wants to make of you another himself, both because you are his vicar, Christ on earth, and because he wants you in bitterness and suffering to reform his dear bride and yours [the church], who has been so pale for so long."

With so little she could do to advance the papal cause, Catherine busied herself with her family of disciples. Whenever she went away her followers in Siena missed her; she was the glue that held them together. In her absence they would neglect prayer meetings or, if they did come together, spend the time chatting instead of praying. She wrote a long letter to Sano di Maco, the Sienese wool worker—but really intended for everyone back home—abjuring them to forsake gossip and lukewarm piety. She wrote several letters to Stefano Maconi, encouraging him to break away from his overly protective family. Don't attempt to untie the knots, she ordered, cut them! Maconi was obviously reluctant to do so. Catherine also used her connections in Rome to secure papal blessings for friends and family in Tuscany—for Stefano, the nuns in Montepulciano, and Francesco di Pipino, the Florentine tailor, and his wife, Monna Agnesa.

Also in December, Catherine's mother came down from Siena to join the Rome famiglia, probably in the company of Francesco Malavolti and Salvi di Pietro, the goldsmith. Why Lapa wasn't in the original party is not clear, but she was there when the year ended. In a note to Stefano dated January 1 Catherine passes along encouragement from "grandma [i.e., Lapa] and Lisa [Colombini] and all the family."

When she first arrived in Rome, Catherine had intended to be like a pilgrim and systematically visit the great shrines. She had grown up listening to stories of the Roman martyrs—Lawrence, Cecilia, Sebastian, and others—and eagerly looked forward to visiting the places where, according to popular belief, they died or were buried. Access to St. Peter's tomb in his basilica was compromised by the siege around Castel Sant'Angelo, but she most likely visited the ancient basilica of St. Paul's Outside the Walls to see the tomb of her beloved Paul, as well as the great basilicas of St. John Lateran and St. Mary Major. Among the other churches she is thought to have visited were San Gregorio Magno al Celio, where her exemplar, Pope Gregory the

Great, once made his residence; Santa Maria in Cosmedin with its famous Mouth of Truth embedded in the portico wall (one wonders if Catherine followed the custom and placed her hand in it); San Sisto Vecchio, rebuilt just the century before by Pope Innocent III; and three churches on the Aventine Hill—Santa Prisca, named for a first-century martyr, Sant' Alessio, and Santa Sabina, whose Dominican prior was an outspoken supporter of Urban VI. Still, she never got around to visiting the various shrines as originally intended. Pilgrims from Tuscany regularly stopped by her residence and often stayed for meals, but she invariably claimed her duties made it impossible to join their tours.

During the seventeen months she spent in Rome, Catherine's dictations overflowed with prayers. In fact, her scribes had been copying down prayers all along. They frequently cropped up in letters when Catherine departed from the gist of the message and spontaneously burst into prayer—one moment she would be addressing her correspondent, and the next moment God. Her two worlds were so interlocked that these asides never became digressions for her. Prayers also abounded in *The Dialogue*, layered with commentaries and prophetic utterances. Still other prayers, though, were dictated by Catherine explicitly *as* prayers, and it is these, collected after her death, that were eventually published as *The Prayers of Catherine of Siena*. They tend to be free-form, usually written in the first person, and long— often running to several pages. Of the twenty-six texts that make up the full collection, as many as nineteen were composed in Rome (two of the others, dictated at Avignon and the Rocca d'Orcia, have already been cited).

The prayers from the Roman period reflect the mature spirituality of her last years. On one hand they reveal her awareness of the vast gulf that existed between her and God:

> You, eternal Godhead,
> are life
> and I am death.
> You are wisdom
> and I am ignorance.
> You are light
> and I am darkness.
> You are infinite
> and I am finite.

You are absolute directness
and I am terrible twistedness,
You are the doctor
and I am sick.

And yet her consciousness of sin and human weakness that seems so medieval to us was leavened by keen attentiveness of God's incarnational connection with humankind, to such a degree that humans had a share in
God's divinity:

If I consider the Word,
through whom we are created anew to grace,
I see you fashioned after us
and us after you
through the union that you, eternal God,
have effected with humankind . . .
So the soul who follows your Truth's teaching
in love
becomes through love
another you.

Unlike *The Dialogue*, which leaned toward the didactic, Catherine's prayers
have a passionate consciousness of God's action in the world, a consciousness that seems to flame up within her. One of her most famous prayers,
composed in mid-February 1379, announces:

In your nature,
eternal Godhead,
I shall come to know my nature.
And what is my nature, boundless love?
It is fire,
because you are nothing but a fire of love.
And you have given humankind
a share in this nature,
for by the fire of love
you created us.
And so with all other people

and every created thing:
you made them out of love.

These are not the prayers of a solitary sitting in a cave. She had departed
from that path years previously. They are the prayers of engagement by a
person thoroughly involved in the world who seeks holiness not for herself
alone but as a blessing on humankind.

We must conform ourselves to you
through suffering and anguished desires.
So through you who are life
we will produce the fruit of life
if we choose to engraft ourselves into you.
It is clear then
that though you created us without our help,
you do not want to save us without our help.

Once we have been engrafted into you,
the branches you gave our tree
begin to produce their fruit . . .
And our will chooses to love and to follow
what our understanding has seen and known.
So each branch offers its fruit to the others.

For Catherine prayer was not separate from social concern. She never
forgot her commitment to support the pope and reform the church even as
she communed with God. For example, in December 1378 she prayed:

And then, director of our salvation,
let this new spouse of the Church [Urban VI]
be directed always by your counsel.
Let him accept
and listen to
and encourage
only those who are clean and pure.
As for these other newest plants of yours [the cardinals],
let them stand before our lord your vicar on earth
just as the angels stand before you in heaven,
for the reform of this holy mother Church . . .

She came back to the theme in late January 1379 in a prayer composed on the feast of the Chair of St. Peter when the papacy was very much on her mind:

> So [God] listen to us
> as we pray for the guardian of this chair of yours,
> whose feast we are celebrating.
> Make your vicar
> whatever sort of successor you would have him be
> to your dear elder Peter,
> and give him what is needed for your Church.
> I am the witness
> that you have promised to grant my desires soon;
> With even more confidence then
> I beg you to wait no longer
> to fulfill these promises. O my God.

Whatever was needed for God's church couldn't happen too soon for her. Time seemed to drag through the winter months. But then, as winter turned into spring, there was a break in the stalemate between the two papal claimants. In April Roman troops surrounding Castel Sant'Angelo stepped up their attacks on the Bretons barricaded inside. The condition of the defenders became desperate as food supplies dwindled. Everyone expected that troops loyal to Clement would attempt to force their way into the city and relieve the siege, but as the weeks dragged on they never came. At last, on April 27, the Bretons laid down their arms. They insisted on making their surrender to the citizens of Rome rather than to the pope. And the Romans—wary lest Urban attempt to use the fortress to expand his power over the city—insisted on keeping it. Urban was annoyed by the terms of surrender, yet pleased he would finally be able to use his basilica. He planned a ceremonial procession to reclaim it.

Before that could happen a climactic battle pitted the Clementine forces in the Alban Hills against Urban's mercenaries under Alberico da Barbiano. The condottieri leader had assembled his troops, supplemented by soldiers from Rome, in the town of Marino, about fifteen miles south of the city. There, on April 30, they were met by a superior force of Bretons and Gascons under Louis de Montjoie, a nephew of Clement. In the daylong battle first Montjoie, then Barbiano, had the upper hand. Finally the French line crumbled. Montjoie and many of his soldiers were taken prisoner; the rest of his army fled toward Naples, while in Fondi Clement waited anxiously for news of the outcome. Reports of the defeat alarmed the Clementines in Naples. Clement and his court quickly prepared for evacuation by sea, and by mid-May they were gone. The French claimant decided Avignon would be a safer place to establish his throne.

In Rome there was rejoicing and great ringing of bells. On the day after the battle, Urban walked barefoot in a procession from Santa Maria in Trastevere to St. Peter's where a *Te Deum* was sung. While her correspondence does not mention her participation, it is likely Catherine joined in the procession and celebration. Certainly she threw off the lethargy that had gripped the Urbanite cause for several months. Believing the victory at Marino made this an ideal time to pursue reconciliation, she addressed letters in the first week of May to leaders on both sides of the schism. She pleaded with Queen Giovanna to "have pity on so many souls who are perishing because of you and for whom you will in the end, at the moment of your death, have to give an account before God. We in fact have the remedy; we have time to return, and [the pope] will receive you very graciously."

Catherine was still grieving over her missed opportunity to visit Giovanna personally. "Oh how blessed my soul would be if I could come there and lay down my life to restore you to the goods of heaven as well as your earthly goods," she wrote. "Oimé! Don't wait for the time you can't be sure of having. Don't make my eyes pour out rivers of tears over your poor little soul and body—for I think of your soul as my own."

Another letter went out to Charles V of France, reiterating her arguments for Urban's legitimacy. As she did with Giovanna, Catherine reminded Charles that one day he would have to stand in judgment before God. "Face up to the fact that you will surely die, and you don't know when. Set your sights on God and his truth, and not on emotion or love for your country. For where God is concerned we must be impartial, since all of us have come forth from his holy mind. "

Her plea to Charles is interesting for the way it stressed the claim of truth above feeling. We moderns may be tempted to believe that Catherine—with her ecstasies, visions, and mortifications—was a prisoner of her emotions. This was not the case, at least not for Catherine in her later years. Adherence to the truth—truth as she understood it—was what really claimed her. Appeals to a truth that was certain and knowable, a truth that brought life and salvation, abound in her letters. In contrast to such surety of truth, she believed that unchecked feelings and sensuality lead people into sin and error. By anchoring her faith in "objective" truth Catherine was very much the daughter of medieval scholastics who placed the loving pursuit of truth above all human occupations. Her reaction to the victory at Marino, for instance, was certainly heartfelt, but the letter she wrote to Alberico da Barbiano and his Company of St. George contained no teary hosannas. It was instead a hard-eyed consideration of the trials that lay ahead. "Oh dearest brother and sons!" she wrote. "You are knights who have gone into the field to give your life for love of life, to give your blood for love of the blood of Christ crucified. Now is the time for new martyrs . . . If you die, you gain eternal life and are set in a safe and stable place. And if you escape, you have made a willing sacrifice of yourself to God and can hold in good conscience what you own . . . And so that we may better call on divine help in this holy work, eternal Truth wants you to enter into this exercise with good and holy intent, making every effort to take as your principle and foundation God's honor, and the defense of our faith and of holy Church and of Christ's vicar, with good conscience."

The road ahead was hard, she was sure of that. And she had no patience for those who took the easy way, as Raymond of Capua discovered to his chagrin. Even before the battle of Marino, Raymond had attempted to enter France in order to present his credentials to Charles V. However, French agents, alerted to his mission, stopped Raymond at the border town of Ventimiglia. His traveling companion was captured, but Raymond, warned by a fellow Dominican, managed to escape and made his way back to Genoa; there he described what happened in letters to Urban VI and to Catherine. The pope told him to stay in Genoa and preach against the schismatics.

Catherine, when she learned of the episode, did not rejoice in Raymond's narrow escape. She promptly shot off a letter to him in which she called him "my wicked little father."

"I long to see you raised this very day above your childishness, a courageous man," she wrote. "Grow beyond liking milk and become a bread-eater, because children who feed on milk are incapable of going into battle; they only enjoy playing games with those of their age. And people who live in selfish love for themselves enjoy the taste of nothing but the milk of selfish consolation, whether material or spiritual. Like children, they have fun with those who are like themselves. But when they become adults, they rise above self-indulgence and selfishness." Mature people, she went on to say, rush into battle. "When they are slashed and torn to pieces by the world, they put themselves back together more perfectly and join themselves to God . . . You weren't worthy to stand for even a little while on the battlefield. No, like a child, you were driven off—and you willingly fled, very happy that God had made concessions to your weakness."

Poor Raymond had to hear from her lips how childishly he had behaved. Yet better her lips than anyone else's, because he knew that beneath her scolding there was love. After reading her letter, he must have been affected by it. Her peroration sounds much like the advice she had given him long ago, after Niccolò di Toldo's execution:

"Immerse yourself in the blood of Christ crucified. Bathe in the blood. Quench your thirst in the blood. Get drunk on the blood. Grieve over yourself in the blood. Be joyful in the blood. Grow and become strong in the blood. Lose your weakness and blindness in the blood. And by the light run like a courageous knight to seek in the blood God's honor, the good of holy Church, and the salvation of souls. I have no more to say to you."

Raymond would never become a knight rushing into battle. He was better cast as Sancho Panza to her Quixote—a good enough standard for most people, although not for Catherine. Meanwhile, back in Rome, the city of martyrs, Catherine dreamed her dream of knights and offered herself to God. She prayed:

> O boundless, gentlest charity!
> This is your garden,
>   implanted in your blood
>   and watered with that of your martyrs,
>   who ran bravely after the fragrance of your own.
> Do you, then, be the one to watch over it.
> For who could prevail
>   over the city you were guarding?
> Set our hearts ablaze
>   and plunge them into this blood
> so that we may more surely conceive a hunger
>   for your honor
>   and the salvation of souls.

13

⁙

CROSSING THE BRIDGE

As soon as the way to St. Peter's Basilica was open, Catherine began to go there nearly every day to pray at the tomb of the apostle. She and her companions would awaken early at their residence on Via del Corso and walk down narrow Via Lata to nearby Santa Maria sopra Minerva. This Dominican church was Rome's only church built in the Gothic style, erected (as the name suggests) over the ruins of a Roman temple. After attending mass and praying in the church's Cappella del Transito, they would continue on to St. Peter's, praying as they went. Catherine certainly was aware and probably took pleasure in knowing that their path generally followed the Via del Papa, the route taken by the pope when on special occasions he processed from St. John Lateran, located beyond the Palatine Hill, to the Vatican. This was not a single road but rather a combination of streets and byways tracing a route from the Lateran, Rome's oldest church and its cathedral, past the Colosseum, and through Piazza della Minerva. Picking it up there, Catherine's party followed it along Via Santa Chiara, with the Pantheon looming on their right, to Piazza della Sant'Eustacchio. Then the route jogged south along Via del Teatro Valle to Via dei Sediari—named after the carriers of the pope's sedan—and across the southern end of Piazza Navona to a place where it was said St. Agnes was put to death in the fourth century. From there, they had a choice. Most often, Catherine and her party forged straight ahead along Via del Governo Vecchio and Via dei Banchi Nuovi until they came to Via del Banco di Santo Spirito angling right to the Tiber and the Sant'Angelo bridge. As they came closer to the river, Rome's maze of streets became more congested. The narrow, fetid alleys, constantly threatened by flooding from the Tiber, were unpaved and frequently muddy. The buildings that crowded in on both sides housed workshops on their lower floors, with living quarters above. The noise and smell of it were overwhelming—coopers or carpenters in the doorways pounded with their hammers as children ran shouting through the throng and peddlers hawked goods from baskets carried on their backs. It was hard to focus on prayer amid the confusion. If this route wasn't chosen, the companions would make their way north from Piazza Navona to Via dei Coronari (an old Roman road called Via Recta in Catherine's time), lined with shops selling bogus relics and cheap religious articles, and which likewise took them to the bridge.

Once across the river, Castel Sant'Angelo loomed. Originally Hadrian's imperial tomb, it was now a fortress and would soon become a place where Urban VI imprisoned and tortured his enemies—of which he had many. By skirting the fortress to the left, Catherine and her party came at last to the Portica (today's Via della Conciliazione), the street leading to St. Peter's Basilica. With their destination finally in sight, they hurried past lodging houses and stables to the square in front of the basilica. The open space was not as imposing in Catherine's day as it is now. It would be three more centuries before Bernini wrapped the vast plaza with his colonnades. In 1379 the place was disorganized and only partially paved, dotted with washhouses for pilgrims and stalls selling badges, candles, and oil for the lamps at the apostle's tomb. Threading their way through the crowds, the companions mounted broad steps and entered the basilica's portico through massive doors. The portico gave way to a large open atrium with a fountain in its center and cloistered walkways on either side. Only at the far end of the atrium did one enter the basilica proper.

It was an awesome space, with the long, dim nave leading to the main altar at the crossing. There were rows of columns along both sides of the nave that partially obscured the side aisles, where one could glimpse more shrines and altars. Light filtered through clerestory windows in the upper walls and illuminated mosaics and rich hangings. Throughout the church, bands of pilgrims huddled in wonder or craned their necks to see the decorations; the steady hum of their murmuring did not cease even when the holy office was chanted. Catherine, one imagines, paid the pilgrims no mind but strode toward the main altar and St. Peter's tomb. Here, when services were not going on, she would plant herself and resume her prayers for the church—the bark of St. Peter that was far more fragile, she knew, than appearances suggested. Just as this majestic basilica, so solid to the casual viewer, had weaknesses in its walls and beams that would lead to demolition and the construction of a completely new basilica two centuries hence, so the human edifice had cracks in its structure, flaws in its design. Catherine earnestly wished to see it rebuilt according to God's plan. Urban VI had pledged himself to the task but once in office did not pursue it, distracted by other commitments. So until real reforms began, Catherine could only bend her head and pray for the church she had.

Praying was one of the few things she could do in these months when she felt herself increasingly powerless to influence events in the church and the world. Urban VI was gracious to her but not open to suggestions. With Raymond in far-off Genoa she was without an advisor schooled in the ways of the papal court. Her confessor and principal mentor in Rome was Bartolomeo Dominici who had little experience with church affairs at this level. She had a useful contact in Tommaso Petra, a lay secretary in the papal household whom she had met in Avignon. Petra was devoted to her, but, it would seem, either lacked real power or did not choose to oppose his employer, the pope. As a consequence, Catherine found herself at a disadvantage in her dealings with the scheming and increasingly mistrustful pontiff.

One of Urban's greatest needs at the moment was money. It took a great deal of money to hire mercenaries and maintain a diplomatic offensive against Clement. Urban did not have the revenue from France and Spain, which was going now to Avignon. The political situation was further complicated by a war that had flared up between the sea powers of Genoa and Venice. Urban, along with King Louis I of Hungary, was backing Genoa, which gave Bernabò Visconti of Milan a fresh opportunity to oppose the pope by casting his lot with Venice. As if that weren't enough, the city-states of Tuscany were behind in their tribute payments mandated by the treaty ending the War of the Eight Saints. So Urban, in effect, put Catherine to work collecting some of his debts.

Back in February she had written to the leaders of Florence to remind them of Urban's largesse in lifting the interdict. "You have been put back at the breast of the holy Church, and can receive the fruits of the blood, if only you want it, from Pope Urban VI, true pontiff and Christ's vicar on earth," she wrote. "The latter has pardoned and absolved you with such great charity, giving you what you had asked and treating you not like children who had sinned, but as if you had never wronged him. And now you see him in such great need, and not only are you not helping him, but you are paying no attention to what you had promised. So you are showing yourselves very ungrateful."

In June she used the same argument with the city fathers of Perugia. "I long to see you coming to the aid of your father," she told them. "You would be helping yourselves as well, since by helping him you are helping along your own spiritual and temporal welfare. You are . . . coming to the aid of this dear bride, holy Church, and Pope Urban VI, you are [i.e., would be] paying what you owe—and by paying it we show our gratitude and appreciation to God, as well as to the pope for all the favors he has continually done for us."

Another political leader constantly on her mind was Queen Giovanna of Naples. Catherine seemed to have a soft spot in her heart for the notorious Giovanna, who had been married four times and taken many lovers along the way. Following the defeat of Clement's forces at Marino, riots had erupted in Giovanna's home city against the presence of French troops. In an attempt to mollify the crowds, she announced she was transferring her allegiance to Urban. As evidence of her change of heart she sent ambassadors to Urban's court and wrote Catherine to reassure her that "the words of a saint" had not gone unheeded. Vastly relieved, Catherine expressed joy to Neapolitan friends that "the heart of Pharaoh is broken—I mean the heart of the queen. She has showed such hardness until now, being separated from her head, Christ on earth, and attached to Antichrist, a member of the devil. She has persecuted the truth and promoted falsehood. Thanks, thanks be to our dear Savior, who has enlightened her heart . . . and has revealed his wonders in her."

Alas, she spoke too soon. No sooner had the people in Naples quieted down than Giovanna recanted her conversion, withdrew her ambassadors, and switched to Clement's side again. Urban was furious, Catherine dismayed. She dispatched Neri di Landoccio Pagliaresi to Naples with a personal plea to the queen. It was a sign of her real concern for Giovanna, as one woman to another, that the message reflected more disappointment than anger. "Oh dearest mother!" she wrote. "I long to see you grounded in this truth [that sin is a form of irrationality]. You will follow it if you live in true self-knowledge, but not otherwise. This is why I said I long to see you coming to know yourself. I invite you to this truth, to come to know it so that you may be able to love it. If you look at the humble Lamb, [you will see] that in his blood is the revelation that this is the truth. This is why it was shed and given as our price, administered within the body of holy Church. What does this truth promise to those who love it? It promises that in the price of the blood, with holy confession and contrition and atonement, they will receive eternal life. It also assures us that every good will be rewarded and every sin punished."

"Dearest mother," she continued, "for love of Christ crucified be sweet to me. For my sake don't be bitter any more. Return to your senses a bit and don't sleep any longer in such a slumber. Wake up in this bit of time that is still left to you. Don't wait for time because time won't wait for you. In true knowledge come to know yourself and God's goodness within you."

By this time Catherine must have known that Urban VI was plotting to overthrow Giovanna. The pope had contacted Charles of Durazzo, a cousin of Louis I of Hungary and second cousin of Giovanna, with the suggestion that Charles march on Naples to claim the kingdom for himself, backed up by the army of Louis. Urban would prepare the way by first excommunicating Giovanna and declaring her throne vacant. Charles found the idea attractive. As a member of the Angevin dynasty, he had a claim on Neapolitan succession, but both Charles and Louis were too busy at the moment to give Giovanna their full attention. As allies of Genoa they were engaged in the siege of Treviso, a town belonging to Venice. Exactly how much of this plot Catherine knew is open to question. Most likely she was aware of its general outline but in her idealism probably did not appreciate the cynical motives of the players. Urban, Louis, and Charles were less interested in advancing the cause of the church than taking control of central Italy. As with many such schemes, soon after it succeeded the plotters had a falling out over the spoils.

But that would not happen for another couple of years. For now, Catherine was intent on supporting the Roman papacy any way she could. She had suggested that Raymond of Capua be sent as a papal delegate to the Hungarian court. In the end he never went, but while the idea was still being considered she wrote to King Louis to thank him for supporting Urban and prepare him for even greater contributions. "The dear God has done you a great favor in not leaving you in darkness but giving you light," she wrote. "And it seems our dear Savior wants you now to be a defender of holy Church just as you have always been a defender of our faith and a champion of the faith in the face of unbelievers [i.e., Ottomans]. Be prepared in everything to defend the truth of holy faith against the lying heretical Christians [i.e., Clementines] who are denying the truth. You must not dally, but very purposefully respond to God, who is calling you to this ministry."

She gave Louis undue credit by wondering if his Angevin family ties with Giovanna would hold him back from attacking her. "Don't let yourself be deceived by emotion in this," Catherine told him. "Don't think . . . that you and your kingdom would suffer dishonor if she were publicly declared a heretic. It is not true that you would be dishonored . . . because her heresy is public and well-known. It would in fact be to your honor to want to see justice done—or to do justice yourself—to this or any other offense by any person whatever, even if that person were your own son."

Catherine was so invested in saving the Roman papacy that she would absolve the king from betraying his relative. She needn't have bothered, since Louis had no scruples in that direction. In retrospect, the whole episode was squalid. It was not Catherine's finest hour.

This was not the only diplomatic move in the summer of 1379. Urban still had hopes of changing the loyalties of Charles V of France. The pope instructed Raymond of Capua to try again to enter France, this time by way of Spain. Once more Raymond set out from Genoa, only to find that his old mentor, Cardinal Pedro de Luna, had become Avignon's legate to the court of Aragon and had nudged Spain into the Clementine camp. Now the route through Spain was closed as well. Raymond reported his attempt to the pope and to Catherine, asking her not to judge his lack of success by her standards: "[You don't] think I should measure you by my standards." She shot back: "So you were suspecting that my love and affection for you had lessened. But you didn't realize—though you showed it to be true— that your love had diminished while mine had grown. For I love you with the same love with which I love myself, and I firmly believe that God in his goodness will provide what is lacking on your part. But it didn't work out that way, for you've found ways of throwing off the load."

Raymond had once more failed to be a martyr. "You ought to be dead but aren't," she told him. "So make an effort to kill yourself with the knife of hatred and love so that you won't hear the mockery and vilification and reproach the world and the persecutors of holy Church may choose to give you . . .

"I tell you, dearest father, whether we want it or not, these times invite us to die—so for my sake, stop being alive! In suffering put an end to your pains. In suffering let your holy desire grow, so that our life may be spent entirely in anguished desire. Let's gladly give our bodies to the wild beasts. I mean, let's gladly, for love of virtue, throw ourselves to the tongues and hands of bestial people. This is what those others have done who have labored in this dead garden, dead, watering it with their blood, but first with tears and sweat. But I, sad as my life is, did not shed water, and so I have [been] refused to shed my blood. I want no more of this. No, let's reform our lives and stoke the fire of desire!"

The fire of her desire had been stoked to a white heat, and it was beginning to burn her up. She was being worn down by the daily trek to and from St. Peter's. She and her party would stay at the basilica until vespers, late in the day. Making their way home through the crowded streets, they would beg food for the supper that was shared in common at their residence. They took turns begging and cooking. On one occasion, when someone—perhaps it was Catherine—forgot to pick up bread, there was great consternation in the house. Pilgrims from Siena were joining them for supper, and there was not nearly enough food to go around. According to the story circulated later, Catherine told the servers to distribute the little bread they had on hand— and lo, there was a miracle! Like the gospel story of the loaves and fishes, they ended with more than they had at the beginning.

Within her famiglia, Catherine was still mamma and provided for its needs. It was the rest of the world and the larger church that weighed on her. Urban VI was a major source of worry. He was supposed to be a shepherd for his people but managed somehow to quarrel with nearly everyone he dealt with. Back in May she had written to remind him to maintain a humble outlook "so that we don't get things out of perspective when we are happy or impatient when we are sad." Conscious of his touchiness, she added a note begging Urban's forgiveness "if I have in any way offended God and your holiness."

He wouldn't listen to advice. In June, Catherine, apparently dissatisfied with some of his appointments, wrote again to ask that when new bishops were being appointed, "let them be persons who are seeking God, not promotions." She went on to remind him that, although he had the power of the papacy, he was not omniscient. "So far as authority is concerned you can do everything, but in terms of vision, you can see no more than one person can." She added, "I know that your holiness really wants assistants who will help you, but you have to have the patience to listen."

In this letter, too, she had to beg the pope's forgiveness. Apparently Bartolomeo Dominici had asked the pope to redress some wrong but had neglected to provide the necessary background. Urban was annoyed, and Catherine had to rush to Dominici's defense. She wrote, "I beg you, holy father, when your foolish son offends you in this way, don't let it upset you. Correct him for his foolishness . . . Both he and I have suffered a great deal on account of it, since he thinks he has offended your holiness. I beg you for love of Christ crucified to punish me for any pain he may have caused you; I am ready for any correction or penance that may please your holiness."

That's the way it was with Urban. He constantly needed to be mollified. That summer he became involved in a bitter dispute with the people of Rome. Raymond of Capua, who mentions the discord, doesn't tell us what it was about, merely that things finally "reached such a pitch that the people began to threaten openly to have the pontiff put to death." Catherine, who lived among the people and heard their anger, feared for the pope's safety. She was worried sick over it. She didn't attempt to mediate but prayed "incessantly" for several days and nights, bringing herself to the point of exhaustion.

She was literally worried sick. Her anxiety concerning the Romans played out inside her psyche as a kind of interior warfare. According to Raymond, "she saw in spirit the whole city of Rome filled with demons busy in every quarter inciting the populace to the murder of their father. As she continued praying they turned on her with dreadful shouts, crying, 'Curse you, it is you who are trying to stop us; but no! we have marked you out for a fearful death, and there is no escape for you.'"

It is fair to wonder why she invested so much of herself in a clearly unstable pontiff. For Catherine, the church was the real focus of her concern; the pope was merely its symbol of unity—although an essential, living symbol: Christ on earth. Her inability to distinguish between the pope's agenda and the church's was not hers alone but to some extent was endemic to the age. Medieval ecclesiology did not provide necessary distinctions between the mystical church and the human institution. And there may have been another reason for her great emotional investment. Already people were whispering that the schism was the end result of bringing the pope back from Avignon before the time was ripe. If this suggestion had weight, then

Catherine, who had leveraged the return, bore some responsibility for the rupture that followed. Whether she heard these rumors or wondered about her share of responsibility we don't know. If she did, then her unstinting support of Urban VI was surely one way she could assert, in the face of rumors, that the true pope was a Roman pope.

The cumulative weight of all these worries—the schism and her own role in it, the neglected reform, the unstable pope, the fury of the Romans, and her inability to do anything except pray—were wearing her out. She was not eating properly. Her fasting, severe even under the best conditions, was becoming more extreme. The little energy she had in her body was expended on the trek of more than a mile through crowded streets to St. Peter's and then back to their home. It became her way of the cross, expressing her belief that pushing ahead was the only way to God. It was her calling, and one that she urged on other people as well. "This very day let's leave the dead to bury the dead," she wrote to Piero Canigiani of Florence, the father of her scribe Barduccio. "As for us let's follow the way of Christ gentle Jesus, persevering in true, solid virtues even to the point of death . . . And let's not dally, because our time is so short that all we can do is perseveringly strip ourselves of this mortal life and head for our goal . . .

"Focus your mind's eye on your God, who is your goal and destination," she told him. "And run with hunger and longing for the virtues, because if you long for them you will long to get to your destination. It's essential that you run with the energy of desire, in remembrance of God, as we are constantly running on toward our end, death, and this course never stops for anything. Whether we are sleeping or eating or speaking or doing anything else, we are always running toward death."

She still had passion for the journey but often lacked the energy for it. There is a curious hiatus in her dictated prayers during the last part of 1379. As far as scholars can tell, no prayers were set down between mid-August and the end of December. Her letter writing slowed as well. During a period in the late summer and early fall when the political situation was still perilous, Catherine wrote no letters to public officials. The few letters she produced went to disciples—to Tora Gambacorta back in Pisa, to Andrea Vanni in Siena—who, after her death, would paint the portrait of Catherine in San Domenico Church—and to poor, sad Neri di Landoccio Pagliaresi in Naples. Neri was going through a period of depression. He felt weighed down by sin. Catherine sent him a number of encouraging notes assuring him of God's love and warning of the deleterious effects of chronic sadness. "You know that discouragement is completely at odds with what you've always been taught," she said. "It's a leprosy that dries up the soul and body, and keeps us in continual torment. It ties the arms of holy desire and keeps us from doing what we would like to do. It makes us unbearable even to ourselves, with our spirit open to all sorts of assaults and imaginings. It robs us of supernatural light and obscures even natural light. And so it brings us to all sorts of unfaithfulness because we don't know the truth with which God has created us."

In October she roused herself again and ventured into the political fray. She was most likely prodded by Urban VI, since Raymond was far from the scene and writing to Charles of Durazzo was not something she would have done by herself. The pope wanted to get his Neapolitan adventure under way. However, its designated leader, Charles, was still engaged in fighting in northern Italy. Catherine wrote him a long letter late that month in an effort to breathe life into the campaign against Queen Giovanna. "God has chosen you to be a pillar in holy Church," she proclaimed, "so that you may be an instrument to root out heresy [i.e., schism], confused falsehood and promote the truth, dissipate darkness and attest to the light of Pope Urban VI. He is the true supreme pontiff, elected and given to us by the Holy Spirit's mercy—in spite of the wicked malicious self-centered people who say the contrary."

In moments such as these Catherine reached back for images of knighthood learned in childhood from books like the *Golden Legend*. She implored Charles to become one of those "courageous knights" who guarded the city from its enemies—the city here being both the church under siege and the individual human soul. Before the knight could undertake such deeds, however, he had to undergo inner purification and come to self-knowledge. So she reminded Charles, "unless we have fought well within, we will fight poorly externally. This is why I said you must first combat your three chief enemies within"—which she identified as the world and its empty honors, the flesh that tempts us with impurity, and demonic, ego-driven disrespect for others. "Try to vanquish them," she said, "by purifying your conscience in holy confession and living a well-ordered life with desire for the virtues."

Also around this time she renewed her plea to the rulers of Siena to pay the indemnity levied on them at the end of the war. The Sienese kept vowing their allegiance to the pope without ever sending him money. Catherine scolded them. "Don't keep throwing words at Christ on earth; give him deeds. Give him back something for what he has given you . . . You are acting like children! He knows, I tell you. He is a man who sees much farther than you think, and who has let both legitimate and illegitimate children rest on his heart. In his own time he will prove that he has known. No more of this now, for love of God! Treat him as Christ's vicar on earth."

She would follow this plea with one more letter to the Sienese in early December. In it, she took the opportunity to reaffirm her own belief in Urban's legitimacy. "I proclaim and will continue to proclaim before the whole world, even to the point of death, that Pope Urban VI is indeed pope, the true supreme pontiff. Oimé! Don't wait any longer to come to the aid of this dear bride of Christ! I trust that God in his infinite goodness will make you do what you should do and are obligated to do."

At some point before the end of the year Catherine and her famiglia changed residences. They moved from their quarters on Via del Corso to a house just off Piazza della Minerva that belonged to Paola del Ferro, described by Raymond as "a pious lady . . . who was very closely associated with Catherine." The building on Via Santa Chiara exists to this day. Catherine's room was on the third floor, reached in medieval times by an exterior staircase. Not only was the new residence nearer to the Minerva Church, it also shortened by a few blocks the walking distance to St. Peter's—a good thing, since Catherine's daily trek was becoming a source of concern to her disciples.

January 1, 1380, was the feast of the Circumcision of Jesus, and Catherine paused to reflect on the marriage of God and humankind. She dictated one of her last prayers:

> Today again in your mercy
> you espouse our souls to you
> with the ring of your flesh,
> the ring of your charity,
> to be espoused to you by law
> if we but recognize these blessing of yours—
> by that law, I mean,
> through which you make us sharers of your eternity.

The day also brought a marked change in her condition. According to Barduccio Canigiani, food and even water had become "so loathsome" to Catherine that she stopped eating and drinking. Deprived of liquids, she developed a thirst so terrible that "her breath seemed to be fire." The symptoms may point to kidney failure, since nausea and bad breath can be signs of malfunctioning kidneys. If so, it was not yet an acute failure. Barduccio said her overall health was "robust and fresh as usual." She continued to dictate letters—two of them to Urban VI that month—and make her way to St. Peter's.

Then, at the end of the month, she had a more serious breakdown. In the evening of Sexagesima Sunday, January 29, Barduccio reported that Catherine had "so violent a stroke that from that day onwards she was no longer in health." Precisely what happened is unclear. Catherine herself, in a letter to Raymond of Capua, described the breakdown as a mystical experience rather than a health issue.

Her letter, written in "a state of some agitation," described an event that resembled her "mystical death" years previously. "The light of my understanding gazed into the eternal Trinity, agitated with grief in the excruciating desire it had once again conceived in God's presence, and in the abyss saw the dignity of human beings and the wretchedness into which we fall when we are guilty of deadly sin," she told Raymond. "I saw, too, the needs of holy Church, revealed by God within his breast, and how no one can come to enjoy God's beauty within the depths of the Trinity except through this dear bride—since we must all pass through the gate of Christ crucified, and this gate is found only in holy Church."

In her vision Catherine asked God, "What can I do, oh immense Fire?" God answered that she and her followers could offer their lives for the church. God seemed to elaborate his reply by endorsing the pontificate of Urban VI, saying, "See his good holy intention . . . And just as the bride is alone, so is he alone. I am allowing him to use immoderately the means he uses, as well as the fear he inspires in his subjects, to sweep holy Church clean."

The divine endorsement was not unqualified, however. In Catherine's telling, God was alluding to Genesis 9 in which Noah's sons covered their father's nakedness with their cloaks: "Tell my vicar that he must make peace as far as he can, and grant peace to whoever wants to accept it. And to the pillars of the holy Church [i.e., the cardinals] say that if they want to repair the great damage they must unite, and together be a cloak that will cover the apparently deficient ways of their father."

Catherine lay prostrate on the floor as the vision played out. Then, she related, "God set me in his presence. True, I'm always present to him because he holds all within himself, but this was in a new way, as if my memory and understanding and will had nothing to do with my body. And I was gazing into this Truth with such light that at that point everything became fresh—the mysteries of holy Church and all the graces I've received during my life, past and present."

That was on Sexagesima Sunday. In the evening of the next day she had another "stroke," to use Barduccio's word. This time it was definitely a physical problem. She had just finished dictating a letter when she became agitated and then collapsed. She was unconscious for some time. Her followers gathered around her, grieving, fearing this was the end. Finally she came to her senses again and actually arose from bed, but she was not the same. "From that hour," said Barduccio, "began new travail and bitter pains in her body."

Calmly she again described this episode to Raymond. On one level she realized these were bodily ailments, but she said it felt like her room was "full of devils" tormenting her. The pain and mental distress as she lay on her bed lasted for two days and nights. Her body, she said, felt as though it were in the grip of an "unclean spirit"; but she stressed that her inner spirit and heartfelt desire did not falter. Finally, after two days of suffering, she expressed the wish to attend mass, most likely celebrated at the small chapel the disciples had created in the second floor of their residence. It was the feast of the Purification of Mary. The service calmed her agitation to the point where she felt she might be able to carry on after all.

Because she didn't know when another attack would occur, she seized the opportunity to leave some parting words and instructions for Raymond. She begged him, first of all, to remain faithful to the "little ship, holy Church" and to the Dominicans, to be cautious in relationships, and to "live within the cell of your heart and carry it about with you."

There were also practical matters to deal with. "I also ask you and Frate Bartolomeo [Dominici] and Frate Tommaso [dalla Fonte] and the master [Giovanni Tantucci] to take care of the book [*The Dialogue*] and any other writing of mine you may find . . . [D]o with them whatever you see would be most to God's honor. I've found some recreation in them. Also, as much as you can, please be shepherd and governor to this family, as a father, and keep them in the love of charity and perfect unity that they may not be cut loose like little sheep without a shepherd. As for me, I believe I can do more for them after my death than I have been able to do during my life . . . I ask you to beg my eternal Bridegroom to let me courageously accomplish what he has commanded and forgive me my many iniquities. And you, please, forgive all my disobedience and disrespect and ingratitude, and all the pain and bitterness I have given you and committed and used against you, and forgive the scant concern I have had for your salvation. And I ask for your blessing. Pray for me earnestly, and have others pray, for love of Christ crucified."

Incredibly, she carried on. In the days following she dragged herself out of bed each morning and attended mass at the chapel downstairs. After communion she would make her thanksgiving by lying prostrate in the Dominican fashion. When she got up again, said Barduccio, she did so "in such a state that anyone who had seen her would have thought her dead, and [she] was thus carried back to bed." But after an hour or two she would rise again and, seemingly refreshed, set out for St. Peter's.

The trek through the city was now more labored. She described herself to Raymond half-jokingly as "a dead woman walking to St. Peter's." Alessa and the other Mantellate, along with male disciples, hovered nearby to support Catherine if she needed help. Slowly the group would make its way through the streets, clutching their mantles close to them and bending against the winter cold. By then she was a well-known figure along the route. Clusters of people would stop and stare as the "saint" passed through this most populated section of the city, then across the bridge to the fortress. (There is a twentieth-century sculpture near Castel Sant'Angelo that shows Catherine in midstride, leaning forward, her right hand pulling her mantle close, her mouth slightly open, her eyes peering up toward the basilica.)

She knew there was little time left. Once inside St. Peter's, she would pray for the two causes closest to her heart, the church and her family of disciples. She worried what would happen to both when she was no longer there. In her very last letter to Urban VI at the beginning of the year, she had tried to steer him away from impulsive behavior: "I want to see you governing holy Church and your little sheep so wisely that it will never be necessary to reverse anything your holiness has done or ordained, not even the least word, so that both God and human beings may always see a firmness grounded in truth."

She also wanted to soften his heart toward the people of Rome. "Forgive me; love makes me say what perhaps needs no saying. For I know that you surely understand how your Roman children are, that they are attracted and held more by gentleness than by sharp words or other force." She pointed out that he needed the Romans and they needed him. Then she added, "And forgive me, dearest and most holy father, for saying these things to you. I trust that your humility and kindness welcome such words, and that you do not scorn and distain them because they come from the mouth of a very contemptible woman. For the humble consider not who is speaking but only God's honor, the truth, and their own salvation."

Always when she left the basilica at the end of the day her eyes would go up to the great mosaic Giotto had created in the atrium earlier that century. The mosaic (which was destroyed during the reconstruction of St. Peter's) pictured the gospel scene in which Jesus, walking on water, rescues Peter who tried to walk on the water's surface with him. Peter is partly submerged, bent over, grasping Jesus's hand, while behind them the anxious apostles look on from their storm-tossed boat. Popularly known as *Navicella* (Little Ship), the mosaic made a deep impression on Catherine. Giotto's perspective was not perfect, and it almost seemed as though the boat pictured in the background was resting on Peter's back.

Leaving the basilica one Sunday late in February she gazed at the mosaic again, and suddenly it seemed as though the weight of the boat was pressing on *her* back. It was too much! She collapsed in the atrium. Alarmed, her companions rushed to her aid, but even when she returned to consciousness her legs would not support her. Somehow they transported her back to their lodging near Piazza della Minerva.

Now she was truly incapacitated. Even after resting in bed Catherine discovered she no longer had the strength to walk. She was experiencing intense physical pain and mental distress. Barduccio declared that for weeks on end she was "both internally and externally tormented . . . unable to lift her head." Her female companions—Alessa, Cecca, Lisa, Giovanna di Capo—and her mother, Lapa, nursed her tenderly. Catherine had told Raymond earlier that her body was surviving "without food—not even a drop of water." Perhaps for short periods that was true, but it would have been impossible to go for eight weeks, as she did, with absolutely no food or liquid. Problems with nourishment surely hastened her end, however. Both Barduccio and Raymond testified that her wasted body became little more than skin and bones.

The word went out to her entire circle that Catherine had little time left. Neri came back from Naples, while Tommaso Caffarini and Stefano Maconi hastened down from Siena. Catherine was especially heartened to see Stefano. Along with young Barduccio, he was a trusted scribe and cherished friend.

At some point they moved her bed from the third-floor room to the little chapel on the second floor of the house. Here Tommaso Petra, the papal secretary, found her when he came to visit in mid-March. It was clear to him, as it was to her disciples, that she was failing. Petra, who had a bureaucratic mentality, asked if she had considered putting her affairs in order. Catherine answered there was no point; she had no possessions. But Petra said he was thinking of a spiritual testament rather than material things. The suggestion may have been seconded by Fra Santi. Many years earlier, Santi had been a disciple of Giovanni Colombini, who famously had dictated a spiritual testament before his death.

Catherine saw the point immediately. The welfare of her famiglia after she was gone had been troubling her. She began almost at once to dictate a final message, speaking in a voice so faint that at times Petra had to bend close to hear it.

The testament is summarized by Raymond of Capua in one of the final chapters of his *Life of Catherine*. The "first and fundamental point" Catherine urged upon her followers, said Raymond, was to seek God single-mindedly and wholeheartedly. They should let no thing and no person come between themselves and God. To attain this end they must pray humbly and recognize that they who pray are nothing and that God is All. This prayer may be vocal or mental; vocal prayer occurs at set times, but mental prayer goes on always.

She spoke of obedience to God's direction. She spoke at length about purity of heart and the danger of judging one another. She spoke of God's providence that will never neglect those who trust in it.

Then, "with great warmth of feeling," she said, "Love one another, my dearest children, love one another."

Following this general discourse, said Raymond, she summoned the women and men present, one by one, to offer direction for their lives after she was gone. She was especially concerned for the Mantellate whom she had served as guide and counselor. She appointed Alessa Saracini to take over that role and commended them to the overall guidance of Raymond when he returned to Rome.

In Raymond's account, these last words of advice took place in a single day, perhaps in just a few hours, after which Catherine died. He was not present, of course, and had to rely on the words of the others. Catherine's testament may actually have been dictated over several days. We know that the process began with Tommaso Petra's visit in mid-March. Catherine lived for six weeks after that and was conscious the entire time, although in great pain.

It was martyrdom at last, endured through the closing weeks of Lent and through Holy Week of 1380. Easter Sunday fell on March 25 that year. Lying in the little chapel, Catherine would have heard bells sounding from all of Rome's churches. It was also her birthday. She was thirty-three years old.

Bartolomeo Dominici, who had gone to Siena, returned to Rome in time for Easter. He celebrated mass in the chapel. To everyone's astonishment Catherine somehow managed to get up from her bed and receive communion. Afterward, she and Dominici spoke. He told her he did not want to go back north but was obliged to do so. She encouraged him to leave. When he came to wish her farewell the next day, he reported her to be "merry and bright."

She clung to life for another month, all the while enduring what Barduccio Canigiani called "terrible and unheard-of agony." In the moments of greatest distress Catherine would thank God for granting her the favor of suffering.

Then, in the early morning of April 29, she underwent what Barduccio called "a great change." Her followers were summoned and crowded into her room. Giovanni Tantucci pronounced the deathbed indulgence granted years earlier by Pope Gregory XI and renewed by Urban VI. After that she was anointed by her old friend Abbot Giovanni di Gano, who years earlier had blessed her monastery of Belcaro and whose abbey of Sant'Antimo in the Orcia Valley she and Raymond had visited.

As Barduccio tells it, Catherine, in a long, rambling speech, then publicly accused herself of sinfulness, of failing to be attentive to God alone, or loving God with all her strength. His account of the confession may be correct. Yet confessing one's sins at the point of death was expected behavior for holy people of that era, so the words may better reflect Barduccio's faith in Catherine than an accurate record of events.

Other details of his description seem authentic: Catherine was lifted to a semi-reclining position, resting against Alessa. Several holy pictures and a crucifix were placed in front of her, but her eyes seemed to focus only on the crucifix. At times she would whisper, "Peccavi, Domine, miserere mei"

("I have sinned, Lord, have mercy on me") or "Sancte Deus, miserere mei" ("Holy God, have mercy on me"). There may have been other words as well; the record is unclear. A period of time passed in this manner. Everyone agrees that toward the end of her agony she cried out at least twice in a loud voice, "Blood! Blood!"

It startled them all.

Then, about noon, she died.

Her disciples tried to keep her death a secret, knowing how the people of Rome revered her and fearing a crowd of believers might arrive searching for relics. But Rome being what it was, news of Catherine's passing was soon all over the city. The sorrowful faces of her followers and the visits of cardinals and other prelates to the house on Via Santa Chiara was announcement enough. Their lodgings couldn't handle all the visitors, so arrangements were made to have the body moved to nearby Santa Maria sopra Minerva. Stefano Maconi was accorded the privilege of carrying the body to its new resting place, most likely in the church's Cappella del Transito. Word quickly spread and soon dozens, then hundreds, of people hurried to the church where they sought to touch the body or snip a fragment of Catherine's clothing. The situation threatened to get out of control, so the body was moved once more, within the church, to St. Dominic's Chapel, where it was placed behind a locked grill.

The funeral was two days later. Catherine's body was brought out of the locked-up chapel and exposed to public view. A restless throng packed the church, its attention focused on the deceased rather than the altar. The more brazen brought sick family members to the bier, hoping for a cure, while others sought to place objects on the body, which could then, by association, become relics. Giovanni Tantucci attempted to deliver a eulogy, but the hubbub increased to such a degree that he couldn't make himself heard. After a short time, he surrendered to the noise and announced, "This holy virgin has no need of our preaching. She preached sufficiently herself."

After the funeral service, Stefano Maconi, with tears and prayers, laid Catherine's body in a cypress coffin that was placed within a stone casket in a chapel near the main altar.

EPILOGUE

༄༅

wo weeks after Catherine's death, Raymond of Capua was elected master of the Dominican order at the general chapter in Bologna—the same meeting for which Bartolomeo Dominici had needed to depart Catherine's bedside so hastily. Raymond took overall charge at a time when the Dominicans were as splintered as the larger church. French and Spanish members of the order continued to accept the Frenchman Élias of Toulouse as master. There were holy and able friars on both sides of the divide. The Spanish-born Dominican Vincent Ferrer was a passionate advocate of Clement VII, even as Raymond continued to champion Urban VI. Part of the new general's task, therefore, was to hold on to friars and provinces that were wavering in their loyalty. Raymond left almost immediately on a long trip to Dominican houses in Germany and Hungary and did not return to Rome until October 1381. One of his first actions on reaching Santa Maria sopra Minerva was to view Catherine's remains. This was easily done, since the body was entombed in the church. When the cypress coffin was opened, the clothing was found damp and mildewed, whether from rain leaking in or from Rome's notorious floods. Raymond decided immediately to transfer the body to a new sarcophagus and to keep it in a safer place. He also proposed to send part of the remains to Siena and appealed to Urban VI for permission.

The medieval practice of dismembering bodies for relics seems grotesque in retrospect, yet from the earliest days of Christianity (and in other religions as well) it has been a point of faith that transparently holy persons manifested blessing through their physical presence. Their bodies in life had been holy vessels and in death still evoked that holiness. When Catherine was first interred, Stefano Maconi desired a relic of her as a way of keeping her close, but knowing she had entrusted the disposition of her remains to Raymond, he paused. After consulting with the famiglia, he removed three teeth, gave one to Alessa, one to Neri, and kept one for himself. When Raymond came to view the body the year after, he knew it was unlikely the Romans would ever let go of her remains completely, but with permission he had the head separated from the rest of the body, encased in a silken cloth, placed in a reliquary, and sent to the church of San Domenico in Siena.

Public fascination with Catherine, so evident during her life, showed no sign of diminishing after her death. A formal declaration of sainthood, however, would have to wait for church action, since by the fourteenth century canonization required something more than popular acclaim. Church law entailed a bureaucratic process—examinations, testimonies, and, most of all, the perspective of time before it could be definitely proclaimed that one had lived a heroic life of sanctity. In Catherine's case there was continued talk that her actions had helped bring on the schism. Whether the allegation was just or not—and probably it was not—a ruling on her sanctity would have to wait until the schism was healed.

That healing was much easier said than done. People on both sides acknowledged the scandal of having two men claiming to be pope, but the claimants themselves and their principal advisors entrenched themselves in Rome and Avignon and would not be moved. It was suggested that both resign in favor of a third party. In principle and at various times both sides accepted that idea, but they could never agree on its details. Who, for instance, would select delegates to elect a new pope?

Pope Urban VI was proving to be, as one historian described him, "violent, overbearing and probably clinically paranoid." His plan to overthrow Queen Giovanna of Naples succeeded in the year after Catherine's death. Charles of Durazzo was crowned king of Naples at St. Peter's Basilica in Rome after promising to turn over part of his kingdom to Urban's nephew. Once on the throne, however, Charles reneged on the promise and sent his army to arrest the pope, forcing Urban to find refuge for a time in southern Italy. A group of Urban's own cardinals, believing he was not in his right mind, secretly considered removing him from power. Discovering the plot, the pope arrested, tortured, and executed several of them. A contemporary witness offered a picture of Urban "walking in the garden calmly reading his breviary while the aged cardinal of Venice, under torture by being raised to the ceiling and dropped to the floor of a nearby room, screamed through the window at the pope whenever he could get breath enough."

It was an age of unexpected endings. Piero Gambacorta, the absolute ruler of Pisa, who had invited Catherine to that city back in 1375, was assassinated by agents of Bernabò Visconti. Bernabò Visconti, in turn, was assassinated by his nephew Gian Galeazzo Visconti. Giovanna of Naples was imprisoned and then strangled by her cousin Charles of Durazzo. And Sir John Hawkwood, the piratical condottiere who pillaged much of northern Italy, lived a long life and died in his sleep in Florence.

Urban VI died in 1389, probably from injuries caused by the fall from a mule, although there were rumors of poison. The cardinals in Rome chose another Neapolitan, Piero Tomacelli, as his successor, and he took the name Boniface IX. Clement VII in Avignon outlived Urban by five years. Then the Avignon cardinals elected Raymond of Capua's old mentor Cardinal Pedro de Luna as their new pope—Benedict XIII. The two new popes turned out to be as stubborn as the old ones. That didn't stop the monarchs who backed them from switching sides freely. Charles of Durazzo rejected the Roman pontiff who had crowned him and transferred his allegiance to Avignon, while the French king disowned the Spanish pope living in Avignon and recognized Rome.

The two-headed, schismatic church continued to exist for another three decades after Urban's death, and all the while the level of disenchantment in Christian Europe rose steadily. Pressure to resolve the schism came at a church council held at Pisa in 1409. Representatives from both sides formally deposed both rivals and instead selected as new pope the archbishop of Milan, who took the name Alexander V. That would have settled matters except that the men sitting in Rome and Avignon refused to accept the authority of the Pisan conclave and would not surrender their offices. So now there were three popes.

If having two popes in the church was awkward, three was positively embarrassing. Still, it took nearly another decade for a church council in the German city of Constance—backed by the muscle of the Holy Roman emperor—to end the schism. The pope in Rome resigned, the successor to Alexander V was deposed and imprisoned, and the aging Benedict XIII (Pedro de Luna) was excommunicated. In their place the electors chose an aristocratic Roman named Oddone Colonna who became Martin V. He accepted the papal tiara and settled at last into St. Peter's Basilica in 1420.

During all this time a formal consideration of Catherine's life and achievements was necessarily shelved. That doesn't mean she was forgotten. Several members of her famiglia who had served as scribes during her life began collecting her letters and jotting down their recollections. It was always understood that Raymond of Capua, when he found the time, would write an account of her life to advance the canonization process. Raymond soldiered on as Dominican general. His health, never strong to begin with, reached a low point in 1385 when he had to cross the Alps twice as well as preside at a chapter meeting in Verona. To regain his strength he went to the hot springs at Vignoni, south of Siena—the same baths Catherine had visited as a girl with her mother. His stay there, close to Rocca d'Orcia and a day's trip from Montepulciano where he had been stationed as a young friar, inspired him to reflect on the wonder-filled years he spent in Catherine's company. He decided to begin work on the story of her life, her *Legenda*. She had been dead then for slightly more than five years, and Raymond planned to mark the anniversary by preaching in Siena. He arranged a celebration that would also provide an opportunity to display the relic of Catherine's head. With the cooperation of the Sienese government, he drew up plans for a procession through the city and festivities at San Domenico Church. Bartolomeo Dominici would also preach. A delegation of Mantellate agreed to march in the procession, along with Stefano Maconi, Neri di Landoccio Pagliaresi, Cristofano di Gano, and Matteo di Fazio dei Cenni, the rector of Misericordia Hospital who had been cured through Catherine's intercession during the plague. When the celebration was finally held that September, one figure in the procession drew special notice. It was Lapa di Puccio di Piagenti, Catherine's mother, then eighty years old.

The Life of Catherine of Siena by Raymond of Capua, written in Latin, was completed in 1395, four years before his death. Translated into many languages, it soon spread Catherine's fame across Christian Europe. The book made Raymond famous, too. It appeared in an English translation during the fifteenth century as the *Lyf of St. Katherin of Senis* and has been retranslated and republished many times since. The *Life* was not a biography in the modern sense, being more of an argument for sainthood than a chronology of her life, yet it was a real advance in the art of hagiography. Instead of simply collecting various pious stories as Jacopo da Varazze had done in the *Golden Legend*, Raymond took time to interview people who had known Catherine. When he dealt with Catherine's early years he leaned on the journal (which has since disappeared) written by Tommaso dalla Fonte. In a prologue to the *Life*, Raymond solemnly declared, "I have recorded in [the book] nothing feigned, nothing fabricated, and, allowing for the human fallibility of my search for the truth, nothing that is false in any way in the substance of the facts narrated." Tommaso Caffarini apparently felt Raymond had been altogether too selective with the record, because after the *Life* appeared, Caffarini put together a collection of stories—called the *Libellus*—that Raymond had left out. Raymond's *Life* contained many accounts of miracles (only a few of which have been retold here), and it gave special attention to the miracles attributed to Catherine's intercession after her death, since posthumous miracles were deemed essential for canonization.

The process for Catherine's sainthood was spearheaded by Caffarini from Venice where he came to live. He solicited testimonies and other documents, completing his part of the work by 1413. Then followed another period of delay. The Council of Constance was over in 1418 and the schism had ended, yet there seemed to be a strange reluctance on the part of church authorities to push Catherine's cause forward. (Perhaps not surprisingly, since canonization depends on the right political climate at least as much as it does on the virtue of a candidate.) Caffarini died in 1434, no doubt a disappointed man. The event that finally put the proceedings on a fast track was the election in 1458 of Enea Silvio Piccolomini as Pope Pius II. The new pope belonged to a prominent Sienese family; in addition to being a diplomat, he was a man of the world, a novelist and poet, and something of a libertine in his younger days. Had she met him, Catherine might have sniffed the air suspiciously. Pius, however, was eager to advance the cause of a local heroine. Two years after his election he presided over a consistory in Siena that reviewed the evidence, and the year after that Catherine was formally declared a saint.

In his bull of canonization, Pius reviewed the young saint's devotion to prayer and ascetical practices, her service to the sick and poor, and her solidarity with two popes. It is interesting to note that—contrary to many popular histories written since then—the document does not give Catherine credit for bringing Gregory XI home from Avignon. It makes a point of recalling how Gregory had already promised to return. Catherine merely reminded him of his vow.

Far more important is Pius's acknowledgment that Catherine enjoyed the direct infusion of knowledge from God. This is the essence of mysticism—an intimate and personal relationship with the transcendent God. In the words of the papal bull, "Her knowledge came down to her from heaven; hence she could teach without having had masters. When Professors of the Sacred Writings, and illustrious Bishops, proposed to her the most difficult questions in Theology, she answered them with so much wisdom and satisfied them so fully that they became gentle as lambs, after having shown themselves to her first as menacing wolves and lions."

The ability of an illiterate laywoman to "teach without having had masters" was a startling admission for the head of a patriarchal church, a church that, over the centuries, had claimed for itself the role of supreme teacher. The existence of mystics, and especially female mystics, is unsettling for an authoritative church, since mystics by definition maintain their own connections with the Divine. Perhaps this factor, as much as any other, explains the delay in declaring Catherine a saint. The church needed time to absorb the significance of her life and her gifts. Fortunately for Catherine, there was no question of her loyalty to the church, to its teachings, or to its hierarchy.

And so Catherine of Siena became a saint of the Catholic Church. Her feast is commemorated each year on April 29, the day of her death. Churches and convents have been named after her, as well as streets, colleges, and entire towns. Today her principal remains rest in a crystal urn under the main altar of Santa Maria sopra Minerva in Rome (the figure displayed on a catafalque is merely a painted statue), and her head is preserved in a reliquary in San Domenico Church in Siena. The house where she grew up, in the Fontebranda neighborhood, has become a shrine attached to a guesthouse run by Dominican sisters. Visitors can peek through an iron gate into the little room, still unspoiled, that Catherine occupied for about three years in solitude. The dye shop downstairs and the kitchen above are both chapels now. The room where she died in Rome, on Via Santa Chiara, was dismantled; its walls were carried down the block to the Minerva Church, where they became a shrine in a small room off the church sacristy.

Her canonization in 1461 was not the final honor accorded to Catherine. In 1940, during World War II, Pope Pius XII named Francis of Assisi and Catherine of Siena as the co-patrons of Italy. Francis was an obvious choice, but public awareness of Catherine had diminished by then, six hundred years after her birth. In 1999, Pope John Paul II expanded on that distinction by naming Catherine one of the six patron saints of Europe.

In the last fifty years Catherine's star, which shone so brightly during her lifetime, has regained much of its luster, although she is honored today more as a truth-teller than as a wonder-worker. The uneducated daughter of a Sienese dyer has become the champion of today's church reformers who use her as a model for plain speaking when confronting authority. Often cited are her words to an unnamed bishop in 1376: "Oimè! No more silence! Shout out with a thousand tongues! I am seeing the world going to ruin because people are not speaking out! I am seeing Christ's bride [i.e., the church] made pallid, her color drained, because her blood is being sucked out from behind her back."

These reformers celebrate the manner in which Mantellate and Beguines in the Late Middle Ages carved out a place for themselves that was connected to the church yet outside its absolute control. Social activists point to the way Catherine and her companions turned their faith into service to the poor. Not to be outdone, Catholic traditionalists honor Catherine's loyalty to the popes and adamant defense of orthodoxy. But perhaps Christian feminists have adopted Catherine of Siena as a role model most ardently. It would be anachronistic to call Catherine a feminist. She would not have understood the term and for cultural reasons would have disagreed with some aims of the feminist movement. Yet just as Catherine looked back on Mary Magdalen as her model, many women today celebrate Catherine as a feisty woman who forged an exceptional place for herself in the world.

An appreciation of Catherine's significance as a teacher—even, one might say, as a theologian—has also grown in recent years, thanks in part to more accessible translations of her great work, *The Dialogue*. In 1970, Pope Paul VI named Catherine a Doctor of the Church, a title given over the centuries to a select few teachers of Christian doctrine. Catherine was one of the first two women—together with Teresa of Avila—to receive this distinction. Reflecting on the papal declaration, one scholar has observed that Catherine "had a genius for applying with a stunning common sense, to real individuals and real life situations, the theological concepts she absorbed . . . She spoke and wrote out of who she was constantly becoming—as woman, friend, caregiver, thinker, mamma and teacher to her expanding *famiglia*, Dominican, and concerned member of a tormented church."

It has taken time for society as a whole to absorb and appreciate Catherine of Siena. During her lifetime, though, members of her spiritual family knew almost immediately after first meeting her that she was someone special. She galvanized them and moved them profoundly. They wanted to be close to her and grew anxious whenever she went away. When she felt death approaching in early 1380, Catherine called the women and men who were with her in Rome to her bedside and gave them directions that became, for each of them, trajectories in their subsequent lives.

Catherine long believed that young Stefano Maconi had a monastic vocation. She badgered him to leave his clinging family and pursue life on his own. After her death Stefano entered a Carthusian monastery near Siena. In 1389 he moved to a monastery in Milan, and he eventually became the prior there. He was elected prior general of the Carthusians in 1398. He died in Pavia in 1424.

Barduccio Canigiani, the son of a Florentine magnate, was ordained a priest shortly after Catherine's death. He was already suffering from tuberculosis, and the Roman weather didn't help. Raymond sent him to live in the hill country of Siena, but Barduccio outlived Catherine by less than two years.

Neri di Landoccio Pagliaresi became a hermit, living first in Florence, then in a hermitage outside Porta Nuova in Siena. He helped to assemble Catherine's letters, wrote verse, and probably always struggled with depression. He died on March 12, 1406, in Santa Maria della Scala Hospital.

Fra Santi, the hermit in whose cell Catherine wrote much of *The Dialogue*, died in Rome a year after Catherine.

Francesco Malavolti, the Sienese nobleman and libertine who was converted by Catherine but who continued to have relapses, was eventually married, was widowed, decided to become a Knight of St. John but was reproved by Catherine who appeared to him in a vision and so joined an Olivetan monastery in 1388. He became a Benedictine in 1413.

Lecceto, the Augustinian monastery outside Siena where Catherine befriended many friars, still exists, operated today by a community of nuns. William Flete lived there into his seventies, counseling Mantellate in the city and regarded as a saint by most Sienese. He died around 1390. Giovanni Tantucci (*il maestro* to Catherine) was also living at Lecceto and died sometime after 1391.

It was the Dominicans, however, who constituted the community that Catherine, as a Mantellata and as a friend, was closest to. The friars and the fellow Mantellate she knew in the order of St. Dominic were brothers and sisters to her, sharing her mission and vision.

The Mantellate who were especially close to Catherine remained in Rome after her death under the care of Alessa Saracini and Raymond of Capua. But Alessa, daughter of a noble family and Catherine's almost constant companion, died the year after her mamma. Francesca (Cecca) Gori died in Rome in February 1383 and was buried in the Minerva Church. Lisa Colombini died around 1400.

Tommaso dalla Fonte, her first confessor and guide, related by blood as well as vocation, survived Catherine by ten years. He spent much of that time as prior of San Domenico Church in Siena.

Bartolomeo Dominici was still a young priest when Catherine died. Eventually he became provincial of the Roman Province of the Dominicans and finally titular bishop of Corona in the Morea. Preaching had always been difficult for Dominici because of his speech impediment, but in 1390, after praying before an image of Catherine, he said that his impediment vanished and never bothered him again.

After Tommaso Caffarini was transferred to Venice, he lived there for forty years, gathering evidence for Catherine's canonization. He was tireless in promoting her cause, at one point producing an abridgement of Raymond of Capua's *Life*. It became known as the *Legenda minore*, after which the *Life* was often referred to as the *Legenda major*. Caffarini also established several convents for Dominican tertiaries in Venice. To one of them he donated Catherine's black mantle. Over the centuries it was lost and found at least twice and finally carried to Milan. It can be viewed there today at the church of Santa Maria della Grazie.

Raymond of Capua continued his labors and travels as the general and the reformer of the Dominican order. Concurrently he undertook several diplomatic missions to Florence and Palermo for the Roman popes. A Dominican historian recounts how in Genoa in 1392, Raymond chanced upon Stefano Maconi and Tommaso Caffarini and how the three men enjoyed a long dinner exchanging stories about their mamma. Raymond's efforts to restore strict observance of the Dominican rule were rewarded in 1391 when a papal decree approved a new rule. He went to Frankfurt in 1397 for a general chapter meeting and then remained in Germany, ailing in health. He was in Cologne during 1398, then went to Nuremberg where he died on October 5, 1399. He was buried in the choir of the Dominican church in Nuremberg, his body remaining there until the sixteenth century. At the beginning of the Reformation his body was quietly moved to the basilica of San Domenico Maggiore in Naples, where today it rests under the main altar. Raymond was beatified in 1899 by Pope Leo XIII and, especially among Neapolitans, is celebrated as Blessed Raymond of Capua.

It is not known whether Raymond preserved anything like a tooth or a mantle to remind him of Catherine. He had his memories, of course. It's nice to think he may have kept one or two of her letters as well. If he did, perhaps it was the letter she addressed to him either late in December 1379 or early January 1380. She was just a few months from her death, and he had just been chosen Dominican provincial of Upper Lombardy. In an effort to confirm him in his new pastoral responsibilities, she wrote to him:

> Drown yourself, then, in the blood of Christ crucified.
> Bathe in the blood; get drunk on the blood;
> have your fill of the blood; clothe yourself in the blood.
> And if you have become unfaithful,
>   be baptized again in the blood.
> If the devil has clouded over your mind's eye,
> wash it out with the blood.
> If you have fallen into ingratitude by not acknowledging gifts,
> become grateful in the blood.
> If you have been a bad shepherd
> and have no staff of justice tempered with prudence and mercy,
> get one from the blood;
> with your mind's eye see it in the blood
>   and grasp it with the hand of love,
> and with restless desire hold it tight.
> In the heat of the blood melt your lukewarmness;
> in the light of the blood let the darkness give way,
> so that you may be espoused to truth,
> a true shepherd and caretaker of the little sheep
> who have been entrusted to you.
> And as much as you can in your position,
> be devoted to your physical as well as your spiritual cell.
> If you dwell in the blood, you will do this; otherwise not.
> So I beg you to do it, for love of Christ crucified.
> Free yourself from every creature—of me first of all—
> and clothe yourself with affectionate love for God
> and for everyone else for God's sake . . .

CHRONOLOGY
ᏔᏍᎣ

1331		Ottoman Turks take Nicaea, advance on Constantinople.
1337		Hundred Years War between France and England begins. Giotto dies.
1343		Chaucer is born (ca. 1343).
1347	Catherine is born in Siena (March 25).	First outbreak of the plague in Europe.
1348	The plague devastates Siena.	
1351		Boccaccio's *Decameron* appears.
1352		Innocent VI is elected pope.
1353	Catherine experiences a vision of Christ in the sky.	
1355	Siena's Council of Nine is overthrown after a lengthy rule. The rule of the Twelve begins.	
1356		The English rout the French at Poitiers.
1362	Catherine's sister Bonaventura dies in childbirth. Catherine defies her parents' wish that she marry, cuts her hair.	Urban V is elected pope.
1363	Her younger sister Giovanna dies. She begins a solitary life in her home.	

1364 /65	Catherine is accepted as a Mantellata.	Charles V becomes French king (1364).
1367	Catherine's "espousal to Christ," gradual end of solitude.	Pope Urban V moves to Rome from Avignon, stays for three years, then returns to Avignon.
1368	Catherine's father dies. The Twelve are displaced in another rebellion. The reformers (Riformatori) come to the fore.	
1370	Catherine's "mystical death." Famine in Siena.	Urban V dies; Gregory XI is elected pope.
1371	Catherine's family of disciples begins to form. Around this time her letter writing commences. She rescues two of her brothers during riots in Siena. The brothers relocate to Florence.	
1373		Birgitta of Sweden dies in Rome. In England, Julian of Norwich records her revelations.
1374	Catherine in Florence for Dominican chapter. Raymond of Capua becomes her mentor. Ministry in plague-ridden Siena. The *Miracoli* appears. Visit to Montepulciano.	Petrarch dies.
1375	Catherine in Pisa and Lucca to promote crusade and support the pope. She experiences the stigmata, is present at Niccolò di Toldo's execution in Siena.	Boccaccio dies.
1376	Catherine goes to Florence on a peacemaking mission, then to Avignon to meet Gregory XI.	Florence placed under papal interdict. War between pope and Florentine league. Gregory XI leaves for Rome in September.

1377	Catherine founds a monastery at Belcaro, visits the Orcia Valley. There she begins to work on her *Dialogue*.	Gregory XI enters Rome. Papal mercenaries massacre citizens of Cesena. Richard II becomes English king.
1378	Catherine, in Florence on a peacemaking mission, narrowly escapes assassination. She goes to Rome in November.	Gregory XI dies in Rome; Urban VI replaces him. The war between church and Florence ends. One group of cardinals elects a second pope.
1379	Catherine works to end the schism, lives in a Rome community with her followers. Her health is failing; she composes prayers.	European powers are divided in allegiance to papal claimants.
1380	Catherine is eating and drinking little. She suffers seizures. In February she can no longer walk. She dies in Rome, on April 29. Raymond of Capua is chosen as master of the Dominican order.	Charles V of France dies.

AUTHOR'S NOTE
ᔕᔕ

In order to make sense of any person's life, it is necessary to see the life against the background of its age. This is especially true in the case of Catherine of Siena, whose life spanned the second half of what Barbara Tuchman has called the "calamitous" fourteenth century—a dismal era of war, plague, famine, and political instability. In Western Europe the carefully structured society of the Middle Ages was coming apart without any clear picture of what would follow. The city-states of Italy, where Catherine was most active, faced particular turmoil. "No people," said Tuchman, "talked more about unity and nationhood, and had less, than the Italians." Unlike France and England, Italy had no ruler to serve as a figurehead. The pope in Avignon had let papal states on the Italian peninsula wither and decay, then attempted to reconstitute them by force. While the independent Italian city-states boasted of cultural achievements and a measure of democracy, political life as a whole was treacherous and brutal.

The main focus of this biography is Catherine's "public" life rather than her private, interior life that pious biographies have focused on in the past. To accomplish that, it has to describe the political and social world she moved in. It is hoped that these details will give the reader a sense of the air she breathed and the ground she walked on.

However much it considers her "public" self, no book on Catherine of Siena can avoid her religious faith. Her motivation for engaging in events of her day flowed out of her conviction that she was called to the task by God. There is simply no way to appreciate her life or gauge her place in history without exploring that conviction. In the process it is necessary to consider the forms of religious expression common among devout Christians, especially women, in the late Middle Ages. Fortunately there have been a number of new studies in that area in recent years by scholars such as Caroline Walker Bynum, John Coakley, Mary Catherine Hilkert, Grace Jantzen, Karen Scott, and Jane Tylus, among others. More than ever before it is possible to appreciate the fervid quality of religious experience in the late Middle Ages. It was an age marked by unusual religious practices—by flagellants, visionaries, and ascetics—all of whom burned with the intuition that the realm of God was separated from the human by the thinnest of membranes. Like daily life itself, religious practice was earthy and physical. Pain and suffering were vestibules for the holy; miracles were evidence of it.

In years past it was common for biographies of saintly figures to describe miracles and visions as though they were historical facts. That kind of assumption is no longer possible. Readers today, both nonbelievers and believers, have stricter evidentiary standards. Today we have more knowledge of the human psyche and its workings and are coming to understand the ways that human virtual reality operates. Yet it would be foolish in the light of this new knowledge to conclude that phenomena such as visions, miracles, and ecstasies are therefore delusions, the products of disordered mental states. To affirm either extreme—to see spiritual phenomena either as absolutely factual or as strictly delusional—would be excessively literalistic and lead down the road to fundamentalism. This book is proposing a more nuanced interpretation, suggesting that these kinds of spiritual phenomena, however strange they may seem to us, are forms of symbolic language that come wrapped in the culture of their age, and that can be understood and have meaning in the same way that any language has meaning. Such phenomena can be revelatory. They reveal relationships between persons and within society generally. If we want to try to understand an era like the fourteenth century, with its paucity of confessional literature, every form of communication, including the inner symbolic language of religion, needs to be heard.

It is difficult to see and feel the life of a private person who lived seven centuries ago. We often lack eyewitnesses, and there are gaps in the record. Catherine did not come from a noble family whose lineage was written down. There are disagreements among historians who have tried to thread the known facts of her life into some sort of chronology. We have the names and a few details about her parents and some of her brothers and sisters, but little of the family history is known beyond that. In addition, she was a woman living in a society where women were commonly devalued. She was unschooled and only semiliterate. This does not mean she was an outsider. Both her family and Catherine herself were involved in public life; therefore we, by following the ebb and flow of civic and ecclesiastical politics, can come to some sense of the forces that shaped her personal history.

There are a number of original sources for Catherine's life story. Most important for understanding her as a person are her own writings—or, in her case, dictations—that preserve her original voice. Nearly four hundred of Catherine's letters and a number of dictated prayers that have come down to us are one of the great treasures of early Italian literature. Her book, *The Dialogue*, is acknowledged to be a seminal work in Christian mystical writing and has never been out of print in the centuries since it was written. All of her works—the letters, the prayers, and *The Dialogue*—have in the last few years received new and excellent English translations by Suzanne Noffke and are now available in annotated editions. No previous biography of Catherine of Siena has availed itself of these fresh, scholarly sources.

The next source is the book written not long after Catherine's death by her mentor, Raymond of Capua. His *Life of Catherine of Siena*, completed in 1395 and still in print, is closer to a memorial than a biography in the modern sense, yet it does recount the principal events of her life based on the author's personal knowledge and supplemented by interviews with those who knew her. Raymond belonged to nobility and was an educated man and an experienced diplomat. During the few short years that represent the crowning period of her life, Catherine and Raymond were close friends and vocational colleagues. Her life was intimately bound to his, and for that reason his book is the record of a participant as well as an observer. Raymond wrote it to promote her canonization as a saint, so his book is both history and personal testament. As a source it is invaluable. Still, readers must approach it with an awareness of its intentions.

Still another source is the so-called *Miracoli* of Catherine of Siena, a collection of stories that were compiled by an anonymous author around the time Catherine was in Florence in 1374. The work makes no claim of being an eyewitness account but repeats stories she and other persons may have related about her youth and early career. Similar to it is the *Libellus de supplemento* by Tommaso d'Antonio Caffarini, the Dominican priest who was one of Catherine's followers. Caffarini became the leading promoter of Catherine's cause for sainthood after her death. His *Libellus*, only partly available in English, recounts miraculous events, healings, and wonders and is more devotional than Raymond's work.

Also among these earliest sources are a few letters and testimonies written after Catherine's death by people who knew her.

In addition to these original sources, I must acknowledge the human sources of inspiration for this biography. The Dominican charism was modeled for me early in life by my late aunt, Macrina Brophy, a member of the Sparkhill Dominicans in New York, and reinforced later by membership in the Dominican parish of St. Mary's on Hillhouse Avenue in New Haven, Connecticut. As an adult I had the pleasure of working with Thomas F. O'Meara, O.P., of the theology faculty at the University of Notre Dame. I am grateful for the hospitality and encouragement of Suzanne Noffke, O.P., at the Siena Center in Racine, Wisconsin. In the course of writing this book I received help from Mary Ann Fatula, O.P., at Ohio Dominican College, Thomas McDermott, O.P., at Kenrick-Glennon Seminary in St. Louis, and from Gabriella Yi, O.P., in Rome.

Turning to non-Dominicans, I am most grateful to Jan-Erik Guerth of BlueBridge for his invitation to explore the life of Catherine and his confidence in the ultimate work. Others who assisted in this project are David Smith and the always helpful librarians at the New York Public Library, Jane Tylus at New York University, Donna Orsuto at the Gregorian University in Rome, and Troy Tower of New York and Baltimore for his help with translations. Last of all I am thankful in a special way for the love and support of my wife, Pat, who listened to stories about Catherine over the dinner table for the last two years without complaining. Catherine tells us that "if you have fallen into ingratitude by not acknowledging gifts, become grateful in the blood." Indeed I am grateful to all the above.

BIBLIOGRAPHY
ༀༀ

PRIMARY SOURCES

Catherine of Siena, *Catherine of Siena: The Dialogue*, edited and translated by Suzanne Noffke, O.P. New York/Mahwah, NJ: Paulist Press, 1980.

____, *The Dialogue of the Seraphic Virgin, Catherine of Siena*, edited and translated by Algar Thorold. Westminster, MD: The Newman Press, 1950.

____, *The Letters of Catherine of Siena*, 4 vols., edited and translated by Suzanne Noffke, O.P. Tempe: Arizona Center for Medieval and Renaissance Studies, 2000, 2001, 2007, 2009.

____, *The Prayers of Catherine of Siena*, edited and translated by Suzanne Noffke, O.P. New York: Paulist Press, 1983.

Coogan, Robert, ed. and trans., *Babylon on the Rhône: A Translation of Letters by Dante, Petrarch, and Catherine of Siena on the Avignon Papacy*. Potomac, MD: Studia Humanitatis, 1983.

Lehmijoki-Gardner, Maiju, ed. and trans., *Dominican Penitent Women*. New York/Mahwah, NJ: Paulist Press, 2005.

Raymond of Capua, *The Life of Catherine of Siena*, edited and translated by Conleth Kearns, O.P. Dublin & Wilmington: Dominican Publications and Michael Glazier, Inc., 1980.

____, *The Life of St. Catherine of Siena*, edited and translated by George Lamb. New York: P. J. Kenedy & Sons, 1960. Rockford, IL: Tan Books, 2003.

SECONDARY SOURCES

Aberth, John, *The Black Death: The Great Mortality of 1348–1350*. New York: Palgrave Macmillan, 2005.

Ariès, Philippe, and Georges Duby, eds., *A History of Private Life*, vol. 2. Cambridge: Harvard University Press, 1988.

Becker, Marvin B., *Medieval Italy: Constraints and Creativity*. Bloomington: Indiana University Press, 1981.

Bell, Rudolph M., *Holy Anorexia*. Chicago: University of Chicago Press, 1985.

Benedictow, Ole J., *The Black Death 1346–1353: The Complete Story*. Woodbridge, England: The Boydell Press, 2004.

Bianchi, Lidia, and Diega Giunta, *Iconografia di S. Caterina da Siena*. Roma: Citta Nuova Editrice, 1988.

Boccaccio, Giovanni, *The Decameron*, 2nd ed., translated, with an introduction and notes by G. H. McWilliam. London: Penguin Books, 1972, 1995.

Bowsky, William M., *A Medieval Italian Commune: Siena under the Nine, 1287–1355*. Berkeley: University of California Press, 1981.

___, ed., *The Black Death: A Turning Point in History?* New York: Holt, Rineheart and Winston, 1971.

Brucker, Gene A., *Florentine Politics and Society, 1343–1378*. Princeton: Princeton University Press, 1962.

Bynum, Caroline Walker, *Holy Feast and Holy Fast: The Religious Significance of Food to Medieval Women*. Berkeley: University of California Press, 1987.

___, *Wonderful Blood: Theology and Practice in Late Medieval Northern Germany and Beyond*. Philadelphia: University of Pennsylvania Press, 2007.

___, "The Blood of Christ in the Later Middle Ages." *Church History* 71, no. 4 (Dec. 2002), 685–715.

___, "Religious Women in the Later Middle Ages," in *Christian Spirituality: High Middle Ages and Reformation*, edited by Jill Raitt, 121–39. Vol. 17 of World Spirituality. New York: Crossroad, 1988.

Byrne, Joseph P., *Daily Life During the Black Death*. Westport, CT: The Greenwood Press, 2006.

Caffero, William, *Mercenary Companies and the Decline of Siena*. Baltimore: Johns Hopkins University Press, 1998.

Cahill, Thomas, *Mysteries of the Middle Ages: And the Beginning of the Modern World*. New York: Doubleday/Anchor, 2008.

Camporesi, Piero, *Juice of Life: The Symbolic and Magic Significance of Blood*, foreword by Umberto Eco, translated by Robert Barr. New York: Continuum, 1995.

Cantor, Norman F., *The Civilization of the Middle Ages*. New York: HarperCollins, 1993.

Cavallini, Giuliana, *Catherine of Siena*. London: Geoffrey Chapman, 1998.

___, *Things Visible and Invisible: Images in the Spirituality of St. Catherine of Siena*, translated by Mary Jeremiah, O.P. New York: Alba House, 1996.

___ and Diega Giunta, *Luoghi Cateriniani di Roma*, 2nd ed. Rome: Centro Nazionale di Studi Cateriniani, 2004.

Cherewatuk, Karen, and Ulrike Wiethaus, eds., *Dear Sister: Medieval Women and the Epistolary Genre*. Philadelphia: University of Pennsylvania Press, 1993.

Coakley, John, "Friars as Confidants of Holy Women in Medieval Dominican Hagiography," in *Images of Sainthood in Medieval Europe*, edited by Renate Blumenfeld-Kosinski and Timea Szell, 222–46. Ithaca: Cornell University Press, 1991.

Collins, Roger, *Keepers of the Keys of Heaven: A History of the Papacy*. New York: Basic Books, 2009.

Connell, William J., ed., *Society and Individual in Renaissance Florence*. Berkeley: University of California Press, 2002.

Costello, M. Starr, "The Mystical Death of Catherine of Siena: Eschatological Vision and Social Reform." *Mystics Quarterly* 13 (March 1987), 19–26.

Currie, Stephen, ed., *The 1300s*. San Diego: Greenhaven Press, 2001.

Douglas, Langton, *A History of Siena*. London: John Murray, 1902.

Drane, Augusta Theodosia, *The History of St. Catherine of Siena and Her Companions*, 2 vols. New York: Longmans, Green & Co., 1899.

Duffy, Eamon, *Saints & Sinners: A History of the Popes*. New Haven: Yale University Press, 1997, 2001.

Falvey, Kathleen, "Early Italian Dramatic Traditions and Comforting Rituals: Some Initial Considerations," in *Crossing the Boundaries: Christian Piety and the Arts in Italian Medieval and Renaissance Confraternities*, edited by Konrad Eisenbichler. Kalamazoo, MI: Medieval Institute Publications, 1991, 33–55.

Fatula, Mary Ann, *Catherine of Siena's Way*. Wilmington, DE: Michael Glazier, 1987.

Fawtier, Robert, *Sainte Catherine de Sienne: Essai de Critique des Sources*, vol. 1: *Sources Hagiographique*. Paris: E[ditions] de Boccard, 1921.

Fines, John, *Who's Who in the Middle Ages*. New York: Barnes & Noble, Inc., 1970.

Gail, Marzieh, *Avignon in Flower, 1309–1403*. Boston: Houghton Mifflin Co., 1965.

Gardner, Edmund G., *Saint Catherine of Siena: A Study in the Religion, Literature, and History of the Fourteenth Century in Italy*. New York: Dutton, 1907.

___, "St. Catherine of Siena." *The Hibbert Journal* (1906), 570–89.

Gatto, Ludovico, "La Roma di Caterina," in *La Roma di Santa Caterina da Siena*, edited by Maria Grazia Bianco. Rome: Edizioni Studium, 2001.

Gies, Joseph, and Frances Gies, *Life in a Medieval City*. New York: Thomas Y. Crowell Co., 1969.

Giles, Mary E., ed., *The Feminist Mystic and Other Essays on Women and Spirituality*. New York: Crossroad, 1982.

Giordani, Igino, *Catherine of Siena: Fire and Blood*, translated by Thomas J. Tobin. Milwaukee: Bruce Publishing Co., 1959; Boston: St. Paul Editions, 1980.

Hackett, Benedict, O.S.A., *William Flete, O.S.A, and Catherine of Siena: Masters of Fourteenth Century Spirituality*. Villanova, PA: Augustinian Press, 1992.

Harrison, Ted, *Stigmata: A Medieval Mystery in a Modern Age*. New York: St. Martin's Press, 1994.

Hay, Denys, *Europe in the Fourteenth and Fifteenth Centuries*, 2nd ed. London: Longman, 1989.

Herlihy, David, *The Black Death and the Transformation of the West*. Cambridge: Harvard University Press, 1997.

Hetherington, Paul, *Medieval Rome: A Portrait of the City and its Life*. London: The Rubicon Press, 1994.

Hilkert, Mary Catherine, *Speaking with Authority: Catherine of Siena and the Voices of Women Today*. New York/Mahwah, NJ: Paulist Press, 2008.

Holloway, Julia Bolton, "Saint Birgitta of Sweden, Saint Catherine of Siena: Saints, Secretaries, Scribes, Supporters." *Birgittiana* 1 (1996), 22–45.

Holloway, Julia Bolton, Constance S. Wright, and Joan Bechtold, eds., *Equally in God's Name: Women in the Middle Ages*. New York: Peter Lang, 1990.

Holmes, George, ed., *The Oxford Illustrated History of Medieval Europe*. Oxford: Oxford University Press, 1988.

Hook, Judith, *Siena, A City and Its History*. London: Hamish Hamilton Ltd., 1979.

Horrox, Rosemary, ed. and trans., *The Black Death*. Manchester: Manchester University Press, 1994.

Housley, Norman, *The Avignon Papacy and the Crusades, 1305–1378*. Oxford: The Clarendon Press, 1986.

Huizinga, Johann, *The Waning of the Middle Ages*. New York: Doubleday, 1954.

Hyde, J. K., *Society and Politics in Medieval Italy: The Evolution of Civil Life, 1000–1350*. London: The Macmillan Press, 1973.

Jansen, Katherine Ludwig, *The Making of the Magdalen: Preaching and Popular Devotion in the Later Middle Ages*. Princeton: Princeton University Press, 2000.

Jantzen, Grace M., *Power, Gender and Christian Mysticism*. Cambridge: Cambridge University Press, 1995.

Jorgensen, Johannes, *St. Bridget of Sweden*, translated by Ingeborg Lund, 2 vols. New York: Longmans, Green and Co, 1954.

___, *Saint Catherine of Siena*, translated by Ingeborg Lund. New York: Longmans, Green and Co, 1938.

Kelly, John, *The Great Mortality: An Intimate History of the Black Death, the Most Devastating Plague of All Time*. New York: HarperCollins, 2005.

Kieckhefer, Richard, *Unquiet Souls: Fourteenth-Century Saints and Their Religious Milieu*. Chicago: University of Chicago Press, 1984.

Kleinhenz, Christopher, ed., *Medieval Italy: An Encyclopedia*. New York: Routledge, 2004.

Levasti, Arrigo, *My Servant, Catherine*, translated by Dorothy M. White. Westminster, MD: Newman Press, 1954.

Lock, Peter, *The Routledge Companion to the Crusades*. Abingdon, Oxon: Routledge, 2006.

Luongo, F. Thomas, *The Saintly Politics of Catherine of Siena*. Ithaca: Cornell University Press, 2006.

Marrone, Gaetana, comp., *Encyclopedia of Italian Literary Studies*, 2 vols. New York & Abingdon: Routledge, 2007.

Marthaler, Berard L., general ed., *New Catholic Encyclopedia*, 2nd ed. Detroit: Thompson-Gale, 2003.

Matter, E. Ann, and John Coakley, eds., *Creative Women in Medieval and Early Modern Italy: A Religious and Artistic Renaissance*. Philadelphia: University of Pennsylvania Press, 1994.

McDermott, Thomas, O.P., *Catherine of Siena: Spiritual Development in Her Life and Teaching*. New York/Mahwah, NJ: Paulist Press, 2008.

McDonnell, E. W., "Beguines and Beghards," in *New Catholic Encyclopedia*, vol. 2, 2nd ed., edited by Berard L. Marthaler. Detroit: Thompson-Gale, 2003.

McGinn, Bernard, *Doctors of the Church: Thirty-Three Men and Women Who Shaped Christianity*. New York: Crossroad, 1999.

____, *The Presence of God: A History of Western Christian Mysticism*, 4 vols. New York: Crossroad, 1991, 1994, 1999, 2005.

____, "Catherine of Siena: Apostle of the Blood of Christ." Sixth Annual de Lubac Lecture in Historical Theology. *Theology Digest* 48 (2001), 329–42.

Meade, Catherine M., C.S.J., *My Nature is Fire: Saint Catherine of Siena*. New York: Alba House, 1991.

Morris, Bridget, *St. Birgitta of Sweden*. Rochester, NY: The Boydell Press, 1999.

Mullins, Edwin, *The Popes of Avignon: A Century in Exile*. New York: BlueBridge, 2008.

Newman, Paul B., *Daily Life in the Middle Ages*. Jefferson, NC: McFarland & Company, Inc., 2001.

Noffke, Suzanne, O.P., *Catherine of Siena: Vision through a Distant Eye*. Lincoln, NE: Authors Choice Press, 1996, 2006.

____, "Catherine of Siena: Justly Doctor of the Church?" *Theology Today* 60 (2003), 49–62.

Okey, Thomas, *The Story of Avignon*. London: J. M. Dent & Sons, Ltd, 1911.

Parmisano, A. Stanley, O.P., "Mystic of the Absurd: Saint Catherine of Siena." *Religious Life Review* (1981), 201–14.

Parsons, Gerald, *Siena, Civil Religion and the Sienese*. Burlington, VT: Ashgate Publishing Co., 2004.

Pastor, Ludwig, *The History of the Popes from the Close of the Middle Ages*, vol. 1, 6th ed. Nendeln/Liechtenstein: Kraus-Thomson Organization Ltd., 1969.

Perrin, J. M., O.P., *Catherine of Siena*, translated by Paul Barrett, O.F.M. Cap. Westminster, MD: The Newman Press, 1965.

Peterson, David S., "The War of the Eight Saints in Florentine Memory and Oblivion," in *Society and Individual in Renaissance Florence*, edited by William J. Connell. Berkeley: University of California Press, 2002, 173–214.

Petrarch, Francesco, *Letters from Petrarch*, edited and translated by Morris Bishop. Bloomington: Indiana University Press, 1966.

Pinto, Giuliano, "'Honour' and 'Profit': Landed Property and Trade in Medieval Siena," in *City and Countryside in Late Medieval and Renaissance Italy: Essays Presented to Philip Jones*, edited by Trevor Dean and Chris Wickham, 81–91. London: The Hambledon Press, 1990.

Pullan, Brian, *A History of Early Renaissance Italy: From the Mid-thirteenth to the Mid-fifteenth Century*. London: Penguin, 1973.

Roberts, Ann M., "Chiara Gambacorta of Pisa as Patroness of the Arts," in *Creative Women in Medieval and Early Modern Italy: A Religious and Artistic Renaissance*, edited by E. Ann Matter and John Coakley, 120–54. Philadelphia: University of Pennsylvania Press, 1994.

Robertson, Elizabeth, "An Anchorhold of Her Own: Female Anchorite Literature in Thirteenth Century England," in *Equally in God's Name: Women in the Middle Ages*, edited by Julia Bolton Holloway, Constance S. Wright, and Joan Bechtold, 170–83. New York: Peter Lang, 1990.

Salimei, Franco, *I Salimbeni di Siena*. Rome: Editalia, 1986.

Schellinger, Paul E., ed., *St. James Guide to Biography*. Chicago: St. James Press, 1991.

Schevill, Ferdinand, *Siena: The History of a Mediaeval Commune*. New York: Charles Scribner's Sons, 1909, 1964.

Scott, Karen, "'Io Caterina': Ecclesial Politics and Oral Culture in the Letters of Catherine of Siena," in *Dear Sister: Medieval Women and the Epistolary Genre*, edited by Karen Cherewatuk and Ulrike Wiethaus, 87–121. Philadelphia: University of Pennsylvania Press, 1993.

___, "St. Catherine of Siena, 'Apostola.'" *Church History* 61 (March 1992), 34–46.

___, "Urban Spaces, Women's Networks, and the Lay Apostolate in the Siena of Catherine Benincasa," in *Creative Women in Medieval and Early Modern Italy: A Religious and Artistic Renaissance*, edited by E. Ann Matter and John Coakley. Philadelphia: University of Pennsylvania Press, 1994.

Singman, Jeffrey L., *Daily Life in Medieval Europe*. Westport, CT: The Greenwood Press, 1999.

Siwek, Paul, "Stigmatization," in *New Catholic Encyclopedia*, vol. 13, 2nd ed., edited by Berard L. Marthaler. Detroit: Thompson-Gale, 2003.

Smith, Daniel B., *Muses, Madmen, and Prophets: Hearing Voices and the Borders of Sanity*. New York: The Penguin Press, 2008.

Smith, John Holland, *The Great Schism: 1378*. London: Hamish Hamilton, Ltd., 1970.

Tuchman, Barbara W., *A Distant Mirror: The Calamitous 14th Century*. New York: Ballantine Books, 1978.

Tylerman, Christopher, *God's War: A New History of the Crusades*. Cambridge, MA: The Belknap Press, 2006.

Tylus, Jane, *Reclaiming Catherine of Siena: Literacy, Literature, and the Signs of Others*. Chicago: University of Chicago Press, 2009.

Underhill, Evelyn, *Mysticism: A Study in the Nature and Development of Man's Spiritual Consciousness*. New York: E. P. Dutton & Co. Inc., 1911.

Undset, Sigrid, *Catherine of Siena*, translated by Kate Austin-Lund. New York: Sheed & Ward, 1954.

Vingtain, Dominique, *Avignon: Le Palais des Papes*. Saint-Léger-Vauban, France: Zodiaque, 1998.

Von Behren, Ruth Lechner, *Women in Late Medieval Society: Catherine of Siena—A Psychological Study*. Doctoral Dissertation. Davis: University of California, 1973.

Weinstein, Donald, and Rudolph M. Bell, *Saints & Society: The Two Worlds of Western Christendom, 1000–1700*. Chicago: University of Chicago Press, 1982.

Wilkins, Ernest Hatch, *Life of Petrarch*. Chicago: University of Chicago Press, 1961.

Ziegler, Philip, *The Black Death*. New York: The John Day Company, 1969.

NOTES

ରେ

General note: The letters of Catherine of Siena have always been difficult to date. Over the centuries different editors have arranged them in different sequences. In her four-volume English translation of the letters, Suzanne Noffke, O.P., imposed her own sequence on the letters but for purposes of identification retained the numbering system of past editors together with their initials. This explains the complex identification that appears in this volume (e.g., T149/G193/DT22). For a more detailed explanation of this system, see Noffke's general introduction in volume I of *The Letters of Catherine of Siena.*

1. THE DYER'S DAUGHTER

3   *A solis ortu usque ad occasum.* Psalm 112 (113) of the Vulgate Bible; it is the first psalm of matins on March 25.

4   With a population of almost 50,000. This estimation is from William M. Bowsky, *A Medieval Italian Commune,* 19.

Siena's walls had to be extended. See Judith Hook, *Siena,* 18–19.

5   All of the streets. For the streets in Siena, see Hook, *Siena,* 25, 28; Bowsky, *A Medieval Italian Commune,* 15.

a housewife . . . by first calling, "*Guarda!*" See Langton Douglas, *A History of Siena,* 121.

6   a dyer named Giacomo di Benincasa. Most Italians during this medieval period did not use family names. Some authors have misidentified Catherine as "Caterina Benincasa," as though Benincasa were her last name; but Benincasa was simply the name of Giacomo's father. Catherine would have been known as "Caterina di Giacomo."

The family of Giacomo. For background on Catherine's parents, see ibid., 30.

7   a master dyer by profession. F. Thomas Luongo points out that Giacomo and his sons were *lanaiuoli,* not *lavoranti*—wool masters rather than wool workers. Noting the civic influence of the wool guild, he adds, "Catherine was born into a family that, while not one of the most wealthy or influential in Sienese society, was nevertheless close to the highest levels of political power." *The Saintly Politics of Catherine of Siena,* 30.

"mixing and manufacture" Raymond of Capua, *The Life of Catherine of Siena* [henceforth *Life*] (I, 1), 21. Unless otherwise noted, page numbers refer to the Conleth Kearns translation of this work.

some disparity in their ages. Caroline Walker Bynum points out that after 1200, the average disparity in age between husbands and wives widened. Men typically married when they were thirty, women at fifteen or seventeen. See *Holy Feast and Holy Fast* [henceforth *Holy Feast*], 226.

"God will show him his mistake" Raymond of Capua, *Life* (I, 1), 26.

The next son after him was Bartolomeo. The early-twentieth-century scholar Robert Fawtier theorized that Lapa had been married previously to a man named Francesco who died leaving her with one son, Bartolomeo; after Lapa married Giacomo, another son was also named Bartolomeo. Fawtier believed it was the first Bartolomeo who married Lisa Colombini. His thesis is not widely accepted today. See Noffke's note in *The Letters of Catherine of Siena*, IV, 190.

8   "I prayed for rain" Hook, *Siena*, 136. Giovanni Colombini was beatified by Pope Gregory XIII in the 1500s. The community he founded, the *Gésuati*, was suppressed in 1668.

Lapa gave birth to twin girls. Fawtier (see above) has argued that Catherine's birth was artificially placed in 1347 to make her the same age as Jesus when she died. He believed she was really born between 1335 and 1337. Today the 1347 date is accepted as reliable. See the introduction to Conleth Kearns's translation of the *Life*, lxiii.

The newborns were weak. See Raymond of Capua, *Life* (I, 2), 26.

9   Dante found the Sienese ardent, vain. See Arrigo Levasti, *My Servant, Catherine*, 86.

10   "Being confined to their own parts" Giovanni Boccaccio, introduction to *The Decameron*, 10–11.

The cloud of plague reached Siena. For Siena during the plague, see John Kelly, *The Great Mortality*, 114–19.

"There are not words to describe … the end of the world" Agnolo di Tura del Grasso, *Cronaca senese*, in Aubrey Threlkeld, trans., Alessandro Lisini and Fabio Iacometti, eds., *Rerum Italicarum Scriptores*, 15/6 (1931–37), 555–56. Cited in John Aberth, *The Black Death*, 81.

11   That number, however. For death estimates caused by the plague in Siena, see Kelly, *The Great Mortality*, 119.

12   Bands of flagellants. See Barbara W. Tuchman, *A Distant Mirror*, 114–16; Kelly, *The Great Mortality*, 255–68.

"[A]ll who survived gave themselves over to pleasures" Aberth, *The Black Death*, 82.

unusable in bad weather. For the condition of Siena's infrastructure in the decades after the Black Death, see Hook, *Siena*, 155–56.

13   They were sued. See Rudolph M. Bell, *Holy Anorexia*, 31.

14   "Medieval people lived as much" Catherine M. Meade, C.S.J., *My Nature is Fire*, 5.

"showed in germ" Raymond of Capua, *Life* (I, 2), 27.

15   There was muttering about the Council of Nine. For a summary of growing dissatisfaction with the Nine in the years after the Black Death, including Fra Moriale's raid,

see Bowsky, *A Medieval Italian Commune*, 304–6. Fra Moriale's full name was Moriale D'Albarno. He was subsequently captured and executed in Rome in 1354.

16   Suddenly Catherine stopped and looked up. Contemporary accounts of Catherine's vision are found in Raymond of Capua, *Life* (I, 2), 29–30; "The *Miracoli* of Catherine of Siena [henceforth *The Miracoli*]," in Maiju Lehmijoki-Gardner, ed. and trans., *Dominican Penitent Women*, 90–91; for a twentieth-century retelling see Johannes Jorgensen, *Saint Catherine of Siena*, 6–7. There is disagreement about Catherine's age at the time. The *Miracoli* states that she was seven; this book supposes it occurred in the summer or fall after Catherine's sixth birthday.

"What are you doing here? . . . wouldn't have disturbed me" Quotes adapted from Raymond of Capua, *Life* (I, 2), 29–30.

"From this moment, she was always tormented" The *Miracoli*, chap. 2, in Lehmijoki-Gardner, *Dominican Penitent Women*, 91. See also Raymond of Capua, *Life* (I, 2), 30–31.

17   Healthy visions. Evelyn Underhill speaks of "healthy ecstasy" and "psychopathic ecstasies," both of which may be manifest in the same person. She maintains that Catherine's ecstasies that occurred when she was young and strong were healthy and produced an "access to vitality," while those that occurred later in life when Catherine was ill and suffered from "nervous instability . . . were not healthy." *Mysticism*, 362.

18   "for the most part took place in her imagination" Raymond of Capua, *Life* (I, 9), 77. Underhill calls such mystical visions products of "subliminal consciousness." *Mysticism*, 270.

dressed in papal vestments. Raymond of Capua states that Christ, in Catherine's vision, was "clothed in pontifical vestments, and wearing on his head a tiara" *Life* (I, 2) 29. By way of comparison, the *Miracoli*, appearing about twenty years before Raymond's *Life*, has Christ "dressed in totally white clothes" and holding a pastoral staff "like a bishop." The *Miracoli*, chap. 2, in Lehmijoki-Gardner, *Dominican Penitent Women*, 90. Popes began dressing in white in the late thirteenth century.

19   She longed to be one of the desert hermits. For Catherine's brief experience as a hermit, see Raymond of Capua, *Life* (I, 2), 27–28, 31–33, and The *Miracoli*, chap. 3, in Lehmijoki-Gardner, *Dominican Penitent Women*, 91.

2. The Mantle

20   "distributed tyranny" Ferdinand Schevill, *Siena*, 197.

21   Charles entered Siena. The visit of Charles of Luxembourg to Siena is described in Bowsky, *A Medieval Italian Commune*, 301–2; see also Schevill, *Siena*, 213–15.

"Long live the emperor" Bowsky, *A Medieval Italian Commune*, 301.

The family of Giacomo was not displeased. For the involvement of Giacomo's sons in Sienese politics, see Luongo, *The Saintly Politics of Catherine of Siena*, 31.

22   "a retired place" Raymond of Capua, *Life* (I, 2), 35.

Catherine's "vow of virginity" is described in Raymond's *Life* (I, 3), 34–37. According to the *Miracoli*, Catherine didn't make her "vow" until seven years later, after the death of her sister Bonaventura. However, most experts accept Raymond's dating.

"life of angelical ... for ever spotless" Ibid., (I, 2), 34.

"the one I long for" Ibid., (I, 3), 35.

Catherine of Alexandria. See Luongo, *The Saintly Politics of Catherine of Siena*, 55, n. 83.

23   intensely physical Christ. Caroline Walker Bynum remarks, "The humanity of Christ, understood as including his full participation in bodiliness, was a central and characteristic theme in the religiosity of late medieval women. Often it had erotic or sensual overtones." *Holy Feast*, 246.

Margery Kempe ... snuggled in bed with the infant Jesus. See ibid., 246.

Catherine's marriage with Christ ... did not lapse into the erotic. According to Bynum, "Catherine's sense of the flesh is extremely unerotic ... In fact, Catherine clearly associated Christ's physicality with the female body, underlying thereby both her capacity for assimilation to Christ and her capacity, like his, for service." Ibid., 178.

"join the mouth of our holy desire" Letter T120/G344 to Monna Rabe, wife of Francesco dei Tolomei, in Suzanne Noffke, ed. and trans., *The Letters of Catherine of Siena* [henceforth *Letters*], vol. II, 439.

While males had a higher status in society. Bernard McGinn, in a private note, points out that medieval men, too, believing that their souls were feminine, claimed marriage with Jesus. Cistercian monks, including Bernard of Clairvaux (1090–1153), held this view. Caroline Walker Bynum writes that for medieval women it went beyond the marriage of souls, that mystical marriage for women was a way of redeeming their bodies. According to Bynum, "They strove not to eradicate body but to merge their own humiliating and painful flesh with the flesh [of Jesus] whose agony, espoused by choice, was salvation." *Holy Feast*, 246.

24   women ... being loci for the transcendent. See John Coakley, "Friars as Confidants of Holy Women in Medieval Dominican Hagiography," in *Images of Sainthood in Medieval Europe*, Renate Blumenfeld-Kosinski and Timea Szell, eds., 234.

"penitent children" They are described in Donald Weinstein and Rudolph M. Bell, *Saints & Society*, 30–34.

"from the age of reason" and "family delights" Ibid., 30–31.

25   The story of the miraculous wine cask. See Raymond of Capua, *Life* (II, 3), 135–36.

"Beat me as you think fit" Ibid. (I, 3), 38–39.

26   "Do you know what your daughter" Jorgensen, *Saint Catherine of Siena*, 20.

Catherine would blame herself. See Raymond of Capua, *Life* (I, 4), 41–42. See also Coakley, "Friars as Confidants of Holy Women in Medieval Dominican Hagiography," in *Images of Sainthood in Medieval Europe*, Blumenfeld-Kosinski and Szell, 235.

27   she began to compare herself to Mary Magdalen. See Raymond of Capua, *Life* (I, 4), 44; Bynum, *Holy Feast*, 81, 166. A different retelling of the medieval legend holds that Mary Magdalen spent her time in the south of France preaching and evangelizing. According to Katherine Ludwig Jansen, people believed that Magdalen, with her sister Martha and brother Lazarus and two servants, were cast adrift in a rudderless boat and were washed ashore in Provence. Magdalen became a Christian missionary to Marseilles and Aix-en-Provence, while Martha evangelized Tarascon. Lazarus became the bishop of Marseilles. "By the twelfth century," says Jansen, "these legendary events were considered the biographical facts of Mary Magdalen's life." *The Making of the Magdalen*, 52–53.

she was being matched. Catherine's proposed marriage to Niccolò is suspected by Bynum, who bases it on a statement in the *Miracoli* (chap. 6) that Catherine's parents were disappointed Bonaventura's husband had remarried so quickly—making it seem as if they were counting on him marrying Catherine. *Holy Feast*, 167. The same idea is also mentioned by Bell, *Holy Anorexia*, 38–39.

she sought counsel from Tommaso. See Raymond of Capua, *Life* (I, 4), 45. Johannes Jorgensen maintains the visit was not Catherine's idea but her family's. See *Saint Catherine of Siena*, 22.

29   "Build yourself a cell" Raymond of Capua, *Life* (I, 4), 47.

a white dove hovering. See ibid., (I, 5), 49.

"It is now a long time . . . supply my every need" Ibid., (I, 5), 50–51.

30   daughters . . . met more parental opposition. See Bynum, *Holy Feast*, 87.

31   Dominicans . . . evoked images of freedom. Jane Tylus has commented that "the preaching friars represented for her a way *out* of the confined spaces of her *quartiere* and, of course, out of the confines of a gender constrained to the invisible spaces of either marriage or the convent." *Reclaiming Catherine of Siena*, 67–68 [italics in the original].

Clare of Assisi. See Bynum, *Holy Feast*, 15.

32   new groups and classes of laypeople into religious life. See ibid., 18.

churchmen . . . grew suspicious of the movement. Caroline Walker Bynum observes that "these movements, which were often labeled 'heresies' for reasons of ecclesiastical politics—not doctrine—expressed many of the basic themes of women's religiosity in its orthodox forms: a concern for affective religious response, an extreme form of penitential asceticism, an emphasis on Christ's humanity and the inspiration of the Spirit, and a bypassing of clerical authority." "Religious Women in the Later Middle Ages," in *Christian Spirituality*, vol. 17, Jill Raitt, ed., 123.

new and creative opportunities of ministry. See Karen Scott, "Urban Spaces, Women's

Networks, and the Lay Apostolate in the Siena of Catherine Benincasa," in *Creative Women in Medieval and Early Modern Italy*, E. Ann Matter and John Coakley, eds., 105–19.

33   15 percent . . . in Cologne lived as Beguines. Statistics cited by Bynum, "Religious Women in the Later Middle Ages," in *Christian Spirituality*, vol. 17, Raitt, 123.

each group of tertiaries . . . free to frame its own association. Maiju Lehmijoki-Gardner maintains that Dominican tertiaries were not entirely subject to male rules but "played a more active role in the creation of the institutional foundations of their form of life than had been hitherto presumed." *Dominican Penitent Women*, 5.

midway between the monastic and the lay state. See E. W. McDonnell, "Beguines and Beghards" in *New Catholic Encyclopedia*, vol. 2, 2nd ed., Berard L. Marthaler, ed., 204–5.

a dream in which St. Dominic appeared. See Raymond of Capua, *Life* (I, 5), 50. See also Thomas of Siena, "The Libellus Concerning Catherine of Siena," in Lehmijoki-Gardner, *Dominican Penitent Women*, 181. A slightly different dream experience is recorded by the anonymous *Miracoli*. That work states that St. Dominic, holding a habit, appeared to Catherine in the midst of a crowd and said, "If you want to pass through this crowd, you will have to hide yourself under something white," adding, "Come and receive my habit." *Dominican Penitent Women*, 93.

34   there she began to practice austerities. See Raymond of Capua, *Life* (I, 6), 54–62.

with a stone as her pillow. Johannes Jorgensen says Catherine used a "log of wood" as a pillow. *Saint Catherine of Siena*, 48. However, Suzanne Noffke states that one can still find in Catherine's little room in Siena the "stone" she used as a headrest. *Catherine of Siena: Vision through a Distant Eye*, 161. Perhaps Catherine used both at different times.

hair shirt . . . thin chain. Jorgensen says that Catherine, who was scrupulous about cleanliness, got rid of the hair shirt because it interfered with washing. He describes the chain as "thin" and studded with small crosses. See *Saint Catherine of Siena*, 48.

a trip to . . . Vignoni. Raymond of Capua, *Life* (I, 7), 64–65. Augusta Theodosia Drane writes that Catherine placed herself under the spout that poured scalding water into the pool. See *The History of St. Catherine of Siena and Her Companions*, vol. 1, 33.

"pious abstinence" Paul B. Newman, *Daily Life in the Middle Ages*, 141. See also Jorgensen, *Saint Catherine of Siena*, 48.

35   "with dovelike simplicity" Raymond of Capua, *Life* (I, 7), 64.

"widows of mature age . . . utmost respectability" Raymond of Capua, *Life* (I, 7), 65. These are Raymond's words.

Catherine became ill. See ibid., 62. Many authorities accept the chicken pox hypothesis. Jane Tylus thinks it was smallpox. See *Reclaiming Catherine of Siena*, 70.

"pimples . . . young people" Raymond of Capua, *Life* (I, 7), 65.

"If you want me . . . to get well" Ibid., 66.

36 "Is she pretty or attractive?" From the George Lamb translation of Raymond of Capua, *Life* (I, 7), 63.

"Come and see for yourself" Quotes adapted from Raymond of Capua, *Life* (I, 6), 66.

her clothing ceremony. The ritual used for the reception of Sienese Mantellate has not been preserved. The account given here follows the *Ordinationes* of Munio of Zamora, written in 1286 for Dominican penitents in Orvieto. See Lehmijoki-Gardner, *Dominican Penitent Women*, 46–56. The Siena ritual was apparently much the same.

3. THE ROOM

37 female anchorites. Elizabeth Robertson points out, "An anchorhold offered a woman a medieval version of Virginia Woolf's room of one's own, because in that place a woman could find privacy, autonomy, and a chance for intellectual development, unavailable in any other sphere." "An Anchorhold of Her Own: Female Anchoritic Literature in Thirteenth Century England," in *Equally in God's Name*, Julia Bolton Holloway, Constance S. Wright, and Joan Bechtold, eds., 171.

38 Tommaso dalla Fonte stated. See Raymond of Capua, *Life* (I, 9), 76.

39 She saw a tree. The vision of the tree is described by Tommaso di Antonio Caffarini, *Libellus de supplemento*, part 1, in Lehmijoki-Gardner, *Dominican Penitent Women*, 181–82.

suffering as a vocation. As Caroline Walker Bynum points out, "Woman's eating, fasting, and feeding others were synonymous acts, because in all three the woman, by suffering, fused with a cosmic suffering that really redeemed the world." *Holy Feast*, 289.

They identified with the godhead through their bodies. See Grace M. Jantzen, *Power, Gender and Christian Mysticism*, 221–23.

40 "bore the mark of exquisite social concern" Marvin B. Becker, *Medieval Italy*, 151. Speaking of the flagellant societies that flourished during this period, Becker states, "Flagellants disciplined themselves not only to gain individual merit but to assist humankind in overcoming its sins. The primary civic function of the confraternities was to reduce the distance between classes and bring peace to the community . . . [R]eligious feeling was not resolved so exclusively in terms of individual morality. Religious sensibilities were less likely to be satisfied by interior or personal renewal and more prone to be realized in abstract and extended schemes for the regeneration of collective life." *Medieval Italy*, 141–42.

"There are two sorts of perfect souls . . . not the same as theirs" Suzanne Noffke, ed. and trans., *Catherine of Siena: The Dialogue* [henceforth *Dialogue*] (99), 186–87.

"dung heap" *Dialogue* (13), 50, and Bynum, *Holy Feast*, 175.

on a staircase. In a letter to Dominican Niccolò da Montalcino, Catherine says, "Out of his very self, that is, out of his body, he has made a stairway so as to raise us up from the way of suffering and set us at rest." Letter T74/G119, in *Letters* I, 313. Then she elaborates on the stages of ascent. The notion of entering Christ's body through his wounds did not originate with Catherine. Aelred of Rievaulx used the image in the twelfth century. See Bynum, "The Blood of Christ in the Later Middle Ages." *Church History*, 687.

41   "I long to see you" Letter T42/G280 to Neri di Landoccio Pagliaresi, in *Letters* III, 266.

Mantellate rule of life. The spiritual practices mentioned here reflect the rule written for Dominican tertiaries in Orvieto, but it was also used in Siena. The rule appears in Lehmijoki-Gardner, *Dominican Penitent Women*, 47–56.

It has also been suggested. According to Suzanne Noffke, in a private note: "I suspect the greatest influence on Catherine in terms of her own entry [into the Mantellate] was her relationship to the friars and her wish to be associated with them and their mission. It was also a way to 'secure' her own determination not to marry, even though the Mantellate did not take a vow of celibacy as such."

42   She entered into God as naturally as a fish enters water. See Raymond of Capua, *Life* (II, 6), 183.

when she was denied. See Raymond of Capua, *Life* (II, 6), 180. This was not the only instance that it seemed to Catherine she was drinking from the side of Christ. On another occasion Jesus showed her his side from afar. When he saw that she longed for it, he smiled and came closer so she could drink. Ibid. (II. 6), 183. Caroline Walker Bynum mentions several other instances of miraculous communion for medieval women who have been denied (*Holy Feast*, 122–33). Nor was the phenomenon limited to women. Henry Suso, the German Dominican mystic (1295–1366), claimed he was nursed at the breast of Christ. Like Catherine, Suso fasted severely.

43   "When the priest came to break the host" *Dialogue* (142), 296.

"taught by God himself" Raymond of Capua, *Life* (I, 11), 105. Reading instructors have long recognized the "whole word" method as an alternative to phonetic systems. Eventually most people become whole-word readers.

44   she never actually read either the Latin psalter. Noffke guesses that Catherine "simply listened and prayed along as the friars sang the Hours, *perhaps* following in the text, and very likely memorizing a good deal of it eventually." *Catherine of Siena: Vision through a Distant Eye*, 38–42.

"When first I began to visit her . . . far more angelic than human" From the process of canonization, quoted by Drane, *The History of St. Catherine of Siena and Her Companions*, vol. 1, 69.

45   "The garment of yours" Letter T104/G92 to Raymond of Capua, in *Letters* II, 654.

"You know that a person who walks with a lamp . . . whatever being they have" Letter T183/G33/DT56 to Archbishop Iacopo da Itri, in *Letters* I, 258–59.

46   "You are she who is not" Raymond of Capua, *Life* (I, 10), 85.

47   "It is no hardship for me" Ibid., (I, 11), 101.

"My daughter Catherine" Ibid.

sleeping time to one half hour. Ibid., (I, 6), 57.

"First you find your cell . . . and never leave" Letter T73/G154 to Suor Costanza of the Monastery of Santa Bonda, in *Letters* I, 306.

48   "from [Lent] until the feast of the Ascension" Raymond of Capua, *Life* (II, 5), 163.

atoning for her own sins. See Richard Kieckhefer, *Unquiet Souls*, 138–41.

Distracted, Catherine glanced up. See Raymond of Capua, *Life* (II, 6), 193.

49   Fasting . . . an instrument of control. Caroline Walker Bynum has fascinating things to say about food as control of oneself and one's surroundings in medieval times. *Holy Feast*, 189–244.

fasting also has the effect of suppressing menstruation. Ibid., 214.

50   exercises in mythmaking. For testimony by Stefano Maconi about Catherine eating bread, cheese, etc., see *Letters* II, 17, n. 23.

food "that had been violently forced down" Raymond of Capua, *Life* (II, 5), 161.

Tommaso would not relent. For this dialogue between Catherine and Tommaso, see ibid.

51   anorexia nervosa. See Bell, *Holy Anorexia*, especially chap. 2.

lesions in the hypothalamus. See ibid., 15.

fixated on food. See ibid., 32–34.

she wrote to another Mantellata. "Be sensitive to your sick, weak body. Eat the food you need every day to restore nature. And if your illness and weakness should get better, take up a well-ordered life with moderation, not with excess." Letter T213/G163 to Daniella da Orvieto, in *Letters* III, 303.

52   "Dearest father . . . will not make light of your prayers" Letter T92/G305/DT19 to a religious person in Florence, in *Letters* I, 160–61.

53   her worldview inevitably widened. The incarnational structure of Christian spirituality tugs at believers even in solitude. According to A. Stanley Parmisano, O.P., "although the Christian mystic may leave the world for a time, may even 'despise' it, in order to draw closer to God in purity and freedom, he or she must always, in act or in affection, return to the world, love it, work in and for it, and return it to [God]." "Mystic of the Absurd." *Religious Life Review* (1981), 202.

last day of carnival. Caffarini, in his *Legenda minore*, points out that carnival in that era was celebrated before Quinquagesima Sunday (i.e., the Sunday before Ash Wednesday), rather than on the eve of Ash Wednesday; see Drane, *The History of St. Catherine of Siena and Her Companions*, vol. 1, 61–62. The anonymous *Miracoli* maintains Catherine spent seven years in solitude (Lehmijoki-Gardner, *Dominican Penitent Women*,

93), but no scholars accept that claim today. Raymond of Capua does not say when the "mystical espousal" occurred, so scholars have argued for 1367 or 1368. Placing the espousal in 1368 preserves the tradition of Catherine spending three years in her cell. This biography, however, has accepted Benedict Hackett's argument that Catherine was already engaged in urban ministry in 1367, so most likely she lived as a hermit for less than three years. See Hackett, *William Flete, OSA, and Catherine of Siena*, 84.

"Behold, I espouse you to me in faith . . . mystical espousal" Raymond of Capua, *Life* (I, 12), 106–9.

54 "One does not live by bread alone" Matthew 4:4.

"On two feet you must walk" Raymond of Capua, *Life* (II, 1), 116.

4. The City

55 "the old pickpocket" Raymond of Capua, *Life* (II, 2), 115 [Lamb translation]. Catherine actually used the local expression, "*Malatasca*."

56 Tommaso . . . in over his head. Benedict Hackett, O.S.A., observes that "Tommaso, a good, honest simple friar, felt completely out of his depth with Catherine." *William Flete, OSA, and Catherine of Siena*, 83.

to meet William Flete. There are differing opinions about when Catherine first met Flete and who introduced them. The author of the *Miracoli* states that in October 1374, the two had corresponded but never met (see Lehmijoki-Gardner, *Dominican Penitent Women*, 98). F. Thomas Luongo points out that "Catherine's early Dominican advisors" [Tommaso dalla Fonte and Bartolomeo Dominici] "clearly knew Flete and held him in high regard" (*The Saintly Politics of Catherine of Siena*, 67, note 35) "much earlier" (ibid., 67) than a documented meeting in 1376. Benedict Hackett believes the encounter took place in the summer of 1367 and the go-between was Tommaso dalla Fonte (see *William Flete, OSA, and Catherine of Siena*, 86). Suzanne Noffke says merely that the two met "very soon" after she emerged from solitude, and that "almost certainly" the link was the Augustinian Giovanni "Terzo" Tantucci (*Letters* I, 155).

Flete was one of the more remarkable men. Jorgensen has a poor opinion of Flete, calling him a "splenetic, misanthropic, taciturn Englishman" and "a romantic, which is the opposite of being a mystic." *Saint Catherine of Siena*, 149, 150. His seems to be a minority view. Luongo notes that Flete was well-connected politically, especially among the Twelve, the party of Catherine's brothers. See *The Saintly Politics of Catherine of Siena*, 67–69.

57 "I . . . commend to your kindness" Letter T92/G305/DT19 to William Flete, in *Letters* I, 158.

"the queen of Fontebranda!" and "with her own hands" Raymond of Capua, *Life* (II, 4), 139 and 141.

58 two crowns. See ibid., 151–52.

the small bowl. See ibid., 148–56. Different English translations of Raymond's work raise questions about what, precisely, Catherine drank. George Lamb's translation describes it as "fetid stuff that had been used to wash the sore, along with all the pus" (Lamb, 147), while Conleth Kearns translates it as "water with which the ulcer had been washed and the corrupt matter which had come away with it" (Kearns, 155).

a communion of sorts. The connection between drinking the liquid from the bowl and holy communion is underscored by Raymond when he reports that Christ, who visited Catherine during prayer that same evening, praised her action, and again invited her to drink from his wounded side. See Raymond of Capua, *Life* (II, 4), 156.

medieval fascination with the eucharist. Caroline Walker Bynum explores this theme in *Holy Feast*, especially in chap. 2.

"Souls are a food" Letter T200/G112/DT9 to Bartolomeo Dominici, in *Letters* I, 21.

60   landed wealth in the city-state. See Giuliano Pinto, "'Honor' and 'Profit': Landed Property and Trade in Medieval Siena," in *City and Countryside in Late Medieval and Renaissance Italy*, Trevor Dean and Chris Wickham, eds., 85.

61   Economic issues. See ibid., 84–88.

62   Little Ice Age. See Tuchman, *A Distant Mirror*, 24–25, 81.

     a dreamy, impractical people. See Arrigo Levasti, *My Servant, Catherine*, 86.

63   Guelph and Ghibelline cities. See Hook, *Siena*, 6, 12.

     King Philip the Fair and Pope Boniface VIII. For a summary of the running battle between the French king and the pope, see Norman F. Cantor, *The Civilization of the Middle Ages*, 492–97.

64   "In [the pope's] absence . . . a shapeless heap of stones?" Petrarch, *Epistolae Seniles* (VII, 1), in *Life of Petrarch*, Ernest Hatch Wilkins, 201.

65   "priests and ordained clerks" Quoted in Johannes Jorgensen, *St. Bridget of Sweden*, vol. 2, 214.

     Giacomo . . . was nearing the end. See Raymond of Capua, *Life* (II, 7), 209–11.

66   the rule of the Twelve was toppled. See Luongo, *The Saintly Politics of Catherine of Siena*, 42–43; Schevill, *Siena*, 218–23; and Jorgensen, *Saint Catherine of Siena*, 87–89. Jorgensen confuses an episode when Catherine rescued her brothers from a mob, which occurred in 1371, and places it during the fall of the Twelve.

5. "Our Most Kind Mamma"

71   her beauty "was not excessive" Drane, *The History of St. Catherine of Siena and Her Companions*, vol. 1, 184.

     Catherine was moderately petite. Recent studies of medieval remains suggest bodily height has varied little over the centuries. Twelfth-century Europeans were nearly as tall as people today, but physical height diminished moderately over the next four centuries due to disease and poor nutrition. Nobles tended to be taller than peasants, and northern Europeans slightly taller than southern Europeans.

Most paintings of Catherine. In addition to the Andrea Vanni portrait, there is a marble bust by Jacobo della Querica, said to be based on a death mask, also on display at San Domenico Church. For a description of the 1947 X-rays of Catherine's skull, see Noffke's *Catherine of Siena: Vision through a Distant Eye*, 164–65.

72   "always kind, always full of clemency" A verse description by Anastagio di Mont 'Altino and Jacomo del Pecora quoted by Drane, *The History of St. Catherine of Siena and Her Companions*, vol. 1, 185–86.

"I might as well be talking to a wall" Raymond of Capua, *Life* (I, 6), 58.

73   two convicted prisoners. See ibid. (II, 7), 215–18. See also *The Miracoli*, in Lehmijoki-Gardner, *Dominican Penitent Women*, 98.

Defensores. During the rule of the Twelve, there were a dozen magistrates called Defensores (Defenders of the People). Later, in the Riformatori government, there were fifteen magistrates, or Defensores. These Defensores served as the Signoria, the executive authority of the commune.

their economic fortunes in the future. F. Thomas Luongo maintains that the family dye business in Siena was still prosperous in 1370, which would suggest its collapse in 1371 was due to political rather than economic pressures. See *The Saintly Politics of Catherine of Siena*, 31–32.

widespread crop failures . . . saw its population shrink from 1,200 people to 100. See William Cafferro, "City and Countryside in Siena in the Second Half of the Four-teenth Century" in *The Journal of Economic History*, 90, 96. Cafferro uses the term "men," not "people."

74   "miraculous multiplication of the loaves" See Raymond of Capua, *Life* (II, 11), 276–78. Some place this miracle during another famine that followed the plague outbreak of 1374.

in a trancelike state. Raymond of Capua reports that during prayer Catherine "lived, practically without interruption in a state of actual contemplation . . . Her mind cleaved so utterly to her Creator that the lower sense-facilities of her soul remained for the most part inactive . . . Any time she was thus absorbed in actual contemplation, we could verify by feeling her arms that they, together with her hands and fingers, had become as rigid as iron bars. It would have been easier to break the bones than to detach her grip from anything she chanced to be holding on to when in this state. Her eyes remained fast closed, her ears impervious to the loudest sounds, and all the senses of her body deprived of their natural operations." Raymond of Capua, *Life* (II, 6), 173–74.

75   "It is a fact, Father" Ibid., 174.

"Don't you notice" Ibid., 176.

"[Christ] who had enkindled" Ibid., 203.

76   "a radical change in the way of life ... the pride of the strong" Ibid., 204–5.

      commissions given in the Hebrew Bible. See Genesis 12; Jeremiah 1; Exodus 3.

      a kind of mountaintop moment. See M. Starr Costello, "The Mystical Death of Catherine of Siena: Eschatological Vision and Social Reform." *Mystics Quarterly*, 19–26.

77   son and daughter of Francesco dei Tolomei. See Raymond of Capua, *Life* (II, 7), 219–22.

78   "never looked back" Raymond of Capua, *Life* (II, 7), 222.

      Neri ... fits of depression. See Drane, *The History of St. Catherine of Siena and Her Companions*, vol. 1, 155.

      Neri ... a courier. He carried personal messages from Catherine to Queen Giovanna of Naples and to the leaders of Perugia. He also served as an "advance man" for Catherine's trip to Avignon. See Luongo, *The Saintly Politics of Catherine of Siena*, 146.

79   "I have already received you" Letter T99/G272/DT7 to Neri di Landoccio Pagliaresi, in *Letters* I, 15.

80   "bold and hot-headed, lascivious and unrestrained" Quoted by Noffke, *Letters* I, 539.

      "when we came into her gracious presence" Quoted by Drane, *The History of St. Catherine of Siena and Her Companions*, vol. 1, 158.

      Nanni di Ser Vanni. See Raymond of Capua, *Life* (II, 7), 223–25.

      "face fell" Ibid., 224.

81   "About what you have written" Quoted by Luongo, *The Saintly Politics of Catherine of Siena*, 123, translated from Misciattelli, *Lettere di S. Caterina da Siena* 6:69 (15 January 1379). For a messianic parallel see Philippians 2:10–11.

82   perhaps as early as 1368. This is the view of Suzanne Noffke, the principal translator of Catherine's letters into English. See *Letters* I, 1. The letter to Neri, cited above, dates probably from 1372.

      It is difficult to date Catherine's letters. Attaching dates has been complicated by the fact that the critical edition of the letters in Italian did not appear until 2002.

      excluded from the canon of great authors. The history of the critical reception of Catherine's letters is detailed in Tylus, *Reclaiming Catherine of Siena*.

83   the letter is a clever forgery. See the note 'the final paragraph ... is a forgery' in the notes for chapter 10 for more background on this letter.

      "excessively mannered, non-literary style ... devotional clichés" A. H. T. Levi, "Catherine of Siena," in *St. James Guide to Biography*, Paul E. Schellinger, ed., 130.

      "Catherine's language is the purest Tuscan ... impassioned words" Edmund G. Gardner, *Saint Catherine of Siena*, 377.

84 dictating three letters. The story is recounted by Gardner, "St. Catherine of Siena." *The Hibbert Journal*, 584.

"Fat Alessa says that you are praying for her" Letter T198/G110/DT4 to Bartolomeo Dominici, in *Letters* II, 81–82.

"she will lead you into her Son's presence" Letter T276/G373 to a prostitute in Perugia, in *Letters* I, 292.

"I Caterina, servant and slave" Letter T142/G242/DT26 to Sano di Maco di Mazzacorno, in *Letters* I, 76.

85 "the sword of divine charity" Letter T144/G371/DT34 to Monna Pavola da Siena, in *Letters* I, 113.

Pope Urban V passed away. Birgitta's warning to Urban and his subsequent death is recounted by many other sources, including Bridget Morris, *St. Birgitta of Sweden*, 117, and Tuchman, *A Distant Mirror*, 251.

an uprising in Siena. The Bruco (i.e., caterpillar) contrada was near the fountain and gate of Ovile, on the opposite side of the city from the Fontebranda neighborhood where Catherine grew up.

86 dispute with the wealthy artisans. Schevill maintains the Bruco uprising was initiated by "starving woolen workers." *Siena*, 223. However, Luongo insists the real cause was a disagreement between the workers and the *lanaiuoli* (wool masters) who were holdovers from the government of the Twelve, now in coalition with the Riformatori. One of the demands of the rioters was that all members of the Twelve be expelled from the coalition. See *The Saintly Politics of Catherine of Siena*, 44–46.

The story of what happened. See *The Miracoli*, in Lehmijoki-Gardner, *Dominican Penitent Woman*, 96.

"wanting to kill them" and "took them directly" Ibid.

87 one of those executed ... a nephew of Tommaso dalla Fonte. See Luongo, *The Saintly Politics of Catherine of Siena*, 47. Throughout his book, Longo documents how Catherine's family members supported the party of the Twelve.

88 "transitory things" and "I ask you, Benincasa" Letter T14/G252/DT13 to her three brothers in Florence, in *Letters* I, 30.

The two women had to sue. See Luongo, *The Saintly Politics of Catherine of Siena*, 48–49.

6. A Time of Testing

90 "unburden your consciences" Letter T202/G226 to Maestro Iacomo, in *Letters* I, 36.

91 "The pope sent his representative here" Letter T127/G117/DT20 to Bartolomeo Dominici and Tommaso d'Antonio, in *Letters* I, 40.

92 "devoid of self-esteem . . . practiced in its perfection" Raymond of Capua in the First Prologue to his *Life*, 11.

anti-Catherine faction . . . in the monastery. See Gardner, *Saint Catherine of Siena*, 95.

"With all your wisdom" Quoted by Igino Giordani, *Catherine of Siena*, 79. The original account of the meeting between Catherine and Friar Gabriele was in a letter by Francesco Malavolti submitted to her canonization proceedings.

93 Franciscan named Lazzarino da Pisa. This story is contained in the *Processo Castellano* prepared by Tommaso Caffarini for Catherine's canonization. It has been recounted in many places, including Giordani's *Catherine of Siena*, 77–78.

94 "Follow humbly in the footsteps" Giordani, *Catherine of Siena*, 78.

Catherine reprimanded. See Raymond of Capua, *Life* (III, 6), 370–71.

"Beware, Catherine my sister, lest" Free translation of a fragment from Bïanco da Siena's "Questa seguente lauda mandò el Bianco alla Beata Caterina da Siena," from *Laudi spirituali del Bianco da Siena*, quoted in Gardner, *Saint Catherine of Siena*, 131.

"Men or women, they all acted . . . to reprimand her" Raymond of Capua, *Life* (II, 5), 162.

95 "But she bore them all victoriously" Raymond of Capua, *Life* (III, 6), 377.

"I don't think it is possible" Letter T30/G150/DT1 to the Abbess and Suora Niccolosa of Santa Marta Monastery, in *Letters* I, 49.

96 Women were believed to represent the material. See Bynum, *Holy Feast*, 261–63.

"How shall this be done?" Raymond of Capua, *Life* (II, 1), 108.

"I am amazed . . . for the love of me" Quoted in Drane, *The History of St. Catherine of Siena and Her Companions*, vol. 1, 300. See also Jorgensen, *Saint Catherine of Siena*, 192, and Gardner, *Saint Catherine of Siena*, 130.

97 "satisfy himself as to her real spirit" Drane, *The History of St. Catherine of Siena and Her Companions*, vol. 1, 216. Jorgensen and Gardner also maintain that Catherine was formally summoned to Florence, just as Luongo states that Catherine was "summoned" (*The Saintly Politics of Catherine of Siena*, 58).

98 casual interrogators . . . Raymond of Capua. Some biographers have assumed Catherine and Raymond never met until after his appointment as her confessor. But given his experience with religious women, it seems far more likely that he would have interviewed Catherine in advance.

its foundress, Agnes. Agnes of Montepulciano (1278–1317) was esteemed for healing and miracle-working and known for her severe fasting. She was canonized in 1726. Raymond was rector and confessor at the convent from 1363 to 1367, during which time he wrote his account of Agnes's life, his first foray into hagiography.

"by sweet Mother Mary herself" Conleth Kearns in the introduction to his translation of Raymond of Capua's *Life*, xvii.

99　"mousy little man" Thomas Gilbey, O.P., in his introduction to the Lamb translation of Raymond's *Life*, 13.

"dearest respected brother" Letter T131/G216/DT33 to Niccolò Soderini, in *Letters* I, 128.

100　the author was a layperson. Maiju Lehmijoki-Gardner theorizes that the anonymous writer of the *Miracoli* was a woman. As evidence she cites three reasons: first, the use of the vernacular in the text (males would have been more likely to employ Latin); second, because its author got to know Catherine through other women; third, because Raymond of Capua felt free to ignore it when writing his *Life* of Catherine. See *Dominican Penitent Women*, 269–70, n. 15.

"came a few times to my house" Ibid., 90.

101　The plague had returned. Medieval Europe suffered from repeated outbreaks of bubonic plague after the initial one of 1347/48. John Kelly, in *The Great Mortality*, 277–79, speaks of the *pestis secunda* in 1361 and the *pestis tertia* in 1369. In addition there were localized outbreaks that infected particular cities.

"These at least I shall not lose" Jorgensen, *Saint Catherine of Siena*, 181.

102　"Get up, Don Matteo" Raymond of Capua, *Life* (II, 8), 234.

"I command you, in the name" Ibid., 239.

"I seemed to feel as if something were being drawn" Ibid., 240.

103　"I was practically alone in my task" Ibid., 239.

There was wonder and astonishment. The incident at Montepulciano is fully reported by Raymond of Capua in *Life* (II, 12), 299–304.

104　"Dearest Sister, we are not asking you" Ibid., 302.

7. "SWEET HOLY CRUSADE"

105　Gambacorta had a daughter, Tora. Tora (probably a diminutive of Theodora) Gambacorta (1362–1419) was married at thirteen and widowed at fifteen. Taking the name of Chiara, she eventually became a Dominican nun and founded an Observant (i.e., reformed) convent of sisters. Although never formally canonized by the church, she is honored as a *Beata* by the citizens of Pisa. See Ann M. Roberts, "Chiara Gambacorta of Pisa as Patroness of the Arts" in *Creative Women in Medieval and Early Modern Italy*, Matter and Coakley, eds., 120–54.

"warmed my heart" and "source of scandal" Letter T149/G193/DT22 to Piero Gambacorta, in *Letters* I, 62.

106　Pisa and . . . Lucca were also being courted. See Luongo, *The Saintly Politics of Catherine of Siena*, 80.

"have lost self-mastery . . . deserving of eternal fire" Letter T149/G193/DT22 to Piero Gambacorta, in *Letters* I, 61.

107 Crusades needed an appropriate historical moment. See Norman Housley, *The Avignon Papacy and the Crusades*, 116.

108 the church of Santa Cristina. Noffke, citing Ambrogio Paganucci, mentions the church as a likely Mantellate meeting place. *Catherine of Siena: Vision through a Distant Eye*, 207.

"I wonder that a creature" Bartolomeo Dominici, *Processes*, 337, quoted in Ruth Lechner Von Behren, *Women in Late Medieval Society*, 166–67.

"sweet holy crusade" Letter T185/G1/DT54 to Pope Gregory XI, in *Letters* I, 248.

"I have written a letter to the holy father" Letter T127/G117/DT20 to Bartolomeo Dominici and Tommaso Caffarini, in *Letters* I, 40–41.

109 "Oh how blessed will our souls be" Letter T66/G125/DT35 to William Flete, in *Letters* I, 156.

"splendid company" Catherine uses this phrase in several of her letters, for instance in Letter T127/G117/DT20 to Dominici and Caffarini, in *Letters* I, 39.

110 "There is no way … So I am inviting you to get ready" Letter T144/G371/DT34 to Monna Pavola da Siena, in *Letters* I, 112–13.

111 usually more than one level of meaning. Christopher Tylerman has noted that the liberation of the Holy Land "provided a spiritual metaphor, both for the liberation of the individual soul from the consequences of sin … and, more widely, for the struggle against the ungodly." *God's War*, 89.

"The business of a crusade" Letter T132/G173/DT48 to Cecca di Clemente Gori, Giovanna di Capo, Caterina dello Spedaluccio, and other Mantellate, in *Letters* I, 202.

112 "Oh dearest gentlest brother … to give your lives for Christ" Letter T140/G220/DT30 to Sir John Hawkwood, in *Letters* I, 80.

113 "Opposing the said Turks" Quoted in Housley, *The Avignon Papacy and the Crusades*, 117.

"Oh what a great joy will it be" Letter T143/G313/DT39 to Queen Giovanna of Naples, in *Letters* I, 148–49. Giovanna's father-in-law had been given the title of King of Jerusalem, although by 1375 the title was empty of significance.

"I would like to ask you to make this holy crusade" Ibid., 149.

114 "I long to see you a true daughter and spouse" Ibid., 147.

"washed away the filth" Ibid., 148.

"sharing in the blood of God's son" Letter T28/G191/DT17 to Bernabò Visconti, in *Letters* I, 132. There is a question about the dating of this letter. Some believe it was written in 1374, but Noffke, citing linguistic evidence, places it in mid-1375.

"No lordship we possess … the city of our own soul" Ibid., 133.

"rebel against your head … to Christ crucified" Ibid., 135–37.

twofold purpose of Catherine's trip to Pisa. The practical political dimension of Catherine's efforts to promote a crusade has been underscored by F. Thomas Luongo. He says, "It . . . represents a misunderstanding to assert . . . that Catherine and Raymond went to Pisa not to keep Pisa and Lucca out of the Florentine league but to elicit support for the Crusade. This distinction is practically meaningless: There could be no Crusade—and no return of the pope [to Rome]—without peaceful consolidation of the papacy's political authority in Italy, and support of the Crusade involved an allegiance to the church that would preclude, theoretically at least, support for the growing movement against the church in central Italy. In this sense, Catherine's discussion of the Crusade in her letters was part of her participation in papal diplomacy . . . not something separate from it." *The Saintly Politics of Catherine of Siena*, 81.

115   "imperious, avaricious, ambitious" These are Noffke's characterizations in her introduction to the letter noted immediately below.

"dearest mother and sister in Christ . . . cease being rebellious" Letter T29/G319/DT18 to Regina della Scala, in *Letters* I, 206–7.

"Up, dearest father!" Letter Gardner I/DT52 to Bartolomeo Smeducci, in *Letters* I, 187.

116   "Urgently ask your son . . . the exaltation of holy Church" Letter T145/G311/DT40 to Queen Mother Elizabeth of Hungary, in *Letters* I, 170.

the village of Calci. Catherine's visit to Calci is related by Jorgensen in *Saint Catherine of Siena*, 204.

117   to the island of Gorgona. The trip to Gorgona is mentioned by Jorgensen in *Saint Catherine of Siena*, 205; he believes the party traveled to the island directly from Pisa. Noffke theorizes they left from Livorno. See *Catherine of Siena: Vision through a Distant Eye*, 209.

"To think the world is opposing us" Letter T139/G106/DT46 to Tommaso dalla Fonte, in *Letters* I, 195.

"Tell them I'm sorry" Letter T283/G104/DT47 to Tommaso dalla Fonte, in *Letters* I, 198.

Caffarini described how people. For Caffarini's description of the Lucca reception see Jorgensen, *Saint Catherine of Siena*, 209. Noffke believes that Catherine stayed in Lucca at a house near the church of San Romano. See *Catherine of Siena: Vision through a Distant Eye*, 211.

118   discern the difference . . . unconsecrated bread. Caffarini's story is repeated by Jorgensen, *Saint Catherine of Siena*, 210. Caroline Walker Bynum observes, "By the thirteenth century the eucharist, once a communal meal that bound Christians together and fed them with the comfort of heaven, had become an object of adoration." She adds, "If anything, food became a yet more powerful and awe-ful symbol, for the bread and the wine that lay on the altar were now even more graphically seen to be God." *Holy Feast*, 53, 54.

"Aren't you ashamed, Father" Jorgensen, *Saint Catherine of Siena*, 210.

119   "I want you to know" Letter T139/G106/DT46 to Tommaso dalla Fonte, in *Letters*
       I, 196.

       In Perugia early that December. The story of the legate's nephew appears in many
       places. The legate's quote is from Tuchman, *A Distant Mirror*, 320.

       "Your unworthy, poor and wretched daughter . . . do it for sure and without delay"
       Letter T185/G1/DT54 to Pope Gregory XI, in *Letters* I, 245–48.

121   "I had been happy, jubilant" Letter T168/G206/DT53 to the Elders of Lucca, in
       Letters I, 243.

8. "THE BED OF FIRE AND BLOOD"

122   "I believe it would be in God's honor" Letter T185/G1/DT54 to Pope Gregory XI,
       in *Letters* I, 250.

       master of the Dominican order. In late medieval times heads of religious orders were
       appointed by the pope instead of being elected by their members. In her letter to
       Nicola da Osimo, Catherine put forward the name of Stefano della Cumba. See *Let-*
       ters I, 256. As it turned out, Élias of Toulouse was never replaced as master general.

123   "Babylon on the Rhône" For a fuller view of Petrarch's opinion, see Robert Coogan,
       Babylon on the Rhône, especially 75–89.

       "predecessors desired the salvation" Boccaccio, *The Decameron* (III, 7), 243.

       "Who are those who are clothed and fattened . . . an account of his little sheep"
       Dialogue (127), 248–49.

124   he lay down his life. See John 10:11.

       "wicked, unbelieving dogs" Letter T145/G311/DT40 to Elizabeth of Hungary, in
       Letters I, 170; "they are our brothers and sisters" Letter Gardner I/DT52 to Bartolo-
       meo Smeducci da Sanseverino, ibid., 189.

       Blood was the coin of payment. Blood in medieval consciousness is discussed by
       Piero Camporesi, *Juice of Life*; see especially chap. 3, 53–76.

125   "frenzy . . . awash in blood" Bynum, *Wonderful Blood*, 2. See also Bynum, "The Blood
       of Christ in the Later Middle Ages." *Church History*, 685–714.

       "I Caterina, servant and slave" Letter T138/G314/DT41 to Queen Giovanna of
       Naples, in *Letters* I, 99.

       "I . . . long to see you" Letter T28/G104/DT47 to Tommaso dalla Fonte, in *Letters*
       I, 197.

       baptism of blood. According to Catholic theology, there are three ways to experi-
       ence baptism: first, the ritual baptism of water; second, a believer who dies before
       undergoing ritual baptism still has a "baptism of desire"; and third, the believer who
       is martyred before being ritually baptized is baptized by his or her own blood.

126 "Give your life to Christ crucified" Letter T100/G95 to Raymond of Capua, in *Letters* III, 43.

"I am inviting you" Letter T131/G216/DT33 to Niccolò Soderini, in *Letters* I, 130.

127 "her face grew radiant" Raymond of Capua, *Life* (II, 6), 185.

"Father, I must tell you" Ibid., 186.

128 "self-authorization" See Luongo, *The Saintly Politics of Catherine of Siena*, 121, 193, 196.

Stigmatists were unknown . . . until Francis of Assisi. Some have maintained that Paul the Apostle was alluding to the stigmata when he said, "I carry the marks of Jesus branded on my body" (Gal 6:17), but the reference is unclear and may refer in a more general way to what Paul suffered for the apostolate.

strong psychological basis. Paul Siwek states, "All scholars agree that stigmata are connected with ecstasy that, considered psychologically, is an emotional state. If it is really God who miraculously produces the stigmata, why would He have imposed ecstasy as an indispensable condition?" "Stigmatization," in *New Catholic Encyclopedia*, vol. 13, 531b.

Preachers . . . sometimes whipping their own bodies. Camporesi mentions a Capuchin in the sixteenth century who scourged his body so violently while preaching the Forty Hours that blood spattered everywhere and people cried out for him to stop. See *Juice of Life*, 57.

129 the desire to replicate in their own bodies. See Bynum, *Holy Feast*, 174.

real instruments of torture as props. Kathleen Falvey has noted that the staged beheading of John the Baptist in the town of Ravello employed the same ceremonial axe (*mannaia*) used for that town's executions. See "Early Italian Dramatic Traditions and Comforting Rituals," in *Crossing the Boundaries*, Konrad Eisenbichler, ed., 48.

in Siena a senator . . . an ally of Catherine. Four of Catherine's letters are addressed to Pietro Marchese del Santa Maria, the earliest around August 1375.

130 at worst as an enemy agent. F. Thomas Luongo, who has made an extensive study of the affair, concludes that "it is reasonable to accept" that Niccolò was an agent of Perugia "and took a position in the court of Pietro [Marchese del Santa Maria] . . . in order to infiltrate the Sienese political world." *The Saintly Politics of Catherine of Siena*, 95.

"certain rash words" The quoted words can be found in Caffarini's *Legenda minore*, cited in Luongo, *The Saintly Politics of Catherine of Siena*, 92.

"the one you know" Letter T273/G97/DT31 to Raymond of Capua, in *Letters* I, 86.

"like a ferocious and desperate lion" From the *Processo Castellano*, prepared by Caffarini for Catherine's canonization inquiry; cited in Luongo, *The Saintly Politics of Catherine of Siena*, 92.

131 *conforteria* ministry. See Falvey, "Early Italian Dramatic Traditions and Comforting Rituals," in *Crossing the Boundaries*, Eisenbichler, ed., 33–43.

"I went to him" Letter T273/G97/DT31 to Raymond of Capua, in *Letters* I, 86.

"Stay with me . . . my gentle spouse Jesus" Ibid., 87.

132 It is a "trick" . . . she thought. "Trick" is described as Catherine's "thought" only in the sense that she didn't speak it aloud to Niccolò. She does use the word "trick" in her letter. See ibid.

"Courage, my dear brother . . . to make one burst at God's goodness" Ibid.

133 "I knelt down and stretched my neck" Ibid., 87–88.

"I waited there in continual prayer" Ibid.

"like a meek lamb" Ibid., 88.

"Down for the wedding . . . my eyes fixed on divine Goodness" Ibid.

134 "stands in for Christ . . . in his execution" Luongo, *The Saintly Politics of Catherine of Siena*, 113.

"bathed in [his] own blood" Letter T273/G97/DT31 to Raymond of Capua, *Letters* I, 88.

"he made a gesture" Ibid., 89.

"Now that he was hidden away" Ibid., 89.

135 concoction of Tommaso Caffarini. The scholar who led the attack on the Niccolò letter was Robert Fawtier in his book *Sainte Catherine de Sienne*. Fawtier initially claimed Caffarini forged the letter. Later he came to believe the letter was authentic but claimed it recorded an interior vision of Catherine's, not a historical event. See Noffke's introduction to the letter in *Letters* I, 82–84, and Conleth Kearns's introduction to his translation of *The Life of Catherine of Siena*, lx–lxx.

"I long to see you engulfed" Letter T273/G97/DT31 to Raymond of Capua, in *Letters* I, 85.

136 "I want you to shut yourself up" Ibid.

9. Encounter in Avignon

137 "You know that a member cut off from its head . . . if it doesn't set itself right" Letter T171/G217/DT60 to Niccolò Soderini, in *Letters* II, 23.

138 "If you should say to me" Ibid., 25.

"I beg you, Niccolò" Ibid., 27. Noffke speculates that this letter was carried to Soderini by Lazzarino da Pisa, the Franciscan who challenged Catherine and became her follower.

139   "I long to see you a good shepherd . . . all of them realize they have done wrong" Letter T19/G4/DT64 to Pope Gregory XI, in *Letters* II, 18–20.

the Eight Saints. The confrontation between Florence and the pope represented just one facet of a long struggle between church and state in the late Middle Ages. For an excellent summary see David S. Peterson, "The War of the Eight Saints in Florentine Memory and Oblivion," in *Society and Individual in Renaissance Florence*, William J. Connell, ed., 173–214.

140   Raymond set off almost at once. The times and places of Raymond's travels are educated guesswork. Suzanne Noffke believes he left Siena around February 17, 1376, and visited Florence before going to Pisa. His party, which included Tantucci, Neri, and Felice da Massa, left Pisa for Avignon, probably by an overland route, in late February or early March. See *Letters* II, 3–4.

141   "With tremendous blazing desire . . . in the way I've described" Letter T226/G89 to Raymond of Capua, in *Letters* II, 7–9.

"on the night of April first . . . 'Is sin blessed now?'" Letter T219/G87/DT65 to Raymond of Capua, in *Letters* II, 91–92.

143   "It is clear that by your disobedience . . . your father's arms!" Letter T207/G198/DT68 to the *Signori* of Florence, in *Letters* II, 141–42.

"brought" Catherine to Florence. See Raymond of Capua, *Life* (III, 6), 381.

"do what you can about seeing" Letter T223/G28 to Cardinal Iacopo Orsini, in *Letters* II, 164.

144   "Come, come," she wrote, "don't resist" Letter T19/G4/DT64 to Pope Gregory XI, in *Letters*, II, 21.

"dearest wish" John Holland Smith, *The Great Schism*, 116.

"joy upon joy" Letter T226/G89 to Raymond of Capua, in *Letters* II, 10, and note 45.

"My dear father! I am begging you" Letter T206/G5/DT63 to Pope Gregory XI, in *Letters* II, 63.

145   "neighborhood of Florence . . . in a most pressing way" Raymond of Capua, *Life* (III, 6), 381. See also the Lamb translation, 376.

there's no mention of such a meeting. See Noffke, *Letters* II, 187.

the old Parte Guelfa. For the list of Catherine's political contacts in Florence see Luongo, *The Saintly Politics of Catherine of Siena*, 66–67.

146   "troupes of buffoons" Marzieh Gail, *Avignon in Flower*, 211.

147   "[There were] the pope's white palfreys . . . by scattering little coins" Ibid., 214.

"From the impious Babylon" Petrarch, *Canzoniere*, 114, A. S. Kline, trans.

148   "a fine house" Gardner, *Saint Catherine of Siena*, 179. According to Jorgensen, the mansion once belonged to Cardinal Gaillard de la Motte (the son of one of the

nieces of Clement V), and later to Cardinal Niccolò di Branca. See *Saint Catherine of Siena*, 227.

"short of stature, pale" Gail, *Avignon in Flower*, 279.

unsettled by the boldness . . . he found her charming. See Gardner, *Saint Catherine of Siena*, 179.

"those merchants" Gail, *Avignon in Flower*, 292.

"have deceived you" Drane, *The History of St. Catherine of Siena and Her Companions*, vol. 1, 364.

"when the holy father finds out . . . they still haven't come" Letter T230/G197/DT72 to the Eight of War, in *Letters* II, 196–97.

149   "He [the pope] doesn't want to make peace" Peterson, "The War of the Eight Saints in Florentine Memory and Oblivion," in *Society and Individual in Renaissance Florence*, Connell, ed., 200. Peterson maintains the amount was one million florins. However, three million is the figure mentioned by Gardner in *Saint Catherine of Siena*, 190.

"When your ambassadors came here . . . always receive mercy" Letter T234/G215/DT82 to Buonaccorso di Lapo, in *Letters* II, 239–40.

Catherine still had a list of things to discuss with the pope. See Gardner, *Saint Catherine of Siena*, 182.

"It is not meet that a wretched . . . he would do this thing" Ibid., 182–83.

150   "Don't make light . . . no one greater [than you] on earth" Letter T255/G13/DT71 to Pope Gregory XI, in *Letters* II, 193.

"Punish my sins, my Lord" Prayer 1 (excerpt), in Suzanne Noffke, ed. and trans., *The Prayers of Catherine of Siena* [henceforth *Prayers*], 20.

152   the archetypal female preacher. See Mark 16:11 and Luke 24:11. In both gospel accounts Mary Magdalen's testimony about the resurrection is not believed because she is a woman. For more on this see Mary Catherine Hilkert, *Speaking with Authority*, 23–29.

"we came into port" Raymond of Capua, *Life* (I, 10), 91.

153   she told Stefano, "You have your wish . . . has given him back to us" Ibid. (II, 8), 244–47.

"I command you, in virtue" Ibid.

154   Lapa was "going to pieces" Letter T240/G169/DT82 to Monna Lapa, in *Letters* II, 250.

"Your poor unworthy daughter . . . his boundless goodness" Ibid., 249–50.

155   not unlike the Apostle Paul. See Karen Scott, "St. Catherine of Siena, 'Apostola.'" *Church History*, 34–46.

10. NEW FOUNDATIONS

160   "a suitable place . . . really good monastery" Letter T12/G66/DT66 to Giovanni di Gano da Orvieto, in *Letters* I, 274.

"ladies of the upper classes" Raymond of Capua, *Life* (II, 7), 226.

161   Belcaro was a Dominican convent. See Jorgensen, *Saint Catherine of Siena*, 254.

"gracious and glorious bridegroom . . . a land of promise" Letter T112/G329 to Countess Bandeçça [Benedetta] Salimbeni, in *Letters* II, 335–37.

162   "Peace! Peace, most holy father!" Letter T252/G11/DT88 to Pope Gregory XI, in *Letters* II, 272.

turned their attention to the town of Cesena. The massacre at Cesena is recounted in many sources, including Tuchman, *A Distant Mirror*, 322.

"the great slaughter of souls . . . as if they were meat" Letter T209/G2 to Pope Gregory XI, in *Letters* II, 298–300.

163   "[T]here are two things . . . the slain, consumed Lamb" Ibid., 301.

"other holy desire" Ibid. Noffke, in a footnote, see ibid., confirms that the "holy desire" is an allusion to the crusades.

164   "tearing [God's servants] apart" Letter T123/G202 to the Defenders of the Commune of Siena, in *Letters* II, 374. This letter was written, probably in July, from Montepulciano.

"prisoners of Siena" and "nursed" at Christ's wounded side. Letter T260/G309 to the prisoners of Siena, in *Letters* II, 318. Nursing from Christ was a frequent motif among medieval mystics. See Bynum, *Holy Feast*, 269–73.

"Keep living in God's holy" Letter T260/G309 to the prisoners of Siena, in *Letters* II, 319.

165   two cousins of the Salimbeni family. For background on the dispute between the Salimbeni cousins, see Noffke, *Letters*, II, 361–63, as well as Franco Salimei, *I Salimbeni di Siena*, 149–58. Luongo refers to Agnolino as the "capo" of the Salimbeni family. See *Saintly Politics of Catherine of Siena*, 179.

166   "preaching mission" Hilkert, *Speaking with Authority*, 22.

the work of reconciliation had already begun. This is the same letter (see above) in which Catherine chided the Defenders for being too suspicious. Letter T123/G202, in *Letters* II, 374.

167   an evil spirit . . . "the news spread" Raymond of Capua, *Life* (II, 9), 255–56.

she healed . . . girl . . . "How can you think I need" Ibid., 252–54.

168   "How can you tolerate . . . the company that is with me" Letter T123/G202 to the Defenders of the Commune of Siena, in *Letters* II, 373, 377.

"opinionated presumption . . . to all my children" Letter T294/G245 to Sano di Maco, in *Letters* II, 381–82.

169   "All the rumors and suspicions . . . the salvation of souls" Letter T122/G304 to Salvi di Messer Pietro, in *Letters* II, 394.

"good children do more" Letter T294/G245 to Sano di Maco about the complaints of the sisters at Belcaro, in *Letters* II, 382.

"I know my presence . . . hard and moldy, if necessary" Letter TT118/G175 to Caterina dello Spedaluccio and Giovanna di Capo, in *Letters* II, 389–90.

"If you think I am staying here . . . longer" Letter T117/G167 to Monna Lapa, in *Letters* II, 442.

170   "evil deeds" and "As for my coming here with my family" Letter T121/G201 to the Defenders of the Commune of Siena, in *Letters* II, 416.

"so many demons are being eaten up . . . souls being saved" Letter TT118/G175 to the goldsmith Salvi di Messer Pietro, in *Letters* II, 390.

"certain church affairs" Raymond of Capua, *Life* (II, 9), 255.

171   "Oimé, Oimé, Oimé . . . with my presence and my words" Letter T267/G91 to Raymond of Capua, in *Letters* II, 474, 475.

172   "a water peaceful, clear and unpolluted" Letter T122/G304 to Salvi di Messer Pietro, in *Letters* II, 393.

"with true knowledge of herself" Letter T272/G90 to Raymond of Capua, in *Letters* II, 496.

"I have very often seen . . . space of time" Caffarini, *Processo Castellano*, quoted by Noffke in her introduction to *The Dialogue*, 14.

173   But if God spoke to them. This point has been made by Karen Scott, who notes, "[W]omen in a patriarchal society and church can acquire an acceptable voice and exert power in religious matters only if the words they speak are considered to be God's words and not their own." "'*Io Caterina*': Ecclesial Politics and Oral Culture in the Letters of Catherine of Siena," in *Dear Sister*, Karen Cherewatuk and Ulrike Wiethaus, eds., 91.

"divine Goodness" and "Oh dearest and sweetest father . . . a follower and lover of truth" Letter T272/G90 to Raymond of Capua, in *Letters* II, 502, 505.

174   writing as a "diversion" The following month Catherine, in a letter to Alessa Saracini, similarly called the act of writing a "distraction": "God has provided for me wonderfully both within and without. Physically he has been very provident this Advent, giving me distraction from my pain in writing." Letter T119/G178 in *Letters*, II, 700. The evidence of this letter is not conclusive, however, since Catherine sometimes spoke of "writing" when she meant dictation. See Noffke, ibid., footnote 6.

"written with my own hand . . . I began to learn in my sleep" Letter T272/G90, to Raymond of Capua, in *Letters* II, 505.

the final paragraph . . . is a forgery. The allegation was first made by a French critic, Robert Fawtier, in the early twentieth century. The fabricator, Fawtier believed, was Catherine's disciple Tommaso Caffarini. See Noffke's general introduction to the letters (*Letters* I, xvi–xviii) and footnote 51 in *Letters* II, 505–6.

why she went back to dictation. There is one other letter, written to Raymond in 1380 (Letter T371/G103; see chapter 13 below, the note "The light of my understanding . . ."), as well as one short prayer (see the last note for this chapter, "O Holy Spirit, come into my heart"), that Catherine supposedly wrote in her own hand. In addition, Caffarini repeated Stefano Maconi's claim that he [Maconi] had seen Catherine physically writing "several pages of the book which she herself composed in her own dialect" (Caffarini, *Libellus de Supplemento* I, I, 9, cited by Noffke in her introduction to *The Dialogue*, 14). None of these handwritten documents are still extant.

"[T]he dream of writing" Tylus, *Reclaiming Catherine of Siena*, 213. For the whole argument, see chap. 4, 164–214.

"at least in an elementary way" Noffke's footnote 51, in *Letters* II, 506.

175   "A soul rises up" *Dialogue* (1), 25.

"Now this soul's will . . . case which had arisen" Ibid., 26.

"to be alert and take down" Raymond of Capua, *Life* (III, 3), 324.

176   careful editing and revision. Noffke, in her introduction to *The Dialogue*, says the work shows "a great deal of painstaking (sometimes awkward) expanding and drawing in of passages written earlier." She believes Catherine herself did the editing, since "it is not an editing in the direction of a more polished style, which it probably would have been had it been the work of any of her secretaries, for they were men whose style reflected their learning." In addition, "they considered the saint's writings too sacred to tamper with." *Dialogue*, 14.

"suffering the weakness" Letter T119/G178 to Alessa dei Saracini, in *Letters* II, 700.

"As for me, if it be" Letter T104/G92 to Raymond of Capua, in *Letters* II, 657.

"O Holy Spirit, come into my heart" Prayer 6, in *Prayers*, 54. Tommaso Caffarini reportedly preserved the original page written by Catherine. After her death he gave it to a convent of Dominican sisters in Venice. The convent was suppressed in 1810. The page has been lost.

11. FULFILLMENT AND DISINTEGRATION

178   "Since you are a courageous man . . . for your salvation" Letter T242/G37 to Bishop Angelo Ricasoli, in *Letters* II, 530.

"A messenger came to me" Raymond of Capua, *Life* (III, 6), 383.

she set off for Florence. Jorgensen, citing a Florentine chronicle, says Catherine arrived in Florence in December 1377, "shortly before St. Lucy's day, December

13" (*Saint Catherine of Siena*, 281); but Noffke believes Catherine did not leave Val d'Orcia until late December or even January 1378 (see *Letters* III, 18). It seems reasonable to put the trip to Florence in mid-January.

179   she lacked the credentials. Stefano Maconi offered testimony, repeated by Drane, that Catherine did meet with Florentine leaders the day after her arrival. The claim is unsupported by evidence.

she made pronouncements on local politics. As Gardner observes disapprovingly, "Catherine did not hesitate to intervene in communal politics." *Saint Catherine of Siena*, 232.

to use her for their own ends. According to Gardner, Catherine in Florence became associated with "a small group of fanatical and overbearing partisans." "From the outset," he adds, "Catherine had fallen into the hands of this faction [of the Parte Guelfa] which by tradition claimed to be that of the Church, and it is clear that its more unscrupulous members were simply making her a tool for their own private ends, dragging her name into their campaign of excluding their own personal enemies from office." Ibid., 236.

180   "it is time to weep and sigh" Letter T126/G270 to Nigi di Doccio Arzocchi, in *Letters* III, 52.

"[God's] providence will not fail" Letter T286/G180/DT57 to Alessa Saracini, in *Letters* III, 55.

"rest and pleasure" and "Those who live in selfish love . . . and those in your charge" Letter T275/G94 to Raymond of Capua, in *Letters* III, 83.

181   "or all the cardinals . . . will be knifed" Smith, *The Great Schism*, 5.

182   "It seems to me the dawn . . . a sweet and lovely sun" Letter T227/G126 to William Flete, *Letters* III, 122.

an abusive and irascible manner. The abusive behavior of Urban VI is discussed by Smith, *The Great Schism*, 140ff, and by Ludwig Pastor, *The History of the Popes from the Close of the Middle Ages*, vol. 1, 121–25. According to Smith, the term Urban used for Orsini was "the dim-witted one."

ten or twelve dioceses. See Pastor, *The History of the Popes from the Close of the Middle Ages*, vol. 1, 123, note.

183   "is beginning courageously" Letter T271/G179 to Alessa Saracini, in *Letters* III, 132.

"this holy father of ours" Letter from the prior of Gorgona quoted by Noffke in the introduction to Letter T293/G26, in *Letters* III, 127.

"discord is arising . . . and to eliminate this scandal" Letter T293/G26 to Cardinal Pedro de Luna, in *Letters* III, 129–30.

184   "This blood and fire" Letter T80/G123 to Giovanni Tantucci, in *Letters* III, 140.

185   "[W]hile she was . . . praying in the garden . . . face to face with her" Raymond of Capua, *Life* (III, 6), 385–86.

186   "Oh! what a disappointment" Ibid., 386.

"my eternal bridegroom . . . prevented by my sins" Letter T295/G96 to Raymond of Capua, in *Letters* III, 149–50.

187   But no one is sure how exactly the book was put together. Suzanne Noffke states that Catherine's original work was "almost certainly one continuous narrative" rather than segmented. This does not mean Catherine had no structure in mind, nor does it mean she always composed earlier parts before later ones. Subsequent editors of the book arranged it into 167 short chapters, then gathered those into "tracts" or "treatises." Giuliana Cavallini, who published the Italian critical edition in 1968, discerned what she believed was Catherine's original structure for *The Dialogue*, and arranged her critical edition under section headings titled Prologue, The Way of Perfection, Dialogue, The Bridge, Tears, Truth, The Mystical Body of Holy Church, Divine Providence, Obedience, and Conclusion. Cavallini's headings are reflected in Noffke's English edition published in 1980 (and in this biography). For more information about the structure of the work, see Noffke's introduction to *Dialogue*, 15–19.

"my chosen children" *Dialogue* (42), 87.

188   "the bridge has walls and a roof" Ibid. (27), 66.

"If [the soul] perseveres to the end" Ibid. (65), 122.

"according to their hunger" Ibid. (61), 116.

"their bed and table" Ibid. (78), 145.

189   "who will really be pillars . . . Bring us a remedy!" Letter T291/G15 to Pope Urban VI, in *Letters* III, 153, 154.

"Oimé! My *babbo!*" Ibid., 154.

190   "Oh dearest children . . . and left the weather fair" Letter T303/G246 to Sano di Maco, in *Letters* III, 167–68. The word "Paterine" was associated with heretics and in Catherine's day was an offensive epithet.

191   "I had wanted to leave" Letter Gardner IV to the *Priori dell'Arti* and the *Gonfaloniere della Giustizia* of Florence, in *Letters* III, 179.

"You want to reform your city" Ibid., 178.

"Anti-Christ, devil, apostate" Tuchman, *A Distant Mirror*, 331.

"fountain of the heart" *Dialogue* (89), 162. Growing up in Siena gave Catherine a particular sensitivity to the value of water and the significance of fountains.

192   "My ministers should be standing" Ibid. (123), 235–36.

"to make her grow in the light of faith" Ibid. (142), 293.

"You responded, Lord" Ibid. (167), 366.

193   "the bitterness in which you find yourself . . . on one's neighbors" Letter T305/G17 to Pope Urban VI, in *Letters* III, 214–15.

"if any are scandalized" Raymond of Capua, *Life* (III, 1), 310.

194 "the cellarer who holds the keys . . . your holiness in person" Letter T306/G18 to Pope Urban VI, in *Letters* III, 284–85. The image of the pope as the keeper of the wine cellar also appears in *The Dialogue.*

"I'll be going to Rome" Letter T290/G293 to Francesco di Pipino and his wife, Agnesa, in *Letters* III, 341.

12. CATHERINE IN ROME

195 "cornfield of towers" Paul Hetherington, *Medieval Rome*, 39. The descriptions of Rome also borrow from Ludovico Gatto, "La Roma di Caterina" in *La Roma di Santa Caterina da Siena*, Maria Grazia Bianco, ed., 13–48.

196 "deserted and without greatness" Gatto, "La Roma di Caterina" in *La Roma di Santa Caterina da Siena*, Bianco, ed., 20. Gatto calls Birgitta's relationship with Rome "misanthropic."

Catherine loved Rome. See ibid., 37.

They found a place to live on Via del Corso. With the exception of the Portica (now Via della Conciliazione), this biography uses today's names for Roman streets. These modern street names will help readers and travelers follow Catherine's footsteps in Rome—for instance, across the city to St. Peter's.

The building on Via del Corso where Catherine stayed no longer exists. The space it occupied is taken up by a sixteenth-century structure, the Palazzo Odescalchi. Jorgensen claims Catherine's first residence in Rome was "at the foot of Monte Pincio," which is not accepted by most historians today. *Saint Catherine of Siena*, 331. See also Giordani, *Catherine of Siena*, 233.

197 with "dear Paul we will glory" Letter T331/G58 to Pietro da Milano, in *Letters* IV, 45. The scriptural allusion is to Gal. 6:14.

198 "Catherine of Monna Lapa has come here" Quoted by Giordani, *Catherine of Siena*, 232.

199 "I long to see you come out . . . there is no way out" Letter T310/G31 to three Italian cardinals, in *Letters* III, 219, 223. The three cardinals were Pietro Corsini, Simone da Borzano, and Giacomo Orsini.

"with an easy flow of language" Raymond of Capua, *Life* (III, 1), 311.

"This weak woman" Raymond of Capua, *Life* (III, 1), 311.

200 discreet stranglings. In 1345, Giovanna's own husband, Andrew, brother of the king of Hungary, was strangled outside the door of her chamber. Although she denied involvement, it was long suspected Giovanna was complicit in the murder.

"If Saint Agnes and Saint Margaret" Raymond of Capua, *Life* (III, 1), 312.

"Dearest mother in Christ gentle Jesus . . . God's holy and tender love" Letter T317/G316 to Queen Giovanna of Naples, in *Letters* IV, 5–6, 9–11.

202 "all other persons except the two" Raymond of Capua, *Life* (III, 1), 313.

"and then she made the sign" Ibid.

"[W]e have seen in the light . . . no more about this" Letter T330/G99 to Raymond of Capua, in *Letters* IV, 42–43.

203 "You will come out of your woods" Letter T326/G127 to William Flete and Antonio da Nizza, in *Letters* IV, 29–30.

"It's my experience . . . all the others my regards" Letter T328/G130 to Antonio da Nizza, in *Letters* IV, 79, 81.

204 "sweet bitterness . . . so pale for so long" Letter T346/G19 to Pope Urban VI, in *Letters* IV, 57.

"grandma [i.e., Lapa] and Lisa" Letter T332/G264 to Stefano di Corrado Maconi, in *Letters* IV, 75.

Among the other churches she is thought to have visited. See Gatto, "La Roma di Caterina," in *La Roma di Santa Caterina da Siena*, Bianco, ed., 32.

205 *The Prayers of Catherine of Siena.* One of Catherine's early editors was Stefano Maconi, who seems to have attached a collection of prayers to his copy of *The Dialogue* and called it an Epitaph. His collection was later detached from the manuscript and lost.

"You, eternal Godhead" Prayer 10 (excerpt), in *Prayers*, 82.

206 "If I consider the Word" Prayer 11 (excerpt), ibid., 90.

"In your nature, / eternal Godhead" Prayer 12 (excerpt), ibid., 104.

207 "We must conform ourselves to you" Prayer 17 (excerpt), ibid., 149.

"And then, director of our salvation" Prayer 7 (excerpt), ibid., 59.

208 "So [God] listen to us" Prayer 8 (excerpt), ibid., 65.

209 Urban walked barefoot in a procession . . . to St. Peter's. Catherine mentions the procession in a May 6 letter to the leaders of the city of Rome. See *Letters* IV, 157–61. Raymond maintains the barefoot gesture was Catherine's idea. See *Life* (III, 2), 320.

"have pity on so many . . . your soul as my own" Letter T348/G317 to Queen Giovanna of Naples, in *Letters* IV, 168–69.

"Face up to the fact" Letter T350/G187 to Charles V of France, in *Letters* IV, 176. In fact Charles died one year later, on September 16, 1380.

210 "Oh dearest brother and sons . . . with good conscience" Letter T347/G219 to Alberigo da Barbiano and the Company of San Giorgio, in *Letters* IV, 163.

"my wicked little father . . . I have no more to say to you" Letter T333/G100 to Raymond of Capua, *Letters* IV, 88–90.

211 "O boundless, gentlest charity!" Prayer 9 (excerpt), in *Prayers*, 71.

13. CROSSING THE BRIDGE

212   As soon as the way to St. Peter's. For Catherine's route through Rome to St. Peter's Basilica, this biography relies on the conjectures of Giuliana Cavallini and Diega Giunta in *Luoghi Cateriniani di Roma*, 54–65. There is disagreement about the exact route of the Via del Papa. Previously it was believed that papal processions went along the avenue now known as the Corso Vittore Emanuele, south of the route described by Cavallini and Giunta. See also Raymond of Capua, *Life* (III, 2), 323.

213   the square in front of the basilica. For a description of St. Peter's Square and the portico in the Middle Ages see Hetherington, *Medieval Rome*, 43.

214   "You have been put back at the breast . . . very ungrateful" Letter T337/G199 to the Priori dell'Arti and Gonfaloniere of Justice of the People and Commune of Florence, in *Letters* IV, 123–24.

215   "I long to see you coming to the aid" Letter 339/G205 to the Lord Priors of the People and Commune of Perugia, in *Letters* IV, 183.

       "the words of a saint" Drane, *The History of St. Catherine of Siena and Her Companions*, vol. 2, 187.

       "the heart of Pharaoh is broken" Letter T353/G337 to Catella, Checcia (called Planula), and Caterina Dentice of Naples, in *Letters* IV, 201.

       "Oh dearest mother! . . . God's goodness within you" Letter T362/G318 to Queen Giovanna of Naples, in *Letters* IV, 223–24, 226.

216   Urban VI was plotting to overthrow Giovanna. Louis of Hungary and Charles of Durazzo had an ancient grievance against Giovanna ever since Louis's brother Andrew (Giovanna's first husband) was strangled just outside her bedchamber in 1345. Louis and Charles believed she was complicit in the murder.

       "The dear God has done you a great favor . . . were your own son" Letter T357/G188 to Louis I, King of Hungary, in *Letters* IV, 240, 241.

217   It was not Catherine's finest hour. According to Edmund G. Gardner, "It is heart-rending to find Catherine involved in this deplorable affair, but it is clear from her letters that she was merely Urban's tool, acting in good faith, without the slightest realization of the extent to which [Louis] and Charles were prepared to carry out their scheme." *Saint Catherine of Siena*, 324.

       "[You don't] think I should measure you . . . stoke the fire of desire!" Letter T344/G101 to Raymond of Capua, in *Letters* IV, 230, 232.

218   "so that we don't get things out of perspective" Letter T351/G20 to Pope Urban VI, in *Letters* IV, 205, 207.

       "let them be persons who are seeking God . . . the patience to listen" Letter T302/G16 to Pope Urban VI, in *Letters* IV, 217.

219   "I beg you, holy father" Ibid., 217–18.

       a bitter dispute with the people of Rome. See Raymond of Capua, *Life* (III, 2),

320–21. Drane, citing Maimbourg (*Histoire du Grand Schisme*, I, 148), claims the Romans actually tried to poison the pope. When that didn't succeed a mob invaded the Vatican but was "overawed" by the papal presence. *The History of St. Catherine of Siena and Her Companions,* vol. 2, 238–39. Gardner says Urban received the insurgents while seated on his throne and "succeeded in appeasing their fury." *Saint Catherine of Siena,* 332.

"reached such a pitch" and "incessantly" Raymond of Capua, *Life* (III, 2), 320.

"she saw in spirit" Ibid.

why she invested so much of herself. Arrigo Levasti makes a slightly different point when he writes about Catherine's investment in the papacy, "it was necessary for her, from now onwards, to convince herself that she had done great harm to the Church, harm for which she could make reparation only by placing herself wholly in the hands of the Pope of Rome." *My Servant, Catherine,* 362.

220   "This very day let's leave . . . always running toward death" Letter Gardner VII to Piero Canigiani, in *Letters* IV, 277, 278.

221   "You know that discouragement" Letter T178/G274 to Neri di Landoccio Pagliaresi, in *Letters* IV, 264.

"God has chosen you . . . with desire for the virtues" Letter T372/G189 to Carlo di Durazzo, in *Letters* IV, 304–5.

222   "Don't keep throwing words" Letter T311/G203 to the Defenders of the People and the City of Siena, in *Letters* IV, 311.

"I proclaim and will continue" Letter T367/G204 to the Lord Defenders of the People and Commune of Siena, in *Letters* IV, 323.

"a pious lady" Raymond of Capua, *Life* (III, 5), 353.

"Today again in your mercy" Prayer 25 (excerpt), in *Prayers,* 215.

"so loathsome" and "robust and fresh as usual" Catherine's breakdown in health is described by Barduccio Canigiani in a letter to Sister Catherine Petriboni at the Monastery of San Piero a Monticelli near Florence. The letter is an appendix to Algar Thorold's translation of *The Dialogue of the Seraphic Virgin, Catherine of Siena* [henceforth *Seraphic Virgin*], 335–36.

223   "so violent a stroke" Canigiani's letter, ibid., 336.

written in "a state of some agitation" This is Noffke's observation, in *Letters* IV, 358.

"The light of my understanding . . . during my life, past and present" Letter T371/G103 to Raymond of Capua, in *Letters* IV, 359–61. Catherinian lore maintains that this letter to Raymond, like the one from Rocca d'Orcia, was written in her own hand. Considering her writing abilities and weakened condition it seems reasonable to question this claim, first put forward by Tommaso Caffarini.

224   "From that hour" Canigiani's letter, in Thorold, *Seraphic Virgin,* 336.

"full of devils . . . for love of Christ crucified" Letter T373/G102 to Raymond of Capua, *Letters* IV, 367, 369.

225   "in such a state" Canigiani's letter, in Thorold, *Seraphic Virgin*, 337.

"a dead woman walking" Letter T373/G102 to Raymond of Capua, in *Letters* IV, 367.

twentieth-century sculpture. The sculpture, set under the trees at the foot of Via della Conciliazione, is by Francesco Messina.

"I want to see you governing . . . and their own salvation" Letter T370/G22 to Pope Urban VI, in *Letters* IV, 355–56.

226   she gazed at the mosaic again. The *Navicella* incident was not reported by Raymond but by Tommaso Caffarini, in his *Legenda minore*. Drane places the incident on Sexagesima Sunday (two Sundays before Ash Wednesday), i.e., January 28, 1380 (see *The History of St. Catherine of Siena and Her Companions*, vol. 2, 240–41), but Gardner says it occurred on the Third Sunday of Lent. See *Saint Catherine of Siena*, 343–44.

"both internally and externally tormented" Canigiani's letter, in Thorold, *Seraphic Virgin*, 337.

"without food—not even a drop of water" Letter T373/G102 to Raymond of Capua, *Letters* IV, 368.

Stefano Maconi hastened down. Caffarini, according to Jorgensen (see *Saint Catherine of Siena*, 387), maintains that Maconi was present for Catherine's last testament. However, Levasti states that Maconi did not arrive in Rome until "a few days after Bartolomeo's departure." *My Servant, Catherine*, 392.

227   The testament is summarized. Catherine's testament is summarized in much greater length in Raymond of Capua's *Life* (III, 4), 334–40.

"first and fundamental point . . . love one another" Raymond of Capua, *Life* (III, 4), 334–40.

228   "merry and bright" Levasti, *My Servant, Catherine*, 392.

"terrible and unheard-of agony . . . Blood! Blood!" Canigiani's letter, in Thorold, *Seraphic Virgin*, 338–43. See also the epilogue of Noffke, *Prayers*, 229.

229   "This holy virgin" Drane, *The History of St. Catherine of Siena and Her Companions*, vol. 2, 276.

EPILOGUE

230   Dominican Vincent Ferrer. Ferrer (1350–1419) was the most famous preacher of his day. He traveled widely across western Europe, converting thousands by his sermons. He was declared a saint in 1455.

231   he had the head separated. Raymond also removed one of Catherine's fingers for Lisa Colombini, as well as the right arm, to be kept in a reliquary in the sacristy of

Santa Maria sopra Minerva. In future years more parts of Catherine's body would be removed, including the left hand, some ribs, and a foot. For details of this dismembering see Noffke, *Catherine of Siena: Vision through a Distant Eye*, 230–32.

Urban VI . . . "violent, overbearing" Eamon Duffy, *Saints & Sinners*, 168.

"walking in the garden calmly" Smith, *The Great Schism*, 151. The witness to the torture scene was Dietrich of Niem, a member of the papal curia.

232   although there were rumors of poison. Roger Collins, *Keepers of the Keys of Heaven*, 301.

council held at Pisa. At the time of the council, in 1409, the pope residing in Rome was Gregory XII, a Venetian. Gregory had promised to resign if his counterpart in France, Benedict XIII, would do the same, but Benedict would not.

233   "I have recorded in [the book]" Raymond of Capua, *Life*, second prologue, 20.

234   The process for Catherine's sainthood. Tommaso Caffarini's augmentation became known as the *Libellus de supplemento*, and his condensation of Raymond of Capua's *Life* was called the *Legenda minore*—after which Raymond's work was commonly referred to as the *Legenda major*. In addition, Caffarini had a hand in pulling together many testimonies and documents for Catherine's canonization process—a collection that became known as the *Processo Castellano*.

"Her knowledge came down" Bull of Pius II, from *Life of Saint Catherine of Sienna* by Blessed Raymond of Capua, edited by E. Carter (1860), 405.

235   the six patron saints of Europe. The other patron saints of Europe are Benedict of Nursia, Saints Cyril and Methodius, Birgitta of Sweden, and Edith Stein.

"Oimè! No more silence!" Letter T16/G38 to a great prelate, in *Letters* II, 117.

236   to call Catherine a feminist. Mary Catherine Hilkert has summarized Catherine's status among women today. She mentions that Catherine's statue flanks the altar at the Washington, D.C., chapel of Opus Dei. See *Speaking with Authority*, 8–15. See also Mary E. Giles, "The Feminist Mystic," in *The Feminist Mystic and Other Essays on Women and Spirituality*, Mary E. Giles, ed., 6–17, 29–36.

Catherine a Doctor of the Church. Thirty-three persons to date have been named by the Catholic Church as Doctors. The third woman to be named as a Doctor was Thérèse of Lisieux, in 1997.

"had a genius for applying" Suzanne Noffke, "Catherine of Siena: Justly Doctor of the Church?" *Theology Today* 62.

238   in Genoa in 1392. The Genoa dinner involving Raymond, Maconi, and Caffarini is mentioned in Kearns's introduction to Raymond of Capua's *Life*, xxix.

239   "Drown yourself, then" Letter T102/G93 to Raymond of Capua, in *Letters* IV, 348.

AUTHOR'S NOTE

244   "No people . . . talked more about unity" Tuchman, *A Distant Mirror*, 248.

INDEX

⑥⑨